Concrete Charlie:

An Oral History of Philadelphia's Greatest Football Legend Chuck Bednarik

By Ken Safarowic
and Eli Kowalski

SPORTS CHALLENGE
Network Publishing

WWW.SPORTSCHALLENGENETWORK.COM

Concrete Charlie:
An Oral History of Philadelphia's Greatest Football Legend Chuck Bednarik

ISBN: 978-0-9819861-3-5

Digital composition and design by Ilene Griff Design

The following individuals and organizations generously gave permission to reproduce photographs in this book:

The private collection of Chuck and Emma Bednarik

The Philadelphia Eagles

The Philadelphia Inquirer and Philadelphia Daily News pages were reprinted with permission by Philadelphia Newspapers, LLC

Urban Archives, Temple University Libraries

Collections of the University of Pennsylvania Archives

Penn Athletics

Publisher
Sports Challenge Network
Philadelphia, PA 19102
www.sportschallengenetwork.com
email: elik@sportschallengenetwork.com

Acknowledgements

Chuck Bednarik is someone that people just like to talk about. Originally we planned on talking to about 70-75 people for this book. There was an exponential effect to so many of interviews with a number of people telling us, "You have to get a hold of this guy; here's his number." The number grew with each phone call.

Special recognition goes out to some of the most helpful and enthusiastic supporters. In no particular order they were:

Bernie Lemonick, the point man for the Munger Men; Larry Kane, who knows everybody around town; Steve Sabol and his assistant Colleen Smith-Grubb at NFL Films; Gene Kilroy, who was known as 'The Facilitator" when he worked with Muhammad Ali and knows just about everyone, everywhere; Pat Williams, who opened his rolodex and reeled off phone numbers; Jimmy Gallagher; the main man for all things Eagles; Nate and Lynare Pipitone for arranging a special day with Steve Van Buren; Derek Boyko, for handing over his files and providing access to the current Eagles administration; Tammy Owens of the Pro Football Hall of Fame, for reaching out to the all-time greats and helping to enlist their support; Bill Margetich, who has an invaluable collection of family pictures and seems to have collected every word ever written about Chuck Bednarik; Larry Kisslinger, Man about Bethlehem; Ernie Montella, for providing access to Philadelphia A's players, Ken Avallon of the Philadelphia Sports Hall of Fame, who loves everything about Philly sports and provided a number of suggestions and contacts; and most important, Emma Margetich Bednarik, for her patience, crisp memory, and never having gotten rid of anything. Her family archives saved a lot of trips to the library.

To the many interviewees without whom, this book would not be rich with first hand information. In alphabetical order they are:

Ernie Accorsi, Dave Anderson, Jim Andrew, Paul Anthony, Neill Armstrong, Joe Astroth, Doug Atkins, Bunny Bankowski, Maxie Baughn, David Bednarik, Upton Bell, Bert Bell, Jr., Jeep Bednarik, Bill Bergey, Yogi Berra, Tom Brookshier, Jim Brown, Mike Brown, Tim Brown, Walt Bruska, Michael Buffer, Patty Burns, Dick Butkus, Bill Campbell, Marion Campbell, Pete Carill, Leo Carlin, John Chaney, Bob Clark, Paul Clymer, Francis Davis, Andy DePaul, Ray Didinger, Dan DiRenzo, Art Donovan, Bob Deuber, Harry Edenborn, Ken Farragut, Bob Feller, Frank Fischl, Dan Fitzinger, Gordon Forbes, Bob Fox, Bob Gain, Harry Gamble, Frank Gifford, Bud Grant, Forrest Gregg, Sonny Hill, Wayne Hillman, Stan Hochman, Paul Hornung, Sam Huff, Dave Jordan, Sonny Jurgensen, Tom Kelleher, Ed Khayat, Dave Klein, Lew Klein, Stan Kotzen, Ed Kreilic, Frank LeMaster, Bob Levy, Marv Levy, Stan Lopata, Dick Lucas, Bill Lyon, Bob Lyons, Bill Mackrides, Gino Marchetti, Monk Matthews, Jack McCallum, Mike McCormack, Tommy McDonald, Hugh McIlhenny, Ed McKeon, Al Meixner, Al Meltzer, Larry Merchant, Walt Michaels, Frank Miller, Mickey Minnich, Lenny Moore, Dean Morrow, Billy Packer, Carmen Palumbo, Vince Papale, Russell Peltz, Bill Piszek, George Piszek, Merrill Reese, Andy Reid, Governor Ed Rendell, Pete Retzlaff, Tom Ridge, Gene Rossides, Andy Russell, Buddy Ryan, Steve Sabol, Dick Scott, Harold Serfass, Bobby Shantz, Don Shula, Greg Sirb, Ed Snider, Bart Starr, Sally Starr, Joe Steffy, Greg Stroble, Jimmy Sturr, Bert Sugar, Pat Summerall, Jim Taylor, Bob Thomason, Joe Timmer, Tom Timoney, Y.A. Tittle, Domonic Toscani, Jim Tunney, Leo Turley, Tim Twardzik, Frank Unger, Steve Van Buren, Dick Vermiel, Tony Veteri, Frank Weaver, Bill Werpohoski Jr., Bill Werpohoski Sr., Jack Whitaker, Jim Williams, Al Wistert, Jerry Wolman, Rob Wonderling, Bill Yeoman, Gus Zernial.

Special thanks to Ilene Griff for her patience and work ethic.

- Ken Safarowic and Eli Kowalski

Table of Contents

Introduction

f there is one thing Charles Philip Bednarik was put on this earth to do, it was to level. Anyone who has watched football or played against him knows what this means when he was on the field. Those who have known him before, during, and after his 18 year run on the Philadelphia football stage are too well aware that he is fundamentally, inherently, and maybe even genetically incapable of giving anything less than a precise and unadorned version of exactly what is on his mind. These lines have never called for an in-between reading.

Since arriving on this earth May 1, 1925, the second most famous son ever born in Bethlehem to a mother named Mary, has leveled on the football field, and has been nothing but level with his words.

This may be the first time that the name Chuck Bednarik ever appeared in the same sentence with words like guile, disingenuous and euphemistic. Some things weren't meant to go together.

A generation or two of football fans, at least those who lack an inclination for historic perspective, may know him only from the Legends version of Madden Football.

'The 60-Minute Man" has morphed into a folk hero legend. His teammates from that improbable 1960 championship team and many of his Hall of Fame contemporaries are still awed by what old Concrete Charlie pulled off that year.

He had actually retired the previous off-season, but decided to come back at age 35 for one more year at center. When Buck Shaw said that they also needed him to stay out on the field and play some defense, Chuck did so because that was what the job called for.

Bednarik discussed his lunch bucket approach to two-way duty with Sandy Grady of the Philadelphia Bulletin before the '60 title game, "Listen, I don't love the idea of going 60 minutes. Like Sam Huff told me, 'They can't pay me enough money to do it.' But with Bob Pellegrini hurt, I know the situation we're in and I'm ready."

It's not that he simply plugged two positions. In the improbable and magical year of 1960, Bednarik made ALL the big plays in the most important games. His foils weren't taxi squad chumps who would be teaching gym in a year or two. At crunch time the opposition put the ball in the hands of their best players, the go-to guys with names like Gifford, Hornung and Taylor—all permanently found in Canton, Ohio—and Charlie Bednarik came out on top every time.

"Ah, Bednarik," said Giants owner Wellington Mara in a New York Times interview,"he flattens anything that moves. He finished Frank Gifford for us and today he sent Paul Hornung to the sidelines, clean, but authoritative."

He was raking in all of $17,000 that historic 1960

season. In fact, 1960 almost didn't happen for him and maybe the Eagles too, as he announced his retirement at the end of '59. Money played a bigger role than any sense of unfinished business in undoing his retirement. He figured one more season of football would be a good side job to supplement his new career as a concrete salesman.

While the money was important in his coming back, he turned down more green from another shade of green when he passed on what he called at the time "an enticing offer" from the New York Titans in the fledgling American Football League. If it were solely about the money, Bednarik would have been playing in Gotham that year. He would have been in the same town as Gifford and the Giants, but their paths would have never crossed. Sorry, Frank.

He's north of 80 now, but there are still a few ways for a questioner to place himself at the wrong end of a fight—tell Bednarik that Deion Sanders played two-ways too; or ask him if he could still play today.

And we're not just talking about Chuck Bednarik in his physical prime. He swears that he could step on the field today and still be the best long-snapper in the NFL.

And you don't want to get him started on salaries. Every record-setting contract for the past 50 years added another level of resentment.

Bitterness didn't come late in the day for Concrete Charlie. In 1971, less than 10 years from Bednarik's exit from the football field; when $400,000 was considered a "when will the madness stop" salary, another legend, James A. Michener, wrote, "Of course a writer could legitimately depict him as a failure who went around trying to relive his days of grandeur. But that would not be the whole truth. Bednarik is a giant with giant resentments but also with a giant capacity to live a good life."

While just about everything has changed in the world around him, not much has changed in the world of Chuck Bednarik.

Nearly 40 years later, Michener's description still works just fine.

The evidence is more than enough to support the legend: the Gifford picture, counting down the clock on top of Jim Taylor, being the star attraction when Franklin Field packed in 80,000 fans for the likes of a Penn-Army game, and of course his reputation as the 60-Minute Man.

If any man has ever done more on the football field, try and find him. Chuck Bednarik gave his best for 60 minutes, and there was never anything better than that.

As a warm-up act for his football career, he flew 30 missions over Germany as the waist gunner in the back of a B-24 fighter plane. The fingers that would become the most famous in football history nursed a .50 caliber machine gun before they ever snapped a ball for the U of P.

Sixty minutes, two-ways, the most famous hit in NFL history, war hero. Reality fades with time and sometimes it may seem like a novelty, or maybe even a fable. Maybe up there somewhere with John Henry and his hammers, Paul Bunyan and his ox. But this all really happened.

The best and only way to understand the man and what he did was to locate the people who played with and against him. These guys are all accomplished in their own right, but they all had a few minutes to talk about Chuck Bednarik.

These voices remind us that Chuck Bednarik didn't just fill two positions on the field, where he was among the very best at both. He was also a teammate and a friend. People use the word exceptional - some in these pages will even say the best - at linebacker. The '50s and '60s were a golden era for linebackers. The names Ray Nitschke, Sam Huff, Bill George, Dick Butkus, and Joe Schmidt come up in many conversations. Bednarik is linked with all of them, and while not everyone says that he was the best, no one says there was anyone better at the position.

They talk about his size and his speed, his reach and his hands, his toughness and his instinct, and no one doubts that he would be just as great a linebacker today.

He played at 6'2", 235 pounds at a time when many linebackers were in the 210-220 range. He was bigger than most guards, and a big tackle weighed in at 250. Weight training, nutrition and off-season conditioning were still a generation or two away.

Salary? Where would it start, $10 million signing bonus, and $4 million a year?

There are those who know him who are sorry that he can't seem to better enjoy, the perks and the perch that should come with being Mr. Eagle. But in reality there are probably few people more content with their lives. He has church, polka music, and Emma, and there really isn't anything that he needs or wants.

Except maybe the adulation. It doesn't matter where he is—Walnut Street, the Ocean City Boardwalk, the farmers market in Quakertown, Lake Harmony in the Poconos, an airport in Houston or even a bus in the Ukraine—someone always knows who he is.

And he never disappoints. Whether it be about Gifford, today's players, Deion, traffic, the weather, or taxes, no one has ever gotten an "excuse me, I don't have the time."

Casual grace was not part of the finishing school education in Bethlehem. Neither is it picked up on a B-24 taking on flak. Chuck Bednarik isn't going any more gently into the night than Dylan Thomas' old man. This old Eagle continues to roar and rage, fighting the light, and everything else in his way. For the most part, Philadelphia football fans won't have it any other way. No one is ever going to have to decipher a mealy mouth rumination that doesn't say anything from Concrete Charlie; Jim Taylor had a better chance of getting up than this ever happening.

They want to hear Chuck being Chuck.

"Mr. Bednarik, you were the best."

"Do you remember Father McCatholic and the time you spoke at my CYO Awards dinner?"

"Chuck, they don't make 'em like you anymore."

He hears a variation of one of these statements almost everyday. If not in person, it may be in one of the 10 or so pieces of fan mail/autograph requests that show up daily.

His body frame still looks like it did in those famous pictures. His is the face of football, with the nose that looks like it was forged into place with an anvil and tong.

If you ask, he's going to tell you. Sometimes it doesn't reflect back all that well. He's criticized the Eagles organization for not buying copies of his last biography before their last Super Bowl appearance. He said he hoped they would lose so that the 1960 team would still be the last championship team in his lifetime. Talk show hosts and print guys have found that they can liven a slow news day by goading Bednarik into complaining about today's salaries and the efforts of the modern players. "Overpaid and underplayed," has been his much-repeated mantra over the years.

Much of this book has been turned over to the people that were there when he was growing up in Bethlehem, serving in World War II, starring at Penn and for the Eagles, and living post-football. This book has taken on the form of an oral history as the memories of these people, related in their own words, seems far more effective than anything any author could write.

It is a project that would have been fuller and richer if it had been started ten, or even five years ago, when more people who remembered his legacy were still around, and the memories of those who are here were less frequently accompanied by a confession of haziness and apologies for not being sharper.

This book, in the words of those who know him, is the story of Concrete Charlie.

Liberty H.S
1943

1947
BEDNARIK
PENNSYLVANIA

A. Ken Steely (#35), Mel Peters (#32) and Chuck (#38)
B. Young Charlie
C. In the backyard
D. Proud parents, Mary and Charles Sr.
E. HS basketball team
F. 1947 All American blanket
G. Chuck today In front of his church, 2009
H. City Catholic League Champs

Chapter | one

Bethlehem

If you talk with anyone who grew up in Bethlehem in the era that spanned from 1920-1960, they are almost certain to tell you that there were five pillars built into everyone's life — steel, church, sports, social clubs, and the music of the old country. It seemed that nearly every family in town was supported by wages earned at Bethlehem Steel and when the workers weren't at the plant, they would be found at church, playing ball, or listening to music at their ethnic hall. Charles Philip Bednarik grew up in Bethlehem and left his hometown in any sense.

His father, Charles Albert Bednarik, was one of the countless European immigrants who came to America to work for Steel. He left Slovakia, a region in eastern Czechoslovakia, in 1921. His only skill was "laborer" and he knew little about his new country and understood even less of its language.

Like almost all of the immigrants, he settled in the neighborhood known as the Southside, and took the only job that he would have for the next 44 years. The 'Southside' was the area south of the Lehigh River that at one time sat at the heart of the Industrial Revolution. Charlie Bednarik saw no need to pay for public transportation when he could walk, and he covered the five-mile roundtrip commute to Open Hearth No. 4 by foot every day. It didn't matter which shift—day; night or middle. He eventually worked his way up to first helper, and in later years was easily identified by the number 60 Penn

Charles Sr. wearing #60 Penn jersey outside Bethlehem Steel plant

football jersey he wore around the mill. As first helper, he earned the honor of being the number one guy standing in front of the open hearth, tossing scrap metal into the flames.

"We finally got him to take the bus," Chuck Bednarik, recalled of his father. "The mills were on the Heights side of town and can you imagine walking at night, in the rain and snow for the 11-7 or 3-11 shift."

In 1923, he married 17 year old Mary Pivovarnicek who had come to the United States following the death of her parents in Czechoslovakia.

Charles Philip was the first son born to Charles Sr. and Mary, arriving May 1, 1925. The youngest of the six Bednarik children, David, arrived in 1946, 21 years after oldest brother Chuck. In between Chuck and David there were two more boys and two girls. Later, when David started playing sports and his brother was starring for the Eagles,

outsiders often assumed that he was a son or younger cousin of Chuck. John 'Jeep' Bednarik, the second of four brothers, was an honorable mention All-American end at William and Mary. He later became one of the best regarded football coaches in northeastern Pennsylvania, first coaching at several high schools and then at Lehigh University. Jeep was enshrined in the Lehigh Valley Chapter of the National Football Foundation Hall of Fame.

The family size came from Mary, a big-boned, stout woman. Charles Sr. was a wiry 5'10", 150 pounds. The worst days of the Depression were as hard on the Bednariks as on anyone else, and even though Pop, as he was known around town, had a steady job at Steel, slowdowns often cut his work week down to one or two days.

In 2009, Chuck revisits 546 E. 5th Street, one of the homes he grew up in.

Chuck Bednarik recalled that his family lived in three of four different houses during the Depression years, because they were "bumped out," as he said, when they couldn't meet the rent.

"There were periods when there was hardly any work and we got used to going to Family Welfare for food and clothing," Bednarik recounts of his childhood.

When the depression ended and Pop was back to pulling regular shifts at the steel mill, the family settled on E. 5th Street, across from SS Cyril and Methodius Church, which was the Slovak parish where the Bednarik children attended grammar school.

Chuck and Jeep played ball in the street using tin cans before graduating to footballs made of stuffed socks. When Chuck was about 10 his mother saved up 25 coupons clipped from coffee bags to send away for the first real football the boys would have. With frequent tape and patch jobs, they squeezed three years of use out of

"Pop signed the permission slip and Chuck showed up in the office of Paul Troxell telling the coach, "I would like to play football."

that ball. Lehigh University featured pristine athletic fields and, when the boys from the Southside wanted some grass to play on, they hiked up to the college and worked their way in by scaling walls and fences.

When they weren't playing themselves, they slipped in to watch the varsity teams play and practice. Down at the Bethlehem Boys Club, they got their first opportunities to participate in organized sports.

Chuck Bednarik's football career began at Broughal Junior High School, on the south side in 1939. Mary had wanted her son to attend Bethlehem Catholic High School, which didn't even have a football program. After a miserable ninth-grade year at "BeCa High," in which he was cut from the basketball team, Chuck and his father convinced Mary to let him transfer to the public school that all his friends attended.

One thing they could not get her to agree to was signing off on the consent form that would allow young Charlie to try out for the football team. "She wouldn't let me play football," said Bednarik, "she said she didn't want anyone hurting me."

Pop signed the permission slip and Chuck showed up in the office of Paul Troxell telling the coach, "I would like to play football."

It was Troxell who kept Bednarik in school when academics weren't going well and a job at the mill didn't seem like a bad idea. Bednarik recalled his junior high days:

1942 Bethlehem HS Football team, Chuck (#38)

"We had a group that used to hang around Tony Kovac's candy store when we were teenagers. We called ourselves the Mountaineers. He used to let us go inside when it was cold. It was a tough life; several of the guys were dropping out of school and going to work at the steel mill to make a few dollars and help out at home."

"When Troxell heard that I was thinking of leaving school, he pressed me up against a wall, he said, 'You dumb Slovak, is that what you want to do with your life. Athletics can get you into college and you can make something of your life.'"

"I had no thought of college; my only thoughts were going to work to help my parents. I wasn't sure I wanted to go to high school. After high school, I probably would have started work at Bethlehem Steel if not for the war."

Mrs. Bednarik didn't attend his games, especially when he entered Liberty High School, which was on the north side of town, about a half-hour ride from their home. Wearing number 38, Bednarik wanted to be a fullback and linebacker for coach John Butler.

Butler had a returning All-State center, but he ran into eligibility problems a week before the first game. The back-up center was too small to play the position, so Butler called Bednarik over and asked if he wanted to be the team's center. Bednarik said "sure," and Butler sent him off to get a larger pair of pants so that it would be easier for him to bend over the ball. He also told him to a take a football home and learn how to snap.

Center, in the single wing, was the toughest position on the field. The center had to look back through his legs and rifle the ball to any of three backs with a pass that would get the play started in the direction it was intended to go. Nearly every defense had their own center, and his main job was to clobber the snapper on every play, with the malicious intent of rattling him so badly that his passes to the backfield would wobble and bounce. To this day, no one who saw him play center at Liberty or Penn, can remember Chuck Bednarik ever making a bad snap.

Liberty finished 5-4-1 Bednarik's first year. He also played baseball and basketball, and would continue with all three sports through high school. College coaches started making a little fuss the following season, but Bednarik had zero interest in continuing on in school once he was done with Liberty.

His most noteworthy athletic moment occurred during a playoff basketball game against Hazleton. Though the game was played on a neutral court in Allentown, the crowd was heavily tilted toward nearby Liberty, with Bethlehem being much closer to the arena than Hazleton.

Hazleton won on a controversial last second basket, and a frustrated Bednarik slugged the opposing team's star center as the teams walked off under the stands. A riot ensued with the Bethlehem steelworkers in the crowd pelting the court with the sandwiches and apples they were carrying to work. Tear gas was needed to break up the riot and several people were taken to the hospital for treatment of injuries.

1949 Mountaineers City Champs

"I still hear about that one,' Bednarik recalled, more than 65 years after the incident. "I don't know why I did it. I didn't have anything against the guy. We had a good rivalry with Hazleton in all sports. The fans used to yell back and forth at the each other, 'What's harder, coal or

> **"When my old friends think I can help them win a ball game and they ask me to play, how can I refuse? After all, they took me off the streets and started me on the way. They want me, I come."**

steel?' I was never proud of starting the riot, but a lot of stories have come out of it over the years."

World War II prevented Bednarik from having a senior season in any sport. He was drafted in May 1943 shortly after turning 18. He was eligible to graduate under the terms of a program called the Dalton Plan. His mother picked up his diploma the following month while Bednarik was training at Fort Indiantown Gap in central

Pennsylvania. This was Bednarik's first trip away from Bethlehem. Two years later, he was a grown man and decorated war hero when he made the first of many return visits home.

He wasn't home long in the fall of 1945 before reporting to the University of Pennsylvania for the second half of the football season. During his four years enrolled at Penn he made the 60-mile trip back to Bethlehem every chance he had. On those early trips home he reunited with the Mountaineers at Tony Kovac's store. Like Bednarik, many of them were returning from the service. High school sports were over, but they were still looking to play ball. With Bednarik taking the lead, they decided to diversify their social activities beyond Mr. Kovac's store and organized baseball and basketball teams that would compete in the City Catholic League.

Lou "Smelly' Bukvics was enlisted to coach the basketball team. Bednarik could have played for any team in the league and indeed was often pressured to play for the Slovak Sokol teams. There was never any doubt that he would suit up with buddies and, for the next 10 or so years, he would make the trip up to Bethlehem for all the big Mountaineer games, even as an All-American at Penn and an All-Pro with the Eagles. Bednarik did play for the Sokols in national tournaments during the period when the Bethlehem squad won eight consecutive national Catholic Sokol championships.

"He sent Bunny Bankowski to dance with me, he was too chicken," recalled Emma.

One of the Mountaineers would drive down to Penn and pick him up for the game. In a 1959 interview in the Bethlehem Globe-Times, he explained his allegiance to the Mountaineers, "When my old friends think I can help them win a ball game and they ask me to play, how can I refuse? After all, they took me off the streets and started me on the way. They want me, I come."

The trip to Bethlehem did not always go as planned. The headline for one game in 1948 proclaimed "Bednarik's Basket Gives Mounts Victory 50-48." The first place Mountaineers came from behind to beat McGovern and Judd on a basket by

Chuck and Emma getting married. June 1948, SS Cyril and Methodius Church

Bednarik with 18 seconds to play. It was also noted later in the article that due to a minor auto mishap in Philadelphia, Bednarik failed to arrive until midway in the third period."

The Mountaineers would win three consecutive Class A City League titles. In addition to being a beast under the boards, Chuck led the team in scoring in 1948, averaging 19 ppg.

In June of 1948, he married Emma Margetich. The wedding was on a Saturday. On Sunday he delayed his honeymoon because the Mountaineers had an important doubleheader. The new groom played catcher that day and took a verbal beating from the rival Hungarian Catholic fans who were seated directly behind him for most of the afternoon. The Mountaineers took both games and were the City Catholic League champs that summer.

Chuck had met Emma Margetich just six months earlier when he stopped by the Croatian Hall for a few beers and some ethnic music. The Margetich family band was playing that night and one of the musicians on the stage attracted the eye of the local football star. Too bashful to approach her himself, Bednarik sent a friend to initiate a conversation.

"He sent Bunny Bankowski to dance with me, he was too chicken," recalled Emma. "After Bunny broke the ice, he came over and we talked and danced. I didn't know anything about him. People were saying, "Look she's with the All-American." I didn't follow football; I didn't know what an All-American was.'

"When we got home, I asked my brother Willie, 'Who is this guy?'" Six months later they were married.

In January of 1948, around the time he met Emma, SS Cyril and Methodius Church sponsored the first of what would be many testimonial dinners for Bednarik in Bethlehem.

In January of 1948, around the time he met Emma, SS Cyril and Methodius Church sponsored the first of what would be many testimonial dinners for Bednarik in Bethlehem. More than 450 people attended, including former coaches Troxell and Butler, as well as Penn's Munger. Most of the Mountaineers were present at the event, which was organized to commemorate Bednarik's selection as a 1947 football All-American.

Bednarik continued to play for the Mountaineers until about 1954. They were one of the best draws in the region, as fans came out to see this nationally-known football star play beer-league basketball and baseball.

The Mountaineers broke up shortly after Bednarik stopped playing. While there were no more sports to be played up in the Lehigh Valley, Bednarik never completely left Bethelehem. He returned for various family functions as both the Bednariks and Margetiches stayed rooted in the area. He was the guest of honor at various testimonial functions including 1960, 1969 and 1988.

With four of their five daughters moved out of the house, Chuck and Emma returned to the Lehigh Valley in 1980, settling in Coopersburg, what was then a farming town 15 minutes outside of Bethlehem.

Bunny Bankowski

A lifelong resident of Bethlehem and Mountaineer teammate, Bunny and Chuck Bednarik were together when they both met their future wives.

Bernard "Bunny" Bankowski is a lifelong resident of the south side of Bethlehem. Bunny was with Chuck the night he met Emma at the Croatian Hall in Bethlehem and Bunny later met his future wife Marie when he accompanied Chuck to pick up Emma at work one day. Bankowski worked 41 years in the machine shop at Bethlehem Steel.

"We've been good friends for a long time. I was an usher at his wedding.'

'He was a tough loser; he didn't like to lose at anything. When he was at Penn, we used to drive down to pick him up for basketball games. We would drive from Bethlehem to Philly, pick him up, play ball, and drive him back all in the same night. One night we lost the keys in the snow down near Penn and we were all crawling around looking for them.'

"When Chuck was in college, he'd tell me to keep an eye on Emma. Me and Fritzi Grginovich were her bodyguards."

'He started hanging around with us in his teens. He lived on Fifth Street, we were over on Fourth. He liked to hang around with us. His buddy was Hips Pecsek, who was quite a guy. We used to hang around the grocery store.'

'Bethlehem south side; we had a lot of good athletes. One year after the war, we won the city basketball championship with the Mountaineers. Chuck was good in hoops, he was the rebounder. He had this hook shot, right hand from the right side. You couldn't push him around.'

'He was okay in baseball. If he got a hold of the ball, it sailed. He hit one of the longest home runs I ever saw, but he struck out more than anything.'

'He took a ribbing; it didn't take much to get him teed off. One woman-a real loud-mouth-she'd sit behind the backstop and ride him mercilessly. She'd yell at him, and he'd strike out. He played hard and he was a bad loser.'

'Our gang all used to hang around the Croatian Club on Saturday night. One night the guys were getting rough with me at the bar, Chuck walked in and they walked away. He's a nice guy, Chuck, but don't get him mad; don't be a wise guy.'

'We used to have a good time at the Croatian Hall on Saturday nights. I was there with him the night he met Emma.'

'After the club, we'd all go to Emma's parents' house, they were very nice people. They had a player piano and we'd sing along Croatian songs.'

'When Chuck was in college, he'd tell me to keep an eye on Emma. Me and Fritzi Grginovich were her bodyguards.'

'When he was at Penn he invited me up to Columbia. He said, 'Bunny, you go up and be with Emma, you're going to be her escort.'

'He intercepted a pass, returned in for a touchdown and threw the ball into the stands. I said to him, 'Chuck, didn't you know where I was sitting?'

1947 Mountaineers City Champs

'He and I were together when I met my wife. He asked me to go with him to pick up Emma from her job in the office at Bethlehem Steel. She was with her friend Marie, and she asked if we could give her a lift.'

'We started dating after that and got married in 1950.'

'He gave us four tickets to go to the Green Bay game when they won the championship. We froze, it was cold…I remember that game.'

'He had strict parents, but his father was so proud. He had a rough job at the mill. He was a thin man, spry, wiry, full of pep. His mother, she was a big woman, that's who he got his size from.'

'Bethlehem was good in those days. Now we have no more steel, the casino will be here in a few weeks.'

'I wouldn't sign a petition for the casinos. They're going to bring nothing but traffic and problems.'

'The only gambling we did, we played craps for nickels and dimes. The cops would come, we would scatter, and they would keep our change.'

'There were no drugs; we didn't even drink until we were drafted.'

'When Chuck was at Penn, we tried to hold a banquet for Chuck. No one influential showed up. The city didn't do enough for Chuck then, and they don't do enough for him now."

"He had strict parents, but his father was so proud. He had a rough job at the mill. He was a thin man, spry, wiry, full of pep. His mother, she was a big woman, that's who he got his size from."

Billy Packer

The most famous announcer in NCAA basketball history, this native of Bethlehem grew up admiring Chuck Bednarik.

Perhaps the most famous college basketball broadcaster ever, Billy Packer became synonymous with the sport while covering 35 Final Fours. Packer grew up in Bethlehem and graduated from Liberty High School. In what might be written off as a 'Bethlehem Thing,' Packer, like Chuck Bednarik, has been involved in several controversies throughout the years. In his case the topics have included, Mid-Major teams in the NCAA tournament, the number one ranking of St. Joseph's, and a misguided comment about Allen Iverson.

"When I was a kid growing up, the Eagles trained in Bethlehem. Bethlehem was a great sports town; guys who were successful like Chuck, Pete Carill, inspired us, gave us local kids people to look up to.'

'Guys like Chuck and Pete, they were the founders; they set the stage. We wanted to emulate what they did; we wanted to be as good as they were in taking it to another level.'

'Bethlehem was great growing up as a kid. We had three elementary schools, and they provided a great feeder system. You got

> **"It was not easy to make a team. My high school class had 800 kids; baseball, basketball, it was competitive to just to get a spot on those teams."**

into sports in 4th, 5th, 6th grade, and we had organized teams with coaches in baseball, basketball track and wrestling. Soccer was big in the Lehigh Valley. You had a lot of eastern Europeans, then people from South America and Mexico. It was excellent soccer. By the time you got into high school, you knew what it was like to be part of a real team.'

"There were always older guys like Chuck who were there to help you. They would taunt you in a good way, teach you to kick ass.'

'The best Chuck story I remember, was when he was asked how he ended up at the University of Pennsylvania. He said that when he was in the service and the war ended, he was given the choice of going to Chapel Hill to play football for a service team, or go home. He went to Chapel Hill, and got cut, so he went home with a job at the mill lined up.'

'He went to see his high school coach, and instead of working at the mill he was on the Penn sideline the next Saturday.'

'He told me, that if not for that he would have been at Bethlehem Steel that Monday. That's the way it was in Bethlehem.'

'Guys stayed home because there were good paying jobs at the mill. You played sports, but there were so many people to compete against. There were a lot of good athletes working at the mill and they provided great competition for the summer leagues.'

It was not easy to make a team. My high school class had 800 kids; baseball, basketball, it was competitive to just to get a spot on those teams. All the high schools were big; we had a great a rivalry with Allentown.'

'In Bethlehem, you didn't look for things to do, you played sports. All the steel towns from that era, 1940-1980; it's incredible how many major athletes came out of them.'

'Very few guys had parents who were academically oriented. Every guy on the south side; either his parents or grandparents came from the old country. At best, they were second generation American.'

'It wasn't a lack of motivation in the families. As a kid, you saw dad making decent wages at the mill, you work 20 years and retire. It was a big deal to have a job in the mill, and the parents passed on the discipline and hard work.'

Chuck goes to 8:00 am mass everyday at St. Joseph's Church in Limeport, PA.

'The last time I saw Chuck was in church. A big guy in a camel hair coat was kneeling in front of me saying his prayers. I sit back, and he's still kneeling. He was a big guy, he looked familiar, he could have been in his 40s, 50s or 60s. The collection plate came and he turned…it was Chuck, he's still a man.'

'If he went of the field now, he looks like he could still give them 30 seconds of absolute hell."

"Very few guys had parents who were academically oriented. Every guy on the south side; either his parents or grandparents came from the old country. At best, they were second generation American."

Pete Carill

The Princeton basketball coach and Bethlehem native formed a future Hall-of-Fame battery when he pitched to catcher Chuck Bednarik for the Mountaineer baseball team.

The legendary collegiate basketball coach was born in Bethlehem in 1930, and was an All-State hooper at Liberty High School. He played baseball and basketball with Chuck Bednarik and the Mountaineers. He is a member of the Basketball Hall of Fame for his work at Princeton Univerisity where he compiled a record of 514-261.

"Chuck Bednarik is a legend in Bethlehem, to say the least. He's always been accessible to his friends.'

'He used to come to the boys club to play basketball when we were growing up. On the Mountaineer baseball team I used to pitch to Chuck. If I knew what I knew today, I would have been more Eddie Lopat-like and thrown junk.'

"Chuck was a war hero. It was hard not to be proud of what he had accomplished."

'Chuck was a war hero. It was hard not to be proud of what he had accomplished. '

'In a steel town, athletics was important. We had a lot of great athletes, Bull Schweder, Hips Pecsek, Fritz Grgiovic. Bethlehem Steel employed about 37,000-38,000 people. On the southside we had the Slavic church, the Irish Church, the Italian Church, the Greek Church.

'There was one game we were playing the Eagles in basketball, Pete Pihos was their high scorer. I was fronting him and he got pissed off. He picked me up and moved me away and told Chuck 'you better get that little guy out of here.'

'Chuck could hit a baseball farther than anyone.

'We were playing at the Bethlehem Boys Club. He threw me through a door.'

'He was a hero, he is a living statue."

Carmen Palumbo

Coached the Mountaineer baseball team and operated a sports-themed bar in Bethlehem that Chuck Bednarik visited with other Eagles players.

Carmen Palumbo was manager for the Mountaineers baseball team in the late 1940s and early 1950s. He often had the luxury of trotting out a future hall-of-fame (albeit not in baseball) battery in pitcher Pete Carill and catcher Chuck Bednarik. Palumbo owned a popular sports bar in Bethlehem and also worked 36 years at Bethlehem Steel. Still spry at 92, he contributes his longevity to a few glasses of red wine every day.

"I knew Chuck most of his life, I played baseball with him. He lived on 5th Street, and played baseball, football and basketball at Liberty High.'

'Later Chuck and some of the guys came and asked me to manage the Mountaineer baseball team. After he joined the Eagles, they wouldn't let him catch any more; they were afraid he would bust up his hands or something. Pete Carill was one of my pitchers. He wanted to catch, but the Eagles wouldn't let him. They said if he was going to play baseball he had to be an outfielder, so he played the outfield. He was a good baseball player.'

'I owned the Sportsman Café at 5th and Buchanan from 1948-52. He used to come to the bar selling pierogies and Pio red wine. Whatever he was selling I bought.'

'After he signed with the Eagles, I used to drive with him to Philadelphia and meet the players. Sometimes he would bring them to the bar.'

'Once he brought one of the guys from the Eagles up with him to play on a Sunday. I went over the signals with the guy before the game. The guy, I can't remember his name, comes up with runners on first and second and I give him the signal to bunt. He ignores me and swings away and hits a home run.'

'I was steaming and I gave the guy hell. Everyone was laughing; I gave the guy hell. Chuck said, "What are you so angry about?" I said, "What the hell are you laughing about, this guy can't obey a signal."

'Chuck also played basketball with the 5th Ward in the City Catholic league. They were all good buddies, Chuck, Bill Werpehowsi, Pete Carill, Hips Pecsek and Fitz Toner, who is in the Moravian Hall of Fame.'

'Chuck is a hell of a good guy; you can't beat him. I said to him, 'How come you're living down in Coopersburg, you belong in Bethlehem?"

'He said, "They never respected me in Bethlehem."

Dan Fitzinger

This bulldozer operator had a newsworthy experience when Chuck Bednarik extricated him from his machine by the throat.

Dan Fitzinger unwittingly became a topic in the news when he was pulled from a bulldozer by Chuck Bednarik while clearing some trees in a lot adjacent to Bednarik's home in 1986. Fitzinger was doing his job into the early evening hours when Bednarik came over to inquire why he was working so late. When the answers were deemed unsatisfactory, Bednarik reached into the cab and extricated Fitzinger by the throat. Despite the experience, Fitzinger remains a Lehigh Valley-based heavy equipment operator today.

"Well, Sports Illustrated sort of made it sound like I was doing the provoking, and he was a tough guy tangling with a bulldozer operator.'

'Had I known how things would turn out, I would have spilled the beans. I could have had him on aggravated assault, but I didn't care about the charges. He threatened to kill me, but I didn't want to press charges. I just wanted satisfaction; I just wanted to go back to my job knowing that he wouldn't bother me again.'

'Sports Illustrated portrayed him as a tough guy. He's a big guy; I wouldn't do anything to provoke him.'

'He didn't like what was going on, that they were building houses behind his property. It had been one big open field.'

'It was about 6:30 in the evening and I was clearing trees. I had no intent of bothering him. I was just doing my job.'

'He threw rocks trying to get my attention. I was pushing a tree and he thought I was pushing the tree on him. He walked into the path. He's yelling, 'You son-of-a-bitch. You tried to kill me.'

"I got off. I didn't know who he was at the time. He grabbed me in a headlock. I was about 6', 170 pounds.'

'I realized how big he was and I wasn't going to try and do anything.'

'When I got home my neck was bleeding. My brother took me to the police. I didn't want to press charges; I just wanted to make sure he wouldn't bother me when I went back.'

'It ended up in court and I told the D.A., I don't want any money, don't want anything; that's not my style. I just don't want him coming after me again. They gave him a misdemeanor and a small fine. I just wanted it to go away.'

'Sports Illustrated ticked me off with the way they played it. Maybe the guy played too many games without a helmet. He was a

> **"He threw rocks trying to get my attention. I was pushing a tree, and he thought I was pushing the tree on him. He walked into the path. He's yelling, 'You son-of-a-bitch; you tried to kill me."**

bit on the edge, but that's what made him a great football player.'

'The next morning I wake up and they mentioned my name and they're talking about it on KYW radio. Dozens of people called me. Some were telling me about fights they got in with him.'

'By no means do I want to make him look like an animal. I know he's done a lot of good things for people, a lot of benefits for kids. I just didn't want people to think I was some tough guy bulldozer operator who instigated things."

Ed Kreilic

A teammate on the Mountaineers, Ed Kreilic remembers Chuck Bednarik not only as the best of the many great athletes who grew up in Bethlehem, but as a guy, even as an NFL star, would hook up with his old friends at every possible chance.

"Chuck was about five or six years ahead of me when I hung out with the Mountaineers. Did anyone mention about when he used to come up and play the City League games when he was with the Eagles?'

'He would get us tickets for the Eagles games and we'd all go down on the bus. When we got to the stadium, he'd be waiting for us.'

'When he was playing at Penn, you would see him at the Croatian Hall after every game. He'd hang out at the bar and listen to the band. My father, played bass in the band with Emma's father Steve Margetich.'

'My father and Steve grew up in the same town in Croatia, Ludoc, and came over on the same boat. You'd see them together outside St. Joseph's, the Croatian Church on 5th Street.'

'We had a lot of good athletes. Chuck,

Pete Carill. Hips Pecsek was as good an athlete as any of them. Even Chuck used to say that Hips was right up there with him. Hips was a natural, he could play any postion in any sport.'

'When Hips owned his hotel near Yosku Park, Chuck used to bring football players in with him all the time. The doorway was so small that these guys and Chuck had to walk through sideways to get in.'

'Chuck and I have always been on the same page. He speaks his mind and so do I. There have been many times when we both hear something and he just looks at me and smiles. He's either on your side or against you.'

'He was something to watch in basketball. He always towered over people and he just cleared the boards. No one touched a rebound when he was on the court. He took down everything. There was a team from Fountain Hill that had the Reyvitz brothers. They were all big guys, 6'5", 6'6", and when Chuck was on the floor there were bodies flying all over the court. He cleared the boards and they couldn't get their hands on anything."

A native of Bethlehem, his father and Chuck Bednarik's father-in-law were best friends, emigrating from Croatia together.

1993 Chuck poses with musicians at the Austrian Village

Frank Weaver

Frank Weaver was a member of the Mountaineers. He was a physician in the Allentown area for many year and now lives in Lancaster.

'I remember going down to Abington to go to the Austrian Village on Saturday night for the polka dances with Chuck and Dick Vermiel.'

'He enjoyed being with Vermiel; he used to protect him from the fans.'

'I knew Chuck from Liberty High in Bethlehem and played with him on the Mountaineers. He always had his opinions.'

'He was an excellent baseball player; pitcher, catcher, centerfield. He usually batted fourth. I batted fifth. He was very enthusiastic. He had to win or he was very upset.'

'Chuck was just a very excellent all around athlete, even in golf. He won the club championship at Whitemarsh.'

"He was always tough and a tough loser at everything. We were playing golf . . . He was losing and on the eight green, he took his wallet out of his pocket slammed in on the ground, and said, 'Here, take everything."

'I was three years younger than most of the Mountaineer guys. They were big guys alright. Chuck used to say. 'If there's a problem, I'll be right behind you.'

'We had a big rivalry with the Hungarian team and Bull Schweder. There was a loudmouth woman on the Hungarian side who used to yell at Chuck to get him upset. The madder he got, the harder he played.'

'He was always tough and a tough loser at everything. We were playing golf at Saucon Valley. He was losing and on the eight green, he took his wallet out of his pocket slammed in on the ground, and said "Here, take everything.'

'We went out to the Hall of Fame in his motor home. He kept it parked outside the Hall and we'd have happy hour in there. Mr. and Mrs. Gale Sayers would come by, Bart Starr, Frank Gifford. It was quite a reunion.'

'We played golf with Paul Brown. We lost and Chuck was really upset that Paul Brown beat us. He always wanted to win. If he didn't win, even if he came in second, it was a problem with Chuck. He showed his emotion when he didn't win."

Greg Stroble

Shortly after he accepted the job to become head wrestling coach at Lehigh University, Greg Stroble met the program's number one fan. Chuck Bednarik had been following Lehigh wrestling since the 1930s when he used to sneak into practices and matches.

When Chuck moved back to nearby Coopersburg, he again became a regular around the Lehigh team. He often traveled with the team to away matches and tournaments, and often brought many of the wrestlers back to his house for dinner or a swim.

"I really enjoyed having him around. I got the job in '95 and he walked in and introduced himself. I didn't know him. I'm from the west coast and didn't know much about east coast professional football.'

'He gave me the handshake and he said, 'Oh, you ruined my pinkie' and stuck those fingers in front of my face.'

'He came to practice quite a bit. I loved having him talk to the wrestlers. He always told them that wrestling was the toughest sport and he never could have done it. The guys enjoyed hearing him. We took him on road trips, it was good for the team.'

"It was important to let the guys on the team know who he was. He was a good motivational speaker. He talked about toughness and had stories of being shot at over Europe in World War II."

'Every year he would introduce himself. He was a legend, but they didn't know who he was. He would tell them about growing up on the south side of Bethlehem and sneaking into the wrestling matches. He helped at motivating the team.'

'I know Chuck enjoyed it and I liked giving him recognition. I believe in honoring the warriors of old. He volunteered, and I said that if Chuck wants to do it, we'll let him speak to the team.'

'It was important to let the guys on the team know who he was. He was a good motivational speaker. He talked about toughness and had stories of being shot at over Europe in World War II.'

'No one remembers or was even aware of one-platoon football. He would talk about what it took to play both ways. Many of our guys, especially the bigger ones, had played high school football and they could relate to what Chuck was talking about when he described playing two-ways for 60 minutes.'

'He asked my permission to give an award at our first banquet. He initiated and made up the "Gutsiest Wrestler" award. We didn't know about it. He was the sole judge. He talked about how impressed he was with wrestlers. He gave his criteria and said 'I picked this guy because at all the matches I went to, he did the job.'

'He could get pretty wild at matches. He yelled at officials. One match he got into a scuffle with a fan from the other school. I didn't see it, but I heard about it.'

'He blended in well with Lehigh wrestling fans. They're rowdy and he's pretty vocal."

Larry Kisslinger

This politically active native of Bethlehem led the effort to have the local youth football field renamed in honor of Chuck Bednarik.

Chuck with Larry Kisslinger at dedication of the Chuck Bednarik Field Complex, May 21, 2005.

arry Kisslinger is a lifelong resident of Bethlehem and graduate of Liberty High School. He has been active in the community most of his life, holding various elected positions, including City Councilman in Bethlehem and president of the School Board. He has produced and hosted talk shows on both local radio and television, and was the public affairs manager for Service Electric Cable TV. He has been active in recent years in trying to get Bethlehem to provide more recognition for Chuck Bednarik and was instrumental in having a local athletic complex renamed Chuck Bednarik Field Complex. He continues to badger local officials about better signage for the project, so it pays appropriate tribute to the city's most accomplished athlete.

"I've known Chuck from, let's see, the early '50s. My uncle, Carmen Palumbo, owned a bar in South Bethlehem, at 5th and Buchanan."

'I was a boy and Chuck used to come up to the bar and bring all the other Eagles players. They would come in to watch the Friday night fights and other sports.'

'In 1980 I ran for state rep, and Chuck came out and gave a speech and supported me at the Bethlehem Club. I'm pretty sure that was the only political speech he's ever given.'

'Another time I brought him to speak to the Lehigh football team. He talked about being a poor kid from the south side who made something of himself because of football.'

'That's one reason that I think he is so underappreciated in the Lehigh Valley. He was never one to get involved with politics or run around town. He's just not flamboyant. He's such a humble and fine guy.'

'All the old timers know of him, but the younger generations don't know who he is. But I can tell you anytime anyone asked him for anything, he did it, whether making an appearance or donating something for a fundraiser or charity.'

'I was instrumental in getting the renaming done. I can tell you the date it became official—May 21, 2005. Now you can't even see the sign from the road. For some reason they moved it inside and there is no recognition from the street.'

'Even the naming of the fields isn't enough. Chuck is top shelf. He doesn't get enough credit for what he has meant to this area. He should have a Rocky-like statue in town.'

'Everyone makes a big deal about Larry Holmes. But Holmes made millions and he had a lot of money to throw around. The most Chuck ever made was $28,000.'

'If he had the money to throw around town like Holmes, people would make a bigger deal of him. He deserves it just as much as Holmes.'

'I don't think people know just what to do for him. He is the best football player from this area and I think he was the best football player of all-time."

Paul Clymer

Paul Clymer has been the State Representative for the 145th District of Pennsylvania since 1980. He grew up in Bucks County as an Eagles fan, and took an opportunity to honor one of his boyhood heroes by initiating a special proclamation for constituent Chuck Bednarik a few years ago.

"I was the primary sponsor of having Chuck honored by the state as a Pennsylvania Sports Legend in 2003. He was an idol for many of us growing up in the Lehigh Valley. He was a household name and we looked to him as the personification of toughness and ruggedness.'

'He loved the game–offense and defense. As the younger generation, we tried to copy him.'

'The first time I met him, I was struck by that hand size, and the grip. As I got to know him, I was impressed with his strength of character and manly toughness. He had done it all, achieved all an athlete can achieve.'

'He is a person who is easy to talk to, but can be intimidating. '

"He was always exemplary, played hard, played by the rules. He never got into mind games and he played hard.'

'On February 10, 2003, along with Pat Brown, I presented him a citation as one of Pennsylvania's great athletes and people. It was the last time speaker Matt Ryan presided over the House. He passed away about a month later; it was a great parting gift for Matt Ryan. It made his last day in the House memorable.'

'I still have a scrapbook from the 1950s with a picture of Chuck from the Bulletin. I remember trying to collect his football cards as a kid. It was unique for the kids in the Lehigh Valley to have a local guy do so well. He's down to earth. The last time I saw him was at a meat counter at the Q-mart in Quakertown.'

'Chuck Bednarik should be recognized for what he is—the American Dream. His parents were immigrant steelworkers. His story is what America should be about. Where he came from, and where he got to is a perfect story."

This Pennsylvania State Representative grew up as a fan of Chuck Bednarik and, when in office, arranged for Chuck Bednarik to be honored by the state.

"He was always exemplary, played hard, played by the rules. He never got into mind games and he played hurt."

Rob Wonderling

Prior to being named President of the Greater Philadelphia Chamber of Commerce, Rob Wonderling was State Senator for the 24th District of Pennsylvania. He was first elected to this office in 2002. He also served as Secretary of Transportation under Governor Tom Ridge. While in office, Sen. Wonderling displayed a great appreciation for the war veterans in his district, including Staff Sgt. Charles Bednarik.

"The first memory of Chuck Bednarik that is seared in my brain comes courtesy of NFL Films. About the time I started to play football, I watched those black and white clips and I came to understand the violence of the game—Frank Gifford—and the reckless abandon. For me, he was someone that inspired my high school gridiron career.'

"In Chuck Bednarik, with concrete feet grounded in faith, family, and devotion to country, we have someone who has made sure to have a positive impact on society for decades."

'As state senator, I met Bednarik as a constituent in 2003 at Harrisburg. He was fully adorned in his Hall of Fame blazer. It was a brief ceremony recapping his service as a citizen of the state.'

'Like so many other people on first meeting, I remember that handshake; he engulfed my hand. It was like a human vice.'

'I got to know him in a ceremonial capacity when he was the featured keynote speaker at an assembly honoring World War II veterans at Lafayette College.'

'It was through that experience that I came to understand his robust citizenship. The crowd came—World War II vets and families—expecting him to offer NFL stories.'

'But, I never forget, it was amazing. He puts himself as one of those in the audience, just one of the guys who got the call to serve. He and the other veterans were just sharing war experiences.'

'I'm not a big guy on ceremony, but you have to give the soldiers their due. He and I were talking to the audience. I will never forget that. I had a one-dimensional view of him from films, but in this setting I got to view his citizenship.'

'The point here, is that he could have fallen back on his rubber chicken football speeches, but here his experience was their experience, and it deserved a more personal approach. It showed the muster of the man.'

'In modern day professional sports in America we give athletes that have feet of clay many opportunities to draw high salaries regardless of their indiscretions, violations, and lawlessness. In Chuck Bednarik, with concrete feet grounded in faith, family, and devotion to country, we have someone who has made sure to have a positive impact on society for decades. We will never have another one like him in Philadelphia."

Bill Margetich

This Bethlehem native is a Mountaineer teammate, brother-in-law, and lifetime chronicler of Chuck Bednarik's achievements.

WWII veteran Bill Margetich visits the Veterans Memorial in DC

Emma Bednarik's older brother, Bill Margetich, has long served as the unofficial family historian, as well as Chuck Bednarik's personal Boswell. Like James Boswell did for Dr. Samuel Johnson, Margetich has saved and recorded nearly everything that was ever written about Bednarik, and includes this information along with his personal memories and insights into letters and missives that he regularly sends to relatives and family friends. The long and lovely hand written letters often arrive as part of a package that includes old family photos, current photos of himself, and copies of news articles or book excerpts. The packages from "Uncle Willie" are always easily identifiable as the envelopes are frequently adorned with postscripts and addendums that simply could not be left out.

Now 87 years old, Bill has had an accomplished life. A disabled veteran of World War II, he served as a petty officer on the U.S. destroyer John W. Weeks, which was charged with shooting down Japanese kamikaze planes.

> **"When he was in training, he would run miles and Emma would run with him. She may not have run the whole way, but she was always there with him. He didn't have to lift weights. He would just go out in the yard and cut trees."**

Like all of the Margetiches, Bill was a talented musician and was playing with the family tamburitzan band the night Chuck met Emma at the Croatian Hall in Bethlehem. It was brother Bill who explained to Emma who this "All-American" was and why everyone was making a fuss over him.

A good athlete, Bill played on several Mountaineer teams with Bednarik. Following the war, Margetich used his G.I. Bill of Rights benefits to attend Moravian Prep, Moravian College, and the University of Miami Law School, where he graduated with honors.

Margetich was a noted investigator for the U.S. House of Representatives for many years. His first big assignment was as investigator in charge of the hearings regarding communist infiltration of U.S. harbors in the 1950s. He was later the investigator in charge of the hearings relating to Puerto Rican terrorism in 1960.

"The whole thing started when Chuck met my sister at the Croatian Hall on a beautiful Saturday evening. Chuck was at the dance with Bunny Bankowski and Fritz Grigovich while Emma was playing Tamburitzan music.'

'It was 10 cent beer night, Chuck was at the bar and he looks around and sees this beautiful Croatian girl playing with the band. I was the bass player and I saw everything as it happened.'

'Emma never knew of or heard of him. He put 25 cents in the jukebox, asked her for a dance, and they were married six months later.'

'We got home that night and Emma asked me who this guy was. Everyone was talking about the "All-American" and she had never heard of him.'

'I knew about him, but I didn't know him. When he started dating Emma, he asked me to join the Mountaineers. Chuck really ran that team.'

'Since that time, Emma has been his alter ego. He came down with pneumonia when he was with the Eagles; he was in bad shape and wouldn't go to the hospital. Emma called and had the doctor come to the house.'

'When he was in training, he would run miles and Emma would run with him. She may not have run the whole way, but she was always there with him. He didn't have to lift weights. He would just go out in the yard and cut trees.'

'When they got home after a game she would rub him down. He would be banged up and she'd ask him, "Why do you do this?"

'He'd say, "I want to be the best. I'm not tired at all".

'Chuck worships the ground Emma walks on. She's an old-time girl and Chuck always admired her. She was engaged prior to meeting Chuck. He was a nice guy, but was too involved with his family. He couldn't make a commitment. She broke it off the engagement with him after meeting Chuck.'

'He'd always have coffee and a candy bar before a game. He said he didn't want to be tired and that was all he needed.'

'He grew up watching wrestling at Lehigh. He used to watch them against schools like Iowa State and Oklahoma, and those were the best programs. He used to work out with the wrestlers and he could have been great.'

'There was a big, Italian guy who went to Penn and was the Ivy League heavyweight champion. He challenged Chuck to a match, said he'd take care of him, would make a fool of Chuck.'

'Chuck pinned him. The wrestling coach wanted Chuck to join the team. He could have been great at any sport at Penn, but Munger told him to concentrate on his studies.'

'The wrestling training helped him in football. In 1960, that was a wrestling hold he put on Jim Taylor. He never let go when he got someone in a wrestling hold. Taylor knocks Don Burroughs down and Chuck wrestles him to the ground.'

'Bobby Mitchell said, "Chuck Bednarik, that guy never lets go," and Jimmy Brown said Chuck's "the only guy who can bring me down alone."'

'He tackled Hornung and knocked him out of the championship game. Hornung said about Chuck, "He talks, but he backs up what he says."'

When Chuck and Paul Brown were inducted into the Hall of Fame, Brown said Chuck "is the best linebacker we ever faced."

Joe Stydahar was inducted the same day as Chuck and Paul Brown, and he said, "My favorite player on the field is Chuck Bednarik."

'He was great in basketball. The Mountaineers, we were champs three years in a row. Chuck could control the boards. He was a great player.'

'He came home from Penn rain, storm, snow for all the tough games. What is that, 60 miles each way?'

'He always came home and we usually won.'

'Chuck loves music. He used to attend the Croatian Hall to listen to the ethnic music. He wanted to play the accordion. Emma was a talented musician and she taught him notes.'

'Emma told him she would get him the top instructor to learn the accordion and, within a year, he knew 20 or 30 numbers.'

'Emma taught him and encouraged him. His family wasn't musically inclined, our family was.'

'He loved music and would play the accordion at any event. When the Eagles trained in Hershey, we used to go over to Steelton. They had a lot of Croatians. He'd play the accordion and harmonica. They loved him.'

'You know the Chuck Noll story, don't you?' Noll was a cocky son-of-a-bitch from Dayton, played guard for the Browns. He wanted to look like a hero, so he played dirty on kickoffs and punts.'

'One play Chuck (Bednarik) says to another guy, 'You get him low, and I'll get him high."

'They wiped out Noll and he didn't like it. He tells Chuck, "I'll see you after the game on the 50 yard line".'

'Chuck (Bednarik) waits for him and he doesn't come out. Chuck goes in to take a shower and Noll has the audacity to come into the locker room and says, "Where is Chuck Bednarik?"

'Noll goes into the shower and Chuck says "Here I am." Noll takes a swing and Chuck floors him with one shot. It cost him a $500 fine. Noll just wanted to make a name for himself by embarrassing Chuck. This happened in Cleveland.'

'Chuck was always the first guy out of the locker room. He'd take a quick shower and be out of there.'

'I saw a game against Penn State at Penn. The Penn State guys were saying all week that Chuck was over publicized. The game starts and they were going to run right at him all day. He stopped everything. One play Sam Tamburo, their All-American end is running with the ball and Chuck running diagonally across the field, caught up to him and stopped the touchdown.'

'Penn won 13-0, and the Penn State guys were all contrite after the game. They told him "You're great. We tried to run at you all day and you stopped us."

'He's a special guy. They don't make them like that anymore."

Bill Werpehowski Sr.

A Bethlehem native, Mountaineer teammate, former brother-in-law of Chuck Bednarik, and basketball star at Moravian College.

William Werpehowski was a Mountaineer teammate of Chuck Bednarik in Bethlehem. He was later a brother-in-law of Bednarik while married to Emma's sister Margaret. An outstanding athlete, Werpehowski held the career scoring record for the Moravian College men's basketball team for many years.

"He was the greatest football player I've ever seen.'

'Back in Bethlehem we started a team called the Mountaineers. Chuck lived on 5th Street. I lived on 6th. We were neighbors by a few blocks. He was one of my idols in both basketball and football.'

'When he came out of the service, we hung at Tony Kovac's grocery store at the corner of 5th and Hayes. We had a gang of friends—Smelly Bukvics was our coach, and we started the Mountaineers basketball team. We were a formidable team.'

'When Chuck was at Penn, he used to come up for all the big games. He was a hell of a good basketball players. He had a great year in high school, playing with guys like Paul Calvo and Allie Saemmeer.'

'He was a great rebounder in basketball, very agile. He always ended up in the right spot.'

'We also played baseball in the Catholic League. Francis Buechin formed the league and it had about eight or 10 teams.'

'Chuck was the catcher for the Mountaineers. He used to work out with the A's. Jimmy Dykes was a coach and he became a good friend of Chuck's. Dykes used to tell him he was wasting his time playing football; he should be playing major league baseball.'

'You know, the Margetiches had a family orchestra. I met my wife Muncy in 1948 while I was playing basketball at Moravian College. I played on the Mountaineer baseball team with Chuck and I met Muncy, Emma's sister, at their wedding. I got married in '51.'

'The Margetiches loved music, especially the Duquesne Tamburitzans. They had a band — the father Steve, brother Willie, Uncle Johnny, Emma, and Muncie played the piano and sang. I played the accordion and we taught Chuck how to play the harmonica.'

'I used sheet music. I wasn't that good. I knew about 12-18 songs. Chuck said, "I'm going to learn to play the accordion."'

'He loved Slovenian and Croatian music. He loved to go to the Austrian Village, have beer and listen to the music. He was a fun-loving guy.'

'I would go to his house in Abington in the morning and we'd go to the White House in Atlantic City for steak sandwiches. We'd get up early, go to the White House, then go to mass. He's a beautiful man.'

'He loved wrestling. We used to meets at places like Cornell, Syracuse, Penn State, Army, Navy and the Palestra. He used to practice with the wrestling team at Penn. He didn't wrestle competitively because he could never face the reality of being pinned. The coach wanted him to wrestle, but he couldn't stand the thought of being pinned.'

'I had some wonderful years with Chuck. I've always loved him and Emma is just a fantastic girl.'

'Chuck came around at the wrong time in life. Vince McNally was tight. Chuck was making All-Pro every year, and they

> **"Chuck came around at the wrong time in life. Vince McNally was tight. Chuck was making All-Pro every year, and they were paying him about $10,000-$14,000. Chuck had been in the league about four or five years, and McNally told him before the season that he was going to have to cut his salary by $500."**

were paying him about $10,000-$14,000. Chuck had been in the league about four or five years, and McNally told him before the season that he was going to have to cut his salary by $500.'

'Chuck was so angry. When he got to training camp, he was like a tyrant. He was hitting and taking it out on everyone. He beat up Jesse Richardson for goofing off in drill; Chuck just knocked him out. He was killing people in preseason and McNally came over and told him to calm down.'

'McNally told him he would give him his $500 back and a $500 raise. His feelings had been hurt and he had to prove to McNally that he was wrong and that he was a cheap son-of-a-bitch.'

'Chuck really loved the little guy. After he retired he used to go down to a famous seafood restaurant in Philadelphia, Bookbinders. The owner, Johnny Taxin, gave Chuck a card saying that he could eat there for free with his family any time. Chuck said, "I can't do that." He didn't want to take advantage. He's a one-in-a-million guy.'

'All of the Mountaineers were great guys. One game the final of the Eye Glass Tournament, the Mountaineers were playing Allentown. Their star was Bill Wanish, who had been an All-State player. Bethlehem lost four games Chuck's senior year, three of them to Allentown. Our coach, Smelly Bucvics, told Chuck to get even with Wanish and beat the hell out of him.'

'He did, and we won the game. Chuck and I both felt like a million dollars, and Smelly was the proudest guy in the world.'

'I'll tell you something about Chuck he was the first and only guy I knew in high school to lift weights. He used to go over to the Bethlehem Boys Club. The Boys Club changed both of our lives, made something out of us. It was because of the Boys Club that we weren't bums on the street. Guys like Johnny Betts taught us to be gentlemen and made something out of us.'

'Do you know the story about the basketball game against Hazleton when Chuck incited the biggest brawl anyone's ever seen?'

'Bethlehem was playing Hazleton at the Palestra in Allentown. It was a night game and Ed Brominksi was the referee. There was three seconds to play and Hunky Moran intercepts the ball in the backcourt and dribbles in for the winning shot. The Bethlehem fans erupted. They were so upset that the basketball was allowed that they were throwing all kinds of food—apples, sandwiches, you name it—on the court. It was hilarious, all of the newspapers—all the Bethlehem Steel people throwing their sandwiches on the court. The steel workers were going to work straight from the game, so they had their lunch pails with them.'

'It all starts because Chuck is so upset about the outcome. He goes under the stands and knocks out Hazleton's star center, a kid named Red Meinhold. The brawl that broke out was legendary. People talked about it for years.'

'Chuck's a funny guy. I'm refereeing a game between the Mountaineers and Lehigh Tavern. Chuck and Pete Carill are on the team. It's a tight game and I make an out of bounds call. Chuck is guarding the guy as he throws the ball in and he turns to me and says, "If we lose this f'-ing fame I'm going to kill you." I laughed my ass off.'

'When he was a member at Saucon Valley, they were holding Seniors Event one year. Chuck was in the clubhouse with the golfers. He sees Bruce Crampton at a table and he goes over and says, "How you doin', I'm Chuck Bednarik." Crampton looks up at him and says, "I don't talk to anyone I don't know."

'Chuck is angry. He's at the second hole and Chuck gets on a bridge as Crampton is coming by and he yells down at him, "You dirty no-good, son-of-a-bitch." The whole club was embarrassed.'

'I remember going down to the games at Franklin Field with Chuck. We used to buy sandwiches outside the stadium. The guy's pitch was "These sandwiches are untouched by human hands; my wife made them this morning."

'I remember when the Giants came down right after the Gifford game. Charley Conerly had been saying terrible things about Chuck all week. First play of the game, Chuck looked over at him and said, "I'm going to break your head."

Bill Werpehowski Jr.

A nephew of Chuck Bednarik and a long time professor at Villanova University.

William J. Werpehowski Jr. is a native of Bethlehem and a nephew of Chuck and Emma Bednarik. He is the Director of the Center for Peace and Justice Education at Villanova University.

"We knew who Uncle Chuck was as we were growing up and we were very proud. My father, Bill Sr., and uncle, Bill Margetich, impressed upon the children what a great thing it was to have him in the family. I really wised up to his career in 1960. Dad got season tickets for the two of us for Chuck's last two years, 1961 and '62.'

'It was a terrific family and Uncle Chuck became very enamored by grandpop's music; he loved the family band. We all participated and he would play the harmonica.'

'I knew what a great player he was while growing up and I have two football-related memories of visiting at his house in Abington. The first was watching the Super Bowl with him and my dad in his room and I remember another Sunday when "Come here, I have something to show you," and it was the letter announcing that he had been elected to the Hall of Fame.'

'We had a lot of low-flying Bethlehem celebrities who served as sports heroes. My dad was a local celebrity; he was the first local college player to score 1,000 points while he was at Moravian College, and he held their scoring record for 14 years. We also had Pete Carill, who is also close friends with my dad.'

'We grew up with a sense of the Bethlehem celebrities. My dad and Pete Carill never let me forget what Chuck meant to our generation in serving the country and coming back from war. They made sure that we know the importance of the Greatest Generation.'

'People knew about my relationship to Chuck and would ask me about him, but I can't say they banged down the door looking for autographs.'

'I remember standing outside Franklin Field, getting autographs—Tommy McDonald, Pete Retzleff, Maxie Baughn…'

'Franklin Field was always a great experience. The Eagles almost won the East again in '61, but Don Chandler took a dive and got a phony roughing the kicker call the last game of the year and the Giants won the division.'

'1962 wasn't a great year, but I remember Chuck getting a game ball for stopping Jimmy Brown on the goal line to save a game against the Browns. The last home game against Pittsburgh, he intercepted two passes.'

'The fact that he was a celebrity was a big thing for me and Chuck was big in the context of Bethlehem.'

'Everything in Bethlehem revolved around steel, sports, church, and music. There was pride and a lot of love for the city. It might not have seemed like a big deal at the time, but in looking back you realize how important growing up there was to you.'

'It was a special place. Pete Carill used to say about the Bethlehem Boys Club that it was the only place where you would leave the balls under the net at night and they'd still be there the next day.'

'There were so many great athletes—Hips Pecsek…Chuck used to say he was the best athlete of all. Rocco and Paul Calvo, my dad, Pete Carill.'

'I remember playing basketball with Chuck. I weighed about 155-160 pounds. It seemed like I was a third his size. I was tall and I played him in the paint and in the post. He was a great passer, terrific in the post, could shoot the hook with either hand…he had formidable skills. He played with his back to the basket and I remember how fluid and smooth he was.'

'I have a few specific memories of Uncle Chuck.'

'One story I like to tell occurred at Christmas, I believe during his final season in 1962. Memory has it that he had just retired. He came over with his family to our grandparents' house for Christmas Eve or Christmas Day. '

'Chuck looked great. He was in a suit and we were giving out gifts. There was a big gift for me. Chuck and Emma had gotten me a Philadelphia Eagles kiddie uniform.'

'I went in the bedroom to put it on, and when I came out Chuck said, 'you look great, just like a player…you look ready to take on a forearm shiver.'

'I said, "What's a forearm shiver?"'

'He flicked his arm and gave me a shot that lifted me off the ground and knocked me into the Christmas tree. It was hilarious. I remember being told that his forearm barely moved.'

'A more general memory of Chuck… I was not a terrific athlete; I did alright, had an okay high school career. I was a brain, always straight A's, knew I would go to an Ivy League college.'

'What I never forget is that he was nothing but supportive—enthusiastically supportive—of what I was doing.'

'I told Uncle Charlie that I wanted to go to grad school and teach at a college.'

'He said, "Teachers are a goddamned dime a dozen. You're so smart you should be a brain surgeon."'

'I always felt he was very supportive and respective, even with music. I played the piano. I was somewhat successful, played a few concerts. He bragged about me as a piano player. He always made me play and when I finished he would say, 'Play something harder."

'He was keen on excellence, wherever he found it. He always got excited about whatever I was doing, and I was always grateful for that. Not many in my family knew how supportive he was. It made me feel good that he marveled at my achievements.'

'Another memory occurred at his Hall of Fame enshrinement in 1967. I was 14 and it was the best time of my life.'

'We got there and they had his uniform on display and we were with Emlen Tunnell, Bobby Layne, Paul Brown and all of those greats.'

'We were staying at a nice motel with a pool. It was a hot day and, after the ceremony, we went for a swim in the pool before dinner.'

'My cousin Billy (Margetich) was skimming pennies across the pool and one of them catches me in the left eye. It hurt. I was screaming.'

'Chuck made sure I saw the team physician and got me to the hospital. I had to stay perfectly still; I was barricaded in the car on the way back so that I wouldn't move.'

'My cousin Billy felt bad, but I felt bad because I thought this was messing up this special day, this event. They were playing the Hall of Fame game thaf night, and my dad had to stay with me in the hotel room.'

'I had to miss the events and I was feeling lousy and getting teary because my dad had to stay back with me.'

"Everything in Bethlehem revolved around steel, sports, church and music. There was pride and a lot of love for the city. It might not have seemed like a big deal at the time, but in looking back you realize how important growing up there was to you."

"I get a phone call before the game, "This is Uncle Chuck, what a goddamned fluke accident that was. I could have been standing at the pool all day skimming pennies and not hit you with one. Don't worry, stay with your dad and listen to the game, you're a man," and that meant a lot to me.'

'There was the time I was at his house in Abington with my cousin Billy. Billy was a quarterback on his high school team; this must have been 1969 or '70. Chuck says to him "Let me give you a pro snap."'

'Billy gets under center and the ball explodes into his hands. He must have had one hand completely flat and the ball broke his fingers."

(Standing) Chuck and David; (sitting) Charles Sr., and Mary

David Bednarik

Chuck Bednarik never had a son but, at 21 years his junior, younger brother David Bednarik had the closest family experience to what it would be like to grow up in the shadow of a legend. A talented athlete, David gave up football to concentrate on basketball in high school and, after a fine schoolboy career, he went on to be a member of the LaSalle College team.

David remained in the Bethlehem area until about 10 years ago, when he moved to Elkton, Maryland.

He has been a manager for various manufacturing companies and has been active as a deacon and elder for his church.

He lost his wife Cindy to cancer six years ago and has remained single. His daughter Joy is a fifth-grade teacher in Maryland.

"Being the brother of Chuck Bednarik had advantages and disadvantages. As a kid growing up, it was great having a big brother who played football. I was interested in sports at a young age and it was such a neat thing.'

'Once a year my family would go down to a game at Connie Mack Stadium and then Franklin Field. I loved it.'

'I was at the championship game. I remember it well. I was disappointed that Chuck didn't get MVP, not just because he's my brother. A lot of people were disappointed. He played the whole game. He made the winning tackle. Nothing against Van Brocklin, but he had an interception returned for a touchdown and he really didn't play that well. Chuck should have had it.'

'I remember another game. I had to be young, about 11 or 12. We were outside the stadium after the game waiting for Chuck. I was with the family. There were about five or six of us.'

'Chuck comes out, then he goes back in, say's he'll be back in a few minutes.'

'He comes back and tells us that there was a guy on the other team he had issues with and he went over and punched him. Why, I don't remember.'

'On the one hand, it was nice having a brother like Chuck. A lot of kids thought it was great, but other resented it, were jealous, you know, "Who's he? Thinks he's a big deal because his brother's a football player.'

'In sports, there was some, "his name's Bednarik, let's see what he's like."

'Once I got to high school, I played football and basketball; I loved basketball. I gave up football as a junior. Chuck didn't say anything, but my brother Jeep, who was a football player too, was upset.'

'There were people who said I chose basketball to get away from football and get away from Chuck's shadow, but I truly just liked basketball better.'

'I think when a lot of people heard my name, because of the age difference, didn't think I was a brother of Chuck. They would think he was an uncle or another older relative.'

'When I was playing basketball, whenever I got a nice write up, they would refer to me as "Dave 'Brother of Chuck' Bednarik." I used to joke that was my middle name, 'Brother of Chuck.'

'What I remember best was the holidays. Every Christmas, Christmas Eve, Chuck would come up to Bethlehem with Emma and the kids; all the brothers and sisters and families would get together. My parents loved it. It was like a revolving door. One year Chuck dressed as Santa I thought it might be him, but I was afraid to be sure.'

> **"As a kid I watched the Eagles on TV and they didn't have a good team every year. What got me was whenever the other team had the ball, all you would hear is "tackled by Bednarik."**

'It was neat in a way because I was so much younger. I was babied. I would go to Chuck's house for a few days and I always had playmates, my nieces and nephews. In fact, I had nieces and nephews who were older than me.'

'Our house was like the typical eastern European home. My mother took care of the house, my father went out and brought home the money. My mother always decided what we would do. My father had his three shots of whiskey a day. I don't think I ever saw him drunk. He said the whiskey was good for him, it helped his metabolism.'

'My father was strict. The older kids tell me I got off easy. He was tough on them, especially Jeep. He got in trouble with my father a lot. They said Chuck was the good boy. By the time I was born, my dad had mellowed. They would tell me, "You got it easy."

'He loved being home. When I got older he would come to visit, stay maybe an hour and say "let's go home now." He always wanted to get back to his castle.'

'As far as Chuck's bitterness, I remember the newspapers started to pick up on the resentment, not long after he retired and the $100,000 contracts were getting started. You

would hear about it from him, what this player is getting.'

'In a way I can't blame him. Those guys are really specialized now. He played 60 minutes.'

'It's a shame, and I've said this to people, but it seems Chuck is remembered for just two things: going two ways in the championship game and Frank Gifford. It's sad. For all the great things he did, those are the only two people talk about. If he had played in New York, they would have built a monument for him.'

'As a kid I watched the Eagles on TV and they didn't have a good team every year. What got me was whenever the other team had the ball, all you would hear is "tackled by Bednarik." As a kid, it bothered me, why aren't the other players making tackles? He was always around the ball. I may have been biased because I was his brother, but I remember thinking, he was always in on the play.'

'I remember when he was doing the sports news on Channel 6. He was good when he was spontaneous.

'Once, I remember he had Mike Caruso of Lehigh on as a guest and he put him in a stranglehold. It was very funny.'

'I've had people say to me many times, 'I heard your brother speak at a banquet and how terrific he was.'

'I remember riding in to games with him and he'd be smoking most of the way. Did you know he smoked? It was nervous anticipation. He didn't have much patience driving to the game."

> **"As far as Chuck's bitterness, I remember the newspapers started to pick up on the resentment, not long after he retired and the $100,000 contracts were getting started. You would hear about it from him, what this player is getting."**

Siblings: Richie, Jeep, Chuck, Betty, Mary, David (Chuck's grandson Sean Davis in back)

Jeep Bednarik

A brother of Chuck Bednarik, Jeep was a renowned high school and college football coach in the Lehigh Valley.

The eldest of Chuck Bednarik's two surviving brothers, John "Jeep" Bednarik played football at Moravian Prep and at the College of William and Mary, where he earned honorable mention All-American status. He became a successful high school coach at several schools in the Lehigh Valley, most notably Dieruff, where he had five winning teams in six seasons. He also served as an assistant at Lehigh University.

He recalls that if not for a failed English class in 9th grade, his brother might have never played organized football.

"As kids, we were all raised to go to Catholic school for the first eight years. In ninth grade, my mother made Chuck go to BeCa (Bethlehem Catholic) High. They didn't have a football program, only basketball, and Chuck wasn't happy. He failed an English class that he could have made up in summer school, but he didn't want to do it.'

'He wanted to transfer to Liberty to play football, but my mother said "No." My father stepped in and said, "I boss, if he vant to play football, I sign."

'Without Pop getting involved, there might have been no football for my brother. If he had passed that English class, my mother might have made him stay. "I, boss;" that's what got Chuck into Liberty.'

'My father was the boss whenever he was home. With him working three shifts at the steel company, we spent most of the time with mom. But he was the boss when he came home.'

'My father had a shot or two of whiskey when he got up in the morning. He'd have a couple of shots before a meal, a shot or two after a meal. He never drank to the point of getting drunk, but that was the way he worked.'

'He always took a flask when he went to the Eagles games. Whenever Chuck made a play he'd take a shot, hold the flask up and say, "That be for my son."'

'I had a lot of pressure playing football because of who my brother was. Opponents would size me up and say "You're Chuck Bednarik's brother; let's see what you're made of."'

'In college I had a sprained ankle and we were playing Wake Forest. I missed the first half and my sub at right tackle wasn't doing real well. The coach asked me if I could go in for the second half.'

'First play they ran a 145, my play, right over me. I moved my guy out of the way for a huge gain and he comes over and takes a swing at me. His name was Bob Gaona, and he swung at me so hard that if he had connected, I would have become the first Sputnik missile. He played for the Steelers and one game against the Eagles he asks Chuck, "Is Jeep your brother?—I owe him one."'

'When we were kids we used to fill socks with leaves, paper, anything we could, and that was our football.'

'Did you ever hear about the first real football we ever had? Lehigh used to have an upper and lower field, and at night we used to climb the fence and play football on the field. There was an old man named Brickley who used to chase us away. One night there was a football left lying around and Chuck grabbed it. That was the first time we had a real football to play with.'

'I didn't even know that Chuck was going to Penn and playing football. The first time I ever hear about him playing football, I was stationed overseas in Japan.'

'One of the radio guys called to ask me, "Do you have a guy named Bednarik playing football; this guy named Chuck Bednarik is playing at Penn" That's how I found out Chuck was playing in college.'

'I guess I did alright as a coach. My only losing season at Dieruff was the last and we had no talent that year. I gave them the first winning seasons they ever had.'

'The biggest thing that I enjoyed; the only team that I really wanted to beat was Liberty. We won six of six against them.'

'When that job was open, I wanted it in the worst way. I had never asked Chuck for help, but I called and asked him to see what he could do to get me that job. "He called to tell me that they were giving it to some guy from a military academy. Whenever we played them, I used to carry a fake gun into the locker room and shout, "They're coming for us!" That was the only game I really wanted.'

'I go to a barber in Allentown who is strictly a football fan. We discuss all of the great players and coaches who have come out of the Lehigh Valley in the past 50 years. We agree, you know who has had the most overall talent come out of the Valley the last 50 years?—Liberty."

"He always took a flask when he went to the Eagles games. Whenever Chuck made a play he'd take a shot, hold the flask up and say, "That be for my son."

Jack McCallum

In 1977, while working as a young sportswriter for the Bethlehem Globe Times, Jack McCallum co-authored with the eponymous subject of the book, "Bednarik Last of the 60 Minute Men."

It would be a little strong to say that I was destined to write Chuck's biography. But only a little. On Christmas Eve, 1960, I reached into my stocking and pulled out a white envelope in which were what appeared to be tickets to the NFL championship game at Franklin Field one week hence.

"These aren't real, are they, Dad?" I asked with bated breath.

"Sure are," he said.

My father, who owned a small grocery store in Mays Landing, a small South Jersey town about 60 miles from Philadelphia, had secured them through a meat company contact that serviced Franklin Field. And so I watched, live, wide-eyed and shivering, as Eagles defeated the Green Bay Packers 17-13. From that moment on, I felt somehow connected to that team.

Two memories stand out, both of them involving leather-lunged fans. After Norm Van Brocklin completed a long pass to Tommy McDonald, the latter gathering it in with outstretched hands, a man stood up, held his hands apart approximating McDonald's stretch, and yelled, "That's the difference between a ham-and-egger and a real quarterback! Right dere!"

"After Norm Van Brocklin completed a long pass to Tommy McDonald, the latter gathering it in with outstretched hands, a man stood up, held his hands apart approximating McDonald's stretch, and yelled, "That's the difference between a ham-and-egger and a real quarterback! Right dere!""

The other occurred just after the game ended with Chuck resting atop the padded body of Packers' fullback Jim Taylor. "There's the toughest son-of-a-bitch who ever put on a uniform," a guy said, pointing onto the field, his eyes misty with triumph. "They'll never be anyone like Concrete Charlie."

Eleven years later, Fate placed me, a recently minted college graduate, in the boyhood home of Concrete Charlie. I heard stories about him from the time I arrived at the Bethlehem Globe-Times, which was located on the south side of the Christmas City, not far from Chuck's old stomping grounds. I fell in love with the ethnic color of the steel-mill town—its myriad churches, its small, neat row houses, its fierce Old World pride. Chuck had been officially gone from Bethlehem for three decades by then, but he was—and still remains—the quintessence of South Bethlehem, or Betlam as it's short-cutted by the citizenry.

I first met him in the pressbox at a Lehigh wrestling tournament. He was standing up and cheering the home team like a wide-eyed freshman. Man, I remember thinking, that is some unusual guy. And so a thought came to me: Book. Chuck's personality intersected with my literary ambition.

I could go on and on about what it was like to work with Chuck, but most of the tales would come down to his incredible intensity. You don't need to hear that again. So I will go in another direction and mention that he actually made the project remarkably easy. Yes, he can be overbearing and intimidating. But he was extremely fair and respectful to me, even though I was a 26-year-old nobody with longish hair. Early on, I showed him a few chapters that included a few curse words.

"I don't want to put those words in," Chuck said flatly. "It makes me look bad."

"Chuck, people know you, they know how you talk. It wouldn't make any sense to have you sound like a librarian," I told him.

It wasn't that simple. But eventually Chuck saw it my way, and much of his colorful language was left in.

During my research, I noticed how enthusiastically everyone responded to Chuck and had some story about the man and his aging-warrior aura. But what he meant to his hometown didn't become clear to me until the day of a book signing at a downtown

Chuck, Mrs. Betty McCallum and Jack, 1977

Bethlehem bookstore in November of 1977, shortly after Last of the Sixty-Minute Men was released. I realized I wouldn't be the main attraction, of course, but I was nervous. An author's biggest nightmare is no one showing up for a book signing.

No need to worry. When I arrived, the line to get into the store snaked around the corner on Main Street.

My first son had been born a few months earlier, and he spent the day being passed around from lap to lap, from my mother (who came up from Mays Landing), to my wife, to various in-laws … and to Chuck. Jamie looked like a doll sitting on Chuck's big knee. Hundreds and hundreds of people bought books and got autographs. They were there mostly to see Chuck, but they spent some time with me, too, and, in retrospect, there is no doubt that the book conveyed a legitimacy upon me in the town. Before I was just a sports writer covering the local high school teams; now I was an author. I never got a chance to tell Chuck how much that day mean to me, both personally and professionally.

Never has a year passed since then that someone doesn't ask me about the book. If they want one, I send it to them. About eight years ago, my supply had dwindled to a precious few, and I called Chuck to see about replenishment. For years—nay, decades—

after publication, he had been carting them around in the trunk of his car.

"Okay," said Chuck. "It'll be twenty dollars a book."

For a moment I thought he was kidding. Then I realized he wasn't.

"Chuck, I wrote the damn thing," I said.

We finally settled on ten dollars. I'm not making that up.

In the three decades since "Last of the Sixty-Minute Men," I've written a few more books, won the odd award here or there, and managed to have a little bit of a rep in the sports writing business. But I have as much pride in that biography of Chuck as anything I've ever done. I was young and unknown, and Chuck was an icon. I thank him for the opportunity he gave me.

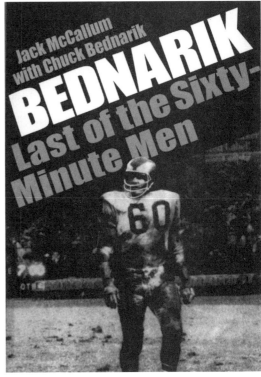

World War II Honoree

World War II Veteran

Charles P. 'Chuck' Bednarik

BRANCH OF SERVICE
U.S. Army Air Forces

HOMETOWN
Coopersburg, PA

HONORED BY
Wife Emma & Friends of American Heroes

ACTIVITY DURING WWII
SERVED WITH THE 467TH BOMB GROUP, 8TH AIR FORCE AS A WAIST GUNNER IN THE B-24 LIBERATOR BOMBER. FLEW 30 MISSIONS OVER GERMANY. EARNED THE AIR MEDAL WITH 4 OAK LEAF CLUSTERS AND THE EUROPEAN-AFRICAN-MIDDLE EASTERN CAMPAIGN RIBBON WITH 5 BATTLE STARS.

Chapter | **two**

WWII

The Consolidated B-24 Liberator was the new aerial machine rushed into production for World War II. An updated, modernized version of the famed B-17 Flying Fortress, it remains today the most widely produced U.S. Military aircraft. While the B-24 offered a higher top speed and greater range, it caused much concern for flight crews because of its tendency to catch fire. The placement of the fuel tanks all along the upper fuselage, combined with lightweight construction. made the aircraft vulnerable to damage and contributed to the bleak nickname of "The Flying Coffin." This was supposed to be an improvement over the B-17, but the crews who flew them had a hard time buying into that logic.

Among its fighting features were .50 caliber M2 Browning machine guns. These guns were usually placed in the hands of the strongest members of the crew and were designed to take on attacking enemy fighters. Strong hands and a true grip were not the only requirements; belt gunners also needed the presence of mind and nimble dexterity to quickly clear a jam with enemy gunners bearing down. A fumble here and the ballgame is over.

Chuck Bednarik's first job out of high school was as a dual gunner-top turret or waist-on a B-24 Liberator, flying for the 467th Bomb Squad of the 8th Air Force out of Rackheath, England.

Bednarik reported to Fort Indiantown Gap in Central, Pennsylvania in July 1943. He was assigned to the Army Air Force. Gunner wasn't his first job choice, but that was the role he settled into during training.

"I wanted to be a pilot," Bednarik recalled, "but I'd get frustrated with all the piston A goes here, piston B goes there stuff. When it came to mechanics, I flunked. They told me "you aren't cut out to be a pilot, and asked if I would like to go to gunnery school. I was just a young kid, and I had never had a gun in my hand, but I said sure."

Gunnery training was provided in Florida and continued in Lincoln, Nebraska, where the B-24 crews were formed. Next stop was Gowen Field in Boise, Idaho where they learned how to fly in formation and perform practice bombings. Final training for the 467th was applied in Ireland and Wales, and it was off to the permanent base in Rackheath, 15 miles off the English Channel, where they reported to Col. Al Showers.

At Rackheath, long days were spent on practice bombing missions, flying formation, short field takeoffs and landings. It was from this home base that all bombing missions would originate.

Mission days began with a 4:00 a.m. wakeup call. After breakfast, the crew would report to a briefing room

The 467th Bomb group, 8th Air Force

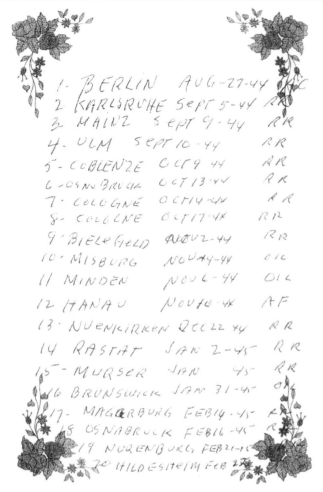

1. BERLIN AUG-27-44
2. KARLSRUHE SEPT 5-44
3. MAINZ SEPT 9-44 RR
4. ULM SEPT 10-44 RR
5. COBLENZE OCT 9 44 RR
6. OSNABRUCK OCT 13-44 RR
7. COLOGNE OCT 14-44 RR
8. COLOGNE OCT 17-44 RR
9. BIELEFIELD NOV 2-44 RR
10. MISBURG NOV 4-44 OIL
11. MINDEN NOV 6-44 OIL
12. HANAU NOV 10-44 AF
13. NUENKIRKEN DEC 22 44 RR
14. RASTAT JAN 2-45 RR
15. MURSER JAN 45 RR
16. BRUNSWICK JAN 31-45 O
17. MAGERBURG FEB 14-45
18. OSNABRUCK FEB 16-45
19. NURENBURG FEB 21-45
20. HILDESHEIM FEB

21. HALLE FEB 27 45 RR
22. INSBRUCK MAR 1-45 RR
23. STUTTGART MAR 4-45 RR
24. RILNABRUK MAR 8-45
25. OSNABRUCK MAR 9-45
26. BRUNSWICK MAR 21-45 RR
27. LECHFELD APR 9-45 AF
28. REGENSBURG APR 17-45 OIL
29. KHRLSBAD APR 17 45 RR
30. ZWIESEL APR 20-45 RR

Handwritten note that Chuck wrote listing all thirty of his bombing missions

where a large map of Europe would be decorated with a stripe of black tape to mark the flight route and final destination. A trip to Berlin or another city in eastern Germany meant 10 hours or more in the air.

Bednarik flew his first mission over Berlin on August 27, 1944. In almost any other year he would have been spending his 19th summer in a college training camp. The required 30 missions were fulfilled before the age of 20.

Every flight came with a prayer that your pilot was more skilled than the Nazi soldiers who were operating the anti-aircraft guns below. For Bednarik, a successful mission meant he was able to stand up and count the bullet holes in the plane after it landed; thirty missions and he never counted less than 100 flak holes.

The act of touching ground didn't mean the mission was safely over. At least three times, Bednarik scampered away from crash landings, like the one where his flak-ridden aircraft skidded off the runway.

"I was in the waist, and I jumped out a window as soon as the plane stopped. I didn't want to be around if it blew up," recalled Bednarik.

The first mission was to Berlin, the heavily fortified Nazi capital. The 11 hour roundtrip flight began on a typically foggy morning. Prior to that flight, Bednarik started a ritual that he was to repeat before every mission.

"I went to the chaplain and got a blessing before we took off, and I did that before every mission. That first mission was that the most anxiety I ever had, oh yeah.'

'Berlin was always rough. That was the capital, loaded with anti-aircraft, all the big guns. Talk about anxious, all the flak, the Fokker fighter planes in the area. Three times we went into Berlin, and three times we came out safely. I'm lucky to be sitting here today."

Between missions they would take a three day pass and go into London or nearby Norwich. "We'd go in and hooch it up," recalled Bednarik. "We were treated well; the English people really respected us."

One of the scariest flights occurred when an engine was knocked out on the return trip over Germany. Bednarik's crew could not keep up with their bomb group formation and proceed back to England alone. They dropped the heavy bomb they were carrying on a "target of opportunity" and radioed for help. Two unidentified fighter planes approached, and it wasn't until they were much closer that they realized they were United States P-51 fighter escort planes.

By the end of 1944, Bednarik had completed about half of his required flights. Just before Christmas, his crew left on a mission. they returned, but two of the crews they shared the barracks with did not.

"I prayed for those guys every day for years. To go out on Christmas Eve and not return."

As he did after every flight, Bednarik kissed the ground and thanked God for bringing him down safely. After the 30th and final mission, he swore that he would never get in a plane again.

The final mission was April 20, 1945 over the city of Zwiesel. For service to his country, Charles P. Bednarik earned the Air Medal with four oak leaf clusters and the European-African-Middle Eastern Campaign Ribbon with five battle stars. The 467th Bomb Group was awarded a Presidential Citation for being the first bomb group to have all three squadrons drop their bombs within a 1000 foot circle. This occurred over Regensburg, a week before Bednarik's final mission. He would be quoted as saying many times over the next 60 plus years that football was easy after this.

While finishing his service commitment in California, Bednarik was not recruited by any of the service football teams playing on the west coast at the time. He was home in Bethlehem in September, and officially discharged October 11, 1945.

He expected to be working at Bethlehem Steel by Halloween.

Dean Morrow

Along with Chuck Bednarik, co-pilot Morrow is the last surviving member of the 467th Bomb Group of the 8th Air Force.

Dean Morrow was co-pilot on 18 of Chuck Bednarik's 30 missions. They are the last two survivors of the 467th Bomb Group, 8th Air Force. Now 87-years old, the retired fireman and contractor resides in Newport Beach, CA and has remained in contact with Chuck and Emma Bednarik.

"He's been out to visit on many of his trips to California over the years. He was very…well, he always believed in church. After every mission he would go to church, and he always said if we got out of there okay, he would go to church every week.'

'During one particular mission there was a mechanical problem that lifted the plane right up. Everyone was quiet. The first words we heard from the back of the plane was "It's a good thing I prayed for you'se guys," that was, Bednarik.'

'One time we came back with a tire blown out. We veered to the left, we veered to the right. We finally landed and there was a big chunk of flak in the tire. Chuck took that flak as a souvenir. I wonder if he still has it.'

'Another time we developed engine trouble. We dropped our bombs on a target of convenience, radioed for help and turned around. Two planes came at us in the distance. We did not know whose planes they were. They could have been Messerschimdts or B-51's.

'They were B-51's coming to our rescue. That was a big relief.'

'I probably got more nervous with each mission. Early on the odds of getting hit were very high. The odds got a little better as we went along because there were more planes in the sky'

'We used to count and compare the numbers of holes in our plane after every mission. I guess it was kind of a badge of courage to compare your holes with the other planes'

"Chuck Bednarik did his job and expected everyone else to do theirs. He was a rough and tough guy.'

'If he was your friend he was your friend.'

'He used to lift me into trucks with one hand. He would grab the back of my belt with one arm and throw me up into a truck. I was about 5'11" and weighed 170 pounds. He was a brute.'

"After the war, when he was playing in the pros he used to call me whenever he came out to California.'

'He would take me in the locker room to meet other players.'

'Later he would come out and stay with us when he came out for celebrity golf tournaments. He could hit it a ton. You know he made himself into a scratch golfer'

'Now he calls me sometimes on Saturday or Sunday and holds up the phone while they're playing polka music on the television. He says to me, "How do like this one?"

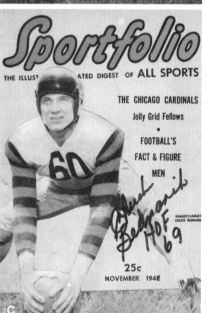

A. All-American center at Penn

B. 1948 Fr. Donnelly watches Chuck receive Catholic Player of the Year Award

C. Cover of Sportfolio, November 1948

D. All-American certificate

E. Chucks residence at Penn was 3743 Spruce St, Newman Hall

F. Franklin Field

G. Dinner reception with Coach Munger

Chapter | three

Penn Years

The plot could pass for a B movie screenplay from the mid-1940s: the decorated war veteran returns home to the gritty industrial city. His buddies are all also coming back, with most of them hoping to join family and friends by drawing a weekly paycheck from the local mills. This vet— maybe even played by the Gipper himself-is facing the same prospects. If things work out well, he might even become the assistant to his father who holds the position of first helper on Open Hearth No. 4. Pop has been a member of Local 2599 for more than 30 years, so the vet has an in.

Before reporting for the first day of work, the vet wanders over to his old high school to visit the coach and kill some time watching the team practice.

In the real-life, September 1945 version of the story, the coach was John Butler of Liberty High School in Bethlehem, PA, and he had the presence of mind to tell his former center/linebacker Chuck Bednarik, "Steel mills nothing, you're taking your GI Bill tuition benefits and going to the University of Pennsylvania to play for George Munger."

"Oh yeah, I was going to work," recalled Bednarik. "I went to see Butler and he said, 'You're going to college.' I said, "What, Where?"

'He said, 'The University of Pennsylvania. I'm going to call George Munger, and you're going to be there tomorrow.'

I said, "Where is it? That was my first trip to Philadelphia."

Chuck Bednarik was barely familiar with Penn. As he reminisced many times in later years, he thought Butler was talking about Penn State. At any other time Butler might have pushed for Penn State, but he was currently at odds with Nittany Lion coach Bob Higgins.

Bednarik admitted in a 1948 interview, "I was all set to go into the steel mill. Hadn't played football since my last season in high school in 1942, and I figured stuff like that was behind me."

The veterans were in the early stages of making their way back into civilian life. Penn was like most non-service academy teams with a roster dominated by 17, 18, and 19-year olds. Many of the Penn players were from the surrounding Philadelphia area.

The cliché 'a man among boys' never fit better than it did on the Penn campus that autumn. The new recruit was midway through his 20th year, stood 6'2", weighed 220 pounds. He was just a few weeks removed from being addressed as Staff Sgt. Bednarik.

"Picture all these high school kids, and me, just out of the service," said Bednarik in remembering the early Penn days. "When Munger saw me," he said "take the entrance exam, take the entrance exam. He rushed me over to the admissions office."

Munger did not need a complete introduction from Butler. In a 1969 letter to commemorate a Bednarik testi-

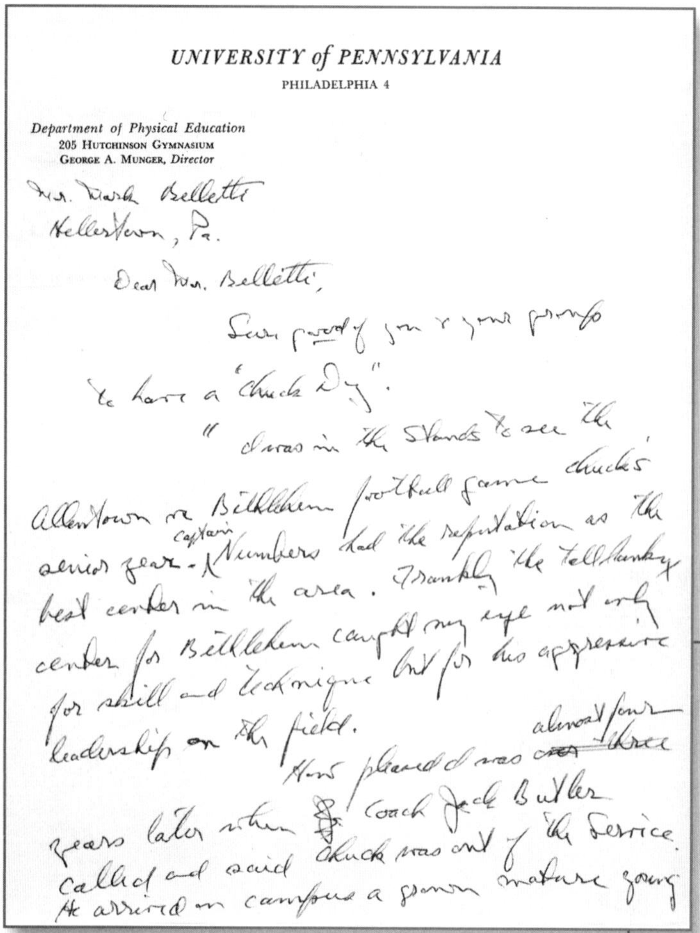

UNIVERSITY of PENNSYLVANIA
PHILADELPHIA 4

Department of Physical Education
205 HUTCHINSON GYMNASIUM
GEORGE A. MUNGER, *Director*

[Handwritten letter reproduced]

many of the mighty Army players would concede that Penn might have been a physically tougher squad. The 'beat 'em up' swagger developed by the Quakers was best personified by Bednarik.

If not the heaviest, (George Savitsky, who later played in the NFL and was inducted into the College Football Hall of Fame, was a monstrous 250 lbs) he was the biggest thing in shoulder pads his teammates had ever seen. The mass— the billboard-sized back, the shoulders, the long arms, hands the size of sewer caps—was accentuated by leonine quickness and preternatural instinct for ending up in the same place as the football. Simply put, he was the best athlete on team and likely the best athlete most of them would see in their lifetimes.

From the moment he stepped out to practice on River Field, with three years of rust since his last competitive game, Chuck did things better and faster than anyone else did.

monial dinner in Bethlehem, Munger wrote, "I was in the stands to see the Allentown vs. Bethlehem football game Chuck's senior year. Captain Numbers (Allentown) had the reputation as the best center in the area. Frankly, the tall lanky center for Bethlehem caught my eye not only for his skill and technique, but for this aggressive leadership on the field."

"How pleased was I almost four years later when Coach Jack Butler called and said Chuck was out of the service. He arrived on campus a grown mature young man and immediately proved an outstanding player."

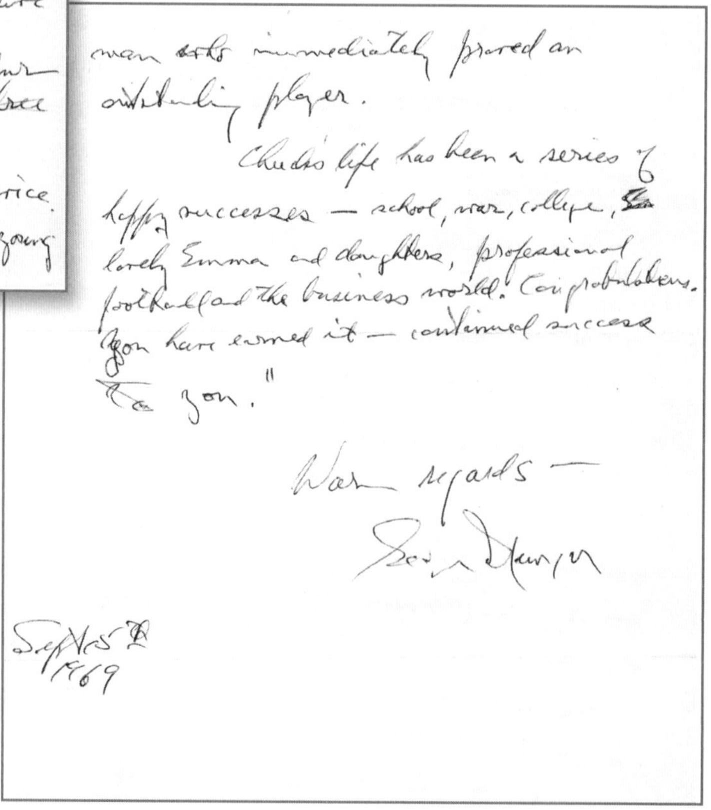

Bednarik started practicing with the team in mid-October, became eligible at the start of the new trimester on November 1, and two days later he suited up against Princeton. Four other veterans – John Curtain, Nelson Harris, Frank Cooney, and Walt Krichling— also became eligible that day. Penn now had 15 former servicemen to provide a grizzled balance to a well-regarded group of younger underclassmen including Skip Minisi, Carmen Falcone, Ed Lawless, and Harry Edenborn.

Penn would become one of most physical eastern collegiate football teams of the post WW-II years. Even

Bednarik and the other four service veterans suited up the first game for which they were eligible, November 3rd against Princeton. The famous number 60 jersey would emerge later. Bednarik was identified as number 17 in the program that year. The first-string center was 180-pound captain Bobby Mosteretz. In the single-wing offense that Penn and most other schools of the era ran, the center was one of the premium spots on the field. The ball was 'tossed' rather than snapped to a fullback, tailback or quarterback. The center was the guy who literally

George Penn 1946

got the offense moving, as he was taught to toss the ball in the direction the play was going in order to give the ball carrier a running start. While not nearly as physical as Bednarik, Mosteretz was a sound and experienced center.

The plan was to have Bednarik finish out the season working at linebacker. Penn beat Princeton 28-0, and then knocked off Columbia 32-7, with Bednarik breaking up a pass that was returned for a touchdown by Carmen Falcone.

Bednarik's first collegiate start came against Army, the most dominant team in college football. Army was number one in the nation the entire season. They were to win all nine of their games by an average score of 45-6, while averaging eight yards gained per snap. They were coming into Franklin Field fresh off a 48-0 crushing of second ranked Notre Dame at Yankee Stadium.

A Time Magazine article that came out the week of the Penn game claimed "...the Army team is a gang of superdupermen who dwell high on the west banks of the Hudson, knock the sawdust out of the tackling dummies all week, emerge from the cave on Saturday afternoon to scare women, children and mere football foes."

Army featured the most famous backfield duo in college history, Felix "Doc" Blanchard" (Mr. Inside) and Glenn Davis (Mr. Outside). They would become the only two Heisman Trophy winners to play together in the same backfield.

The opponents may been Cadets, but they were not going to intimidate a guy who was addressed as Staff Sgt. Bednarik less than two months prior. Before the game, Bednarik told reporters, "Just let that Doc Blanchard try to run through me."

The final score, Army 61, Penn 0. - the first start of his career and the worst defeat Bednarik would suffer in college or the pros.

The Quakers came back to beat Cornell 59-6 to close out the season on Thanksgiving Day. They would finish ranked sixth in the nation with a record of 6-2, losing only to Army and Navy.

George Munger, the man who took Bednarik at the recommendation of Coach Butler, looked like the classic Ivy League coach. About 6' tall, trim and solid (he had been a sculptor's model at an earlier age), he wore rounded eye glass frames and a receding hair line. He was noted for his calm demeanor, not rip-the-roof-off speeches. The lifelong resident of the Philadelphia area was promoted from freshman coach to varsity coach in 1939. He was the only serious candidate for the job. The only question about Munger was wether he was too young for the job at age 28.

Nevertheless, he would lead one of the nation's most powerful football programs for the next 16 years. Eleven times during Monger's career, Penn led the nation in attendance. The Franklin Field experience was so great

MUNGER LETTERMEN 1938-1953

embellished on blocking sleds for more than 70 years, and those are probably the last two words many an overweight lineman has seen before passing out on a hot summer afternoon. It was Crowther who developed the concept and later manu-factured/sold the dreaded sleds. Bednarik remembers him as just the type of person who would devise this line-man's instrument of torture.

"He was tough and could be mean," recalled Bednarik. "As a person he was nothing like George [Munger]."

On campus, Bednarik spent his first year at Memo-rial Hall, before moving to Newman Hall the dormitory for Catholic students. Father John Donnelly was in charge of the hall and he would become Bednarik's most trusted adviser. He was the priest the day Chuck and Emma were married in 1948. He also assisted in negotiat-ing Chuck's first professional contract.

"We used to hang around in Father Donnelly's office," said Bednarik. "We'd sit in his office and watch sports. That was the first time I had ever seen a TV."

and so lucrative that Penn played most of its games at home. Teams opted for the road trip, calculating that their visitor's share of the gate was substantially more than they could earn with a home date. The headlines of the day commonly blasted out attendance figures of 60,000, 70,000, even 80,000 for Franklin Field games.

While the Ivy League was not yet a formal confer-ence, Munger had an overall career record of 82-42-10, going 52-7-4 against other Ivy schools and winning nine mythical league championships. Penn did not play Yale, Harvard, or Brown during Bednarik's career. Munger had two top 10 rankings, 4 second 10 rankings, and developed 14 All-Americans. He was to be joined in the College Football Hall of Fame by five of his players.

Penn also had a line coach of note, and his is a name familiar to nearly anyone who has played the line at any level of football. The words "Rae Crowther" have been

The rust fell off more easily on the football field than it did in the school. Never a natural student and three years removed from a classroom, he forced himself into several hours of repetitive rote drilling almost every night. While not the best student on campus, Chuck was among the most serious, never cutting class while seated in the front row. The determination and doggedness that he used to get through college would remerge in later years. Several of his post-football employers in both sales and broadcasting would comment about how hard he worked to improve at his job.

Socially, Bednarik had little interest in campus or city life. He never missed a chance to get back to Bethlehem. One would be hard pressed to find someone who disliked being in a city more than Chuck Bednarik. Given a choice of hitting the nightclubs downtown or having one of the

Mountaineers drive down and pick him for a ballgame, the ballgame always won.

The summer following freshman year was spent at home. Bednarik played catcher, outfield, and even pitched for the Mountaineer baseball team. Offseason workouts consisted of muscle development by way of loading beer trucks at Banko Distributors.

The Penn roster was loaded with talent as Bednarik prepared for his first full collegiate season in 1946. He and Savitsky were getting some All-American whispers and the very talented running back, Skip Minisi, had transferred back to Penn following a season at Navy. Army, with Davis, Blanchard, and quarterback Arnold Tucker, appeared to be the only team in the East with more talent.

Bednarik was now officially a two-way man, starting at center as well as linebacker. The Quakers won their first three games against Lafayette, Dartmouth, and Virginia by a combined scored of 145-6. Week four brought Navy into town and Penn avenged one of its two losses from the previous season with a 32-19 victory.

The next toughest games on the schedule would be Columbia and Army. Prior to taking on those two teams, Penn had what figured to be an easy game with Princeton. Penn had risen to #3 in the country and the Tigers were lightly regarded. The Quakers took the week of mentally and the result was a stunning 17-14 upset loss.

"We used to hang around in Father Donnellys' office," said Bednarik. 'We'd sit in his office and watch sports. That was the first time I had ever seen a TV."

Penn took this game out on Columbia the following week, smashing a good Lions team 41-6. This set the Quakers up for Army, the biggest game of this and every other season in Bednarik's college career.

Army was ranked first in the nation and Penn was fifth as the game approached.

Even at 21 years old, Bednarik spoke nothing less than what was on his mind. In an article for the Evening Bulletin, Dick Cresap reported, "The 220-pound center is so sure of victory, in fact, he has even the score figured out.

"It'll be 20-13," said Bednarik, "although we may make the other extra point."

Bednarik backed up his words with two interceptions and the defense gave Blanchard and Davis one of the toughest games of their careers, holding the two to about 125 total rushing yards. Despite their best efforts, Penn came up short once again to the Cadets, 34-6.

Penn closed the season by beating Cornell 26-20 in the annual Thanksgiving Day game. A 6-2 record earned the Quakers #13 a ranking in the final national poll. Bednarik was named to the All-East team.

He also started gathering national attention as he and fellow sophomore Carmen Falcone were selected to play in the Blue-Gray game.

Penn was looked at as one of the best team's in the east going into the 1947 season. They would have Bednarik and Anthony "Skippy" Minisi, a future enshrinee in the College Football Hall of Fame. As a freshman in 1944, he had been a star on both sides of the ball for the Quakers. He transferred to the Naval Academy for the 1945 season and intercepted a pass that helped the Midshipmen defeat the Quakers 14-7 that season.

There was no limit on Penn's expectations going into the 1947 season. Army was almost mortal now that they were minus two legends and one All-American quarterback with the graduations of Doc Blanchard, Glenn Davis, and Arnold Tucker. The Cadets were regarded as the only team that could keep Penn from being the top ranked squad in the East.

The first national rankings came out the first week in October. Penn at 2-0 had beaten Lafayette and Dartmouth by a combined 91-0 and were ranked seventh in the nation. Dartmouth was a rare road game for the Quakers, and the Big Green though they had a chance to steal one, playing in front of a friendly crowd that would be only about 50,000 people smaller than the typical Franklin Field Saturday. Coach Tuss McLaughry told the press, "his boys were going to play it to win." With Minisi and Bob Deuber scoring two touchdowns apiece, Penn won 32-0

The initial national rankings for the season were published the first weekend in October. With that 2-0 record the Quakers were ranked seventh. Fifth-ranked Army was the only eastern team ahead of them.

Next up was Columbia. While never a consistent football power, the Lions in 1947 were enjoying one of the best runs in their history. An 8-1 record in 1945 was followed by 6-3 the next year. They had a Hall of Fame Coach in Luigi Piccolo, better known as 'Lou Little' and

> **"News reports called it simply a "chest injury." Bednarik later revealed that it was a punctured lung."**

some great players in Bill Swiacki, Lou Kusserow and Gene Rossides. This started as an eventful week for Bednarik when it was decided that he would not also kick extra points in addition to kicking off. It would end with Bednarik suffering the only injury of his collegiate career and the Quakers survived a late Lions comeback and held on 34-14.

As reported by Art Morrow in the Philadelphia Inquirer, "...the big center removed himself from the game, came trotting off the field and stretched out beside the bench. "Don't you think you'd better go in and make this kickoff?" George Munger asked. Bednarik struggled to his feet. "Gosh coach," he gasped, "I can't breathe."

X-rays taken at the time showed no fractured ribs. News reports called it simply a "chest injury." Bednarik later revealed that it was a punctured lung. Navy was the next game and, up until Friday, pre-game reports wavered as to whether or not Bednarik would play. Navy had a center named Dick Scott who was considered Bednarik's only eastern rival for All-American honors.

Bednarik ended up sitting the game out. Penn won anyway 21-0 and Bednarik's replacement, Charlie Hassler neutralized Scott. It took a punctured lung for Bednarik to miss a game, and only one game at that.

Even more important that week Columbia, spurred by their gallant though failed comeback against the Quakers, upset Army. Penn moved up to fourth in the nation and were now the top-ranked team in the east.

Revenge was the theme of the next game, and no one was going to keep Bednarik on the bench for another week. The 17-14 upset loss to Princeton the previous year was stilled viewed as "catastrophic" on the Penn campus. An Inquirer headline read, "50,000 to See 'Revenge' Game; Bednarik Ready." Revenge accomplished, final score Penn 26, Princeton 7.

Undefeated Virginia traveled up to Philadelphia the following week, with Army on deck. If there was any point in the season the Quakers could be vulnerable to an upset, this was it. Penn had beaten them 40-0 the previous season, turning this into revenge week for the Cavaliers. The score was tied at the half, but Deuber scored on two long touchdown runs in the second half. Bednarik intercepted two passes and also stopped fullback Grover Cleveland Jones, Jr. at the goal line to thwart a touchdown. Virginia was tough, but Penn prevailed 19-7 and, as reported in the Inquirer, the Cavaliers, "...went down with the Confederate flags of its followers still flying high in the crowd of 79,000."

Bednarik was named national lineman of the week by both the Maxwell Club and the Associated Press, and Virginia coach Art Guepe said, "I think we would have scored more than twice—in fact, I feel sure of it—except for one man. That Bednarik. We knew he was good, but we didn't believe any center in the country was that good."

The game of the year in the east was played November 15, at Franklin Field. The third-ranked and undefeated Quakers were a slight favorite over 13th

> **"Army coach Bob St. Onge said "Chuck Bednarik is the best center in the country, including the professionals."**

ranked Army, which had already suffered two losses and was tied by Illinois 0-0.

Minisi told the press, "A one point victory would be plenty. We just want to beat them."

It was widely acknowledged that Penn had more talent. Army coach Bob St. Onge said, "Chuck Bednarik is the best center in the country, including the professionals." Several players from both squads would say in later years that Army always beat Penn in the mental game. Penn played its worst game of the season. Each team scored once in the first half and the final score ended 7-7.

The Quakers did close out their first undefeated season since 1908 by beating Cornell 21-0 in the annual Thanksgiving Day matchup. They were ranked 7th in the final poll. Bednarik was named to at least nine All-American teams and won several linemen of the year awards, including that of the Maxwell Club.

Bednarik entered his senior season as one of the most publicized players in college football. He was the cover boy for at least one national publication, the 1948 Illustrated Football Annual. Veterans on the GI Bill flooded campuses throughout the country and more young men than ever before were playing college football. With the added bodies, more schools were moving away from the one-platoon system and some players were found on only one side of the ball.

Army, loaded with talent, started deploying players on either offense or defense in 1946. Army head coach Col. Blaik is credited with using adapted military terminology to coin the 'platoon system.'

Chuck enjoying pre-game breakfeat with Coach Munger and teammate Dolph Tokarczyk.

Munger started dallying with the two-platoon system in '48. Five or six guys played only one-way, but Bednarik was not among them. In a preseason article, Munger told Art Morrow of the Philadelphia Inquirer, "He (Bednarik) could play any position on the team and he would be outstanding wherever he played." At times during the season, Munger seemed determined to have Bednarik play every position; he was of course back at center and linebacker, but he also occasionally carried the football, in addition to kicking off, punting and kicking extra points.

While Penn had more bodies than ever before, the talent level was down. Twenty-two lettermen from the previous season were gone, including linemen George Savitsky, Ed Marshall, Rod Adams, and Art Littleton. The backfield was missing Minisi, Bill Luongo, and Bob Evans.

"Search the nation and you won't find a greater center than Chuck Bednarik, Penn's rough-and-tumble pivot pin," proclaimed the Illustrated Football Annual. The inside of the offensive line would be strong with Bednarik flanked by two veteran guards, his old Bethlehem friend John "Bull" Schweder and Dolph Tokarczyk.

Along with one-platoon football the single wing was also declining in popularity among major football programs. The T-formation was the rage of offensive football, and Munger started to mix it in with the reliable single wing. Carmen Falcone lined up on center and took the snaps in the "T," while Bill Talarico served as quarter-

back in the single wing. The electrifying Minisi had graduated, but Deuber provided breakaway speed. Fullback Ray Dooeny brought the power and newcomer Reds Bagnell would come off the bench and be a major contributor by the end of the season.

The Quakers beat Dartmouth 26-13 to open the season in front of new university President Harold Stassen. Munger surprised the Big Green by lining up in the T formation before shifting into the wing. He also introduced Bednarik as a ball carrier, with the senior running 35 yards from punt position on a third down their first series of the game. Bednarik also blocked a punt in the second half.

The following week Penn overpowered Princeton 29-7 in front of the usual Franklin Field crowd of 60,000. Bednarik again got to run the ball from punt formation and gained 17 yards. After the game, Princeton Coach Charlie Caldwell told the Inquirer's Morrow, "This Penn team may never be a great one, but as long as they have that big boy up front they'll be no pushovers." The 'big boy' was of course Bednarik.

Penn carried a 14-game unbeaten streak into one of their biggest games of the season at Columbia. The Lions hadn't beaten the Quakers since 1937, but they had one of the highest scoring offenses in the east and two of the best players in fullback Lou Kusserow and quarterback Gene Rossides.

Columbia charged out to a 14-0 lead at the half, but Bagnell threw a three-yard touchdown pass to Bob Sponaugie with about 30 seconds to play to complete a 17-14 Quaker comeback victory. The touchdown was set up by a pass interference against Rossides, who has maintained for more than 60 years that it was a bad call.

Penn had pulled to within 14-13 early in the fourth quarter when Bednarik scored the only touchdown of his college career when he carried a blocked punt three yards into the end zone. He celebrated by heaving the football into a stadium crowd that included one of his old bosses from World War II, Columbia president Dwight Eisenhower. Penn was penalized 15 yards on the next kickoff and Bednarik was admonished by an official who told him, "You shouldn't do that, it doesn't look nice." After the game Munger said, "How could anyone be angry with Bednarik? He was entitled to his fun." Earlier in the game he completed the first pass of his career when he faked a punt and threw for a 50-yard gain.

Bagnell again supplied the late dramatics with two fourth quarter touchdown runs as Penn came back from a 14-7 deficit to beat Navy 20-14. Bednarik was named Associated Press Lineman of the Week for his efforts and the Quakers remained undefeated. However this was to be his last collegiate win, as Penn dropped their last three games to teams that would all finish in the Associated Press' Top 20.

Penn State came into Franklin Field undefeated for what was billed as "The Battle of Pennsylvania." Penn State won 13-0, but Bednarik made 10 tackles including one that is still talked about by the people who witnessed it. In the fourth quarter with the Nittany Lions up 7-0, Bednarik ran down All-American end Sam Tamburo following a 52-yard gain and dropped him with a one-hand tackle from behind. Penn State's Dave Coulson said at the time, "It was Bednarik's greatest game in a long series of great games. For years to come, I'll carry that picture of him coming from behind to tackle Sam Tamburo. It will be one of my most vivid recollections of what super effort means in football."

The Quakers narrowed the gap mightily against Army since losing 61-0 Bednarik's freshman year, but the Cadets still came in for their annual visit to Franklin Field favored by as many as 20 points. Penn played their best game of the year and came within 30 seconds of walking off with an upset win, but a late 15-yard pass from Arnie Galiffa to Jack Trent gave the Cadets a 26-20 victory.

Bednarik, as usual, led the team in tackles and averaged almost 42 yards on five punts, including a spectacular 70-yarder that Army return man Frank Fischl would later say was the highest and deepest kick he had ever seen. Army center Bill Yeoman was considered in some circles to be a rival for All-American honors, but was clearly outplayed by Bednarik.

Penn 20-Columbia 14, 1948

The letdown from this game carried over to Thanksgiving, when Cornell scored a 23-14 upset victory that brought them the Ivy League title. The Big Red had been lightly regarded coming into the season, but lost only to Army and finished the season ranked 19th in the nation, just behind Penn State. Army was sixth with a record of 8-0-1.

Bednarik made every All-American team that year, was named United Press Lineman of the Year, and Football Digest's Player of the Year. He also became the first lineman to win the Robert W. Maxwell Award as the nation's most outstanding player and was third in the voting for the Heisman Trophy, behind winner Doak Walker and Charlie "Choo Choo" Justice. The same day that he was named the Maxwell winner, November 29, it was also announced that the Philadelphia Eagles had utilized their 'bonus pick' to make him the first player selected in the NFL draft.

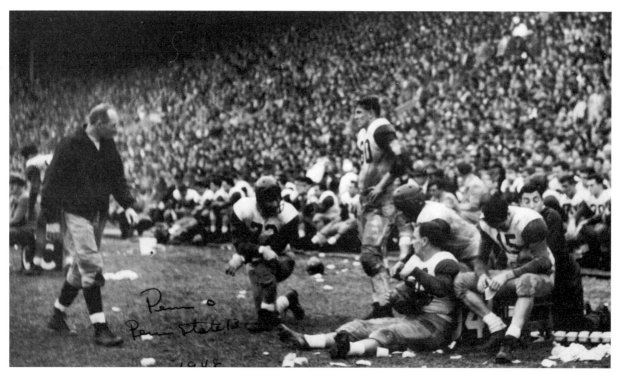

Bill Yeoman

Bill Yeoman played center for Army during the glory years of Doc Blanchard and Glenn Davis. He was touted as a rival to Penn center Chuck Bednarik and was named a second team All-American. He later became the most successful coach in the history of the University of Houston, winning 160 games in 25 years. He made history when he became the first coach from a major Texas university to bring in a black player with his 1964 recruitment of Warren McVea. Yeoman was elected to the College Football Hall of Fame as a coach in 2001.

"Well, I'll tell you what, I talked a good game, and Chuck Bednarik played one.'

'He was a great player. He was a dominant figure on the field — physically very capable, very intense.'

'They were serious games, a serious rivalry. We had more speed. They had that Dooney kid; he was an armful. They also had that big Savitsky kid. They were physical, but mentally we had an edge on them.'

'They thought they had a chance to beat us in '48. Munger came down to greet Col. Blaik at the train station. We nearly died laughing. That really ticked old man Blaik off. Munger thought he could get into Blaik's head. It was tough to get to Blaik's mind; this really fired him up.'

'This was a serious, physical game. We waited a long time to pull it out; we needed a late touchdown to win. That Minisi, damn gum coach, he could run.'

'Those games filled Franklin Field all the time. It was a serious rivalry.'

'Penn was physically as good as anyone. They seemed psyched out when they played us. We were not imposing physically, but our guys could execute.'

'Playing Penn was a mental exercise, not physical. I was 190 pounds; the guys across from me were significantly bigger than that. Physically it wasn't a contest.'

'But Bednarik, he was physical and extremely capable. He was a stud duck walking around out there.

'He was the one guy, I could say, we never got to his head."

Dick Scott

Dick Scott was an All-American center at Navy and was later inducted into the College Football Hall of Fame. During the 1947 season, he was considered to be Chuck Bednarik's main competition for All-East honors.

Bednarik was injured and missed the Navy game that year and his replacement Charlie Hassler was widely-viewed to have held his own against Scott during a 21-0 Penn victory. This helped elevate Bednarik's status among football observers.

"Those games were 60 years ago. They come in kind of faintly, but I sure remember the Penn, Army and Notre Dame games.'

'Franklin Field had long grass, like a wheat field. Our punter had a tough time. The grass was high and made it tough to punt on. It was also tough to run around on. We beat Penn in '45 and '46. I remember Bednarik was hurt for the '47 game and we didn't have a very good team that year.'

'Chuck and I both played center and linebacker. I remember him coming over after we beat them in '46. He wanted to know who we were playing next week; I told him Notre Dame. He expressed his condolences and said "that's too bad."

'Penn was a physical team. Civilian colleges had more leniencies on the size and strength of recruits. Penn wasn't known as an Ivy League team. They were a football power.'

'Chuck and I shared Lineman of the Week once in '46. We were considered the two best centers in the east. I saw him at the Hall of Fame dinner in New York one year. We exchanged pleasantries."

Frank Miller

A running back for Cornell who had a good day when the Big Red upset Penn for the 1948 Ivy League championship.

f Chuck Bednarik had a serious flaw in his linebacker game, it wasn't exposed until the final game of his senior year. A sharp scouting report tipped Cornell's football team on how to attack the two-time All-American. A Cornell team that was lightly regarded coming in to the season pulled an upset that captured the unofficial Ivy League championship in 1948.

The Ivy League as it exists today was not formally recognized in 1954. For 20 or so years prior, the eight schools that now make up the league had an informal alliance. The University of Pennsylvania was a dominant east coast football power through the most of the 1940s and regularly beat up on those schools that would become their brethren league members when the Ivy was officially christened.

Cornell was one of the least successful of these Ivy schools and, going into the 1948 season, Chuck Bednarik's senior year, little was expected of the Big Red.

Frank "Moose" Miller, a schoolboy sprint champion in Georgia, played a season at Georgia Tech before transferring to Cornell in February, 1948. He was a three-year starter at halfback and from his Atlanta home, the retired financial planner well remembers the Penn game that took place on Thanksgiving Day 1948.

"I played against Bednarik in 1948 and it was perhaps the worst game of his college career.'

'This was the first time I saw Franklin Field and there must have been about 85,000 people at the game.'

'It was perfect weather, unlike the next two years when it rained.'

'I grew up in Decatur, Georgia and we played in the state championship game my junior and senior years. I was the fastest guy in Georgia in high school and speed made my game.'

'I had visited Cornell in high school, but went to Georgia Tech for half a year. I was unhappy at Tech, basically the coaches told us not to worry about studying.'

'I had fallen in love with Cornell when I visited, and transferred there in February '48.'

'I get to Cornell and I pick up a sports magazine and find out that we were picked unanimously to go winless that year.'

'Well, we were the Cinderella team of that season.'

'We beat Dartmouth the second to last game of the season and the next Monday we prepared to play Penn for the league championship.'

'I was the starting right halfback and that Monday our coach Lefty James tells us that he is putting in a play that looks like an end run, but instead you are going to cut off left tackle and run at Bednarik.'

'I weighed 162, Chuck Bednarik weighed 235. The guy I had blocking in front of me was a guard named John Jaso, who was very tough, but he weighed about 185.'

'Chuck Bednarik, I'll never forget Chuck Bednarik. He's lined up about five yards off the line. He had his hands on knees and he was watching all the faking in backfield. The left half went straight ahead on a fake and the fullback went right into the middle.'

'I was the right half and the ball was handed to me. Bednarik is off the line and reading what's going on in the backfield. Jaso runs out on him, and he couldn't move him an inch, but he shielded him, and I ran around Jaso. We went wild with that play.'

'I had a big run and I remember, within two seconds of getting tackled, Bednarik piled on. We moved the ball all day. Jaso couldn't block or move Bednarik, but he got in front of him just enough to shield him.'

"After that game I thought Bednarik was the most overrated player I ever played against, and at a reunion 10 years later I found out why."

'We won 22-14 and won the Ivy League title. That game was crucial. We had been voted to go winless. The only game we lost that season was against Army.'

'After that game I thought Bednarik was the most overrated player I ever played against and at a reunion 10 years later I found out why.'

'I was talking to Hal McCullough, who had played at Cornell around '39-41, and I was telling him about the brilliant play we ran against Bednarik in the Penn game '

'And McCullough says, 'That was my scouting report. I was scouting Penn and I saw that Bednarik had great lateral speed, but didn't move as well straight ahead." He said that he noticed that Bednarik was looking in the backfield instead of the linemen and the best way to beat him was to go straight at him.'

'When he got to the pros, they must have taught him to read the blockers, but in college he was always reading the backs.'

'Oh yeah, he was the guy we had to stop, an All-American two years. Physically he was so impressive.'

'Ten years later I was still marveling that we ran at

Chuck Bednarik and it worked. The only way to get around him was to go right into him. I'm confident that it was the worst game he played in college.'

'Thanks to Hal McCullough, we ran right at him. Lefty James put that play in based on his scouting report.'

'The next year Bednarik was the Rookie of the Year or something with the Eagles and Furman Bisher wrote an article about him for the Atlanta paper. He called me and I told him that against us, he was ineffective, that he didn't know how to diagnose line play."

Frank Fischl

The former mayor of Allentown, was an opponent of Chuck Bednarik while playing for Army in the 1940s.

The Mayor of Allentown, from 1978-1982, Frank Fischl was born and raised in the city, and played football at West Point from 1948-1950. He was on the field for the epic 1948 game in which Army beat Penn 26-20 on a late touchdown pass.

Fischl was later part of a foursome put together by Ed McKeon in which the 1948 game became a topic of conversation among other subjects.

"I remember a lot about Chuck, but as great an all-around football player as he was, not many people remember that he punted for Penn. He could really boot the ball.'

'I was back to receive a punt and it was so high and so far, I backed up to catch it and I was tackled right away. I was amazed, it was the highest punt I had ever seen. I played on offense and we knew that Chuck was a great linebacker, but people may have forgotten what a great punter he was.'

'We used to beat Penn, but the games were always tough. We played all the games at Franklin Field. For whatever reason we didn't play home and home with them.'

'The games were close and Penn was one of the better teams we played. We beat Michigan handily compared to Penn.'

'I remember the golf tournament we played in together at Saucon Valley. We rode in the cart together.

We always beat Penn when he played for them, but I don't think I joked about it too much. He would have knocked me out of the cart."

Monk Matthews

A Penn teammate of Chuck Bednarik, Matthews served in the Navy during World War II.

A reserve guard for Penn, Matthews was long associated with the Penn athletic program.

He taught physical education at the school and was the head lacrosse coach for 21 years.

"Chuck was a great guy. He used to tell us about his war experience and gave us a lot of great information about his service in World War II.'

'I was in the service too, with the Navy in the Pacific. We were there on the GI Bill and we were glad we didn't have to pay out of our pockets.

'Chuck was well-known to everyone. As a teammate, he taught us a lot of things —

how to pay attention to a play, how to keep up with the other team. He always knew the other team's plays.'

'He did everything so well. He was so good. We felt we had to do things as well as him. He was the campus football hero and we did many activities together.'

'Chuck has a lot of respect for guys who did well. We had a lot of World War II vets and we all respected each other.'

'He always liked wrestling and many years later we used to get together at the Palestra to watch wrestling.'

'Once I brought one of my grandsons, I have 11 grandchildren, and Chuck shook his hand and did that thing with his bent finger where he says, "Ouch, look what you did to me.'

'And my grandson says "get out of here, you've had that for years."

Gene Rossides

The Columbia quarterback from 1945-48, he called Chuck Bednarik the best college lineman of all time.

Gene Rossides was the quarterback for Columbia University during its "Golden Era" of football, 1945-48. Together with fullback Lou Kusserow, he made up half the school's 'Gold Dust Twins' backfield. After getting drafted by the New York Giants, he passed on a career in professional football to enter Columbia Law School.

He later became the assistant attorney general for New York State and then served as an undersecretary of treasury in the Nixon administration. Today he is president of the American Hellenic Institute and is recognized as a leading authority on Greek and Turkish issues.

"Do I have memories of playing against the best college lineman of all time? I have many memories of Chuck Bednarik. Yes, he stood out.'

'In those days Penn was the second best team in the country to West Point and they probably had better overall talent except for Glenn Davis.'

'They had the best lineman in Bednarik and great players like George Savitsky, Skip Minisi, and Reds Bagnell.'

> **"I threw a good pass and that goddamn ham hand (Bednarik) reaches out and intercepts it. I never thought he could reach it; he was so quick, and that long reach."**

'One memory—I was 18 years old and we had won six straight. That was big news. Columbia hadn't won much in recent years.'

'We ran out onto Franklin Field and it was double-tier, 60,000 people. I had real butterflies. The first and only time I had butterflies. In the second half they beat us handily, they had a much better team. We scored on the opening kickoff and gave them a game for a half.'

'I was playing left half in the wing-T, but I was like the quarterback. I called the plays for four years. Not like today, we called the plays on the field.'

'I threw a pass, short, to the right end coming across the field. Lou Little and Buff Donelli had always told us that the down and out was the best pass in football. It will either be completed or it can't be intercepted. Don't throw

to your man directly, throw it away from the defender. Sid Luckman used to tell me the same thing.'

'I threw a good pass and that goddamn ham hand (Bednarik) reaches out and intercepts it. I never thought he could reach it; he was so quick, and that long reach.'

'In '46 they beat us handily again. Then in '47, at Penn, we made a couple of mistakes and were down about 21-0 at the half. We outplayed them in the second half. We really moved them around. This was a great Penn team and we gelled that game. That really helped us as a team and the next week we beat Army and ended their 32-game winning streak.'

'In '45 we started about five or six freshman. In '46 the veterans came back from the war. We had Lou Kusserow, myself, and for the first time we had some strength.'

'That Penn game made us a real unit. We upset Army. The next three games we held the other teams scoreless.'

'Chuck was all over the field that day.'

'In '48 we had a chance to beat them. I got a bad pass interference call. I had touched the ball, but they missed the call. Bednarik was all over the place that game too.'

'We played together once. In 1949 we upset the Giants in an exhibition game. It was the Eastern All Stars Herald Tribune Fresh Air Game. Joe Steffy from Army was on that team too. We beat the Giants. I tried to get the film from that game but the Giants said it was lost in a fire. They didn't want anyone to see it.'

'Chuck was on the squad. What a hell of a fun loving guy. He joked around during practice. He was a joy to be with.'

'Originally, I was going to go Penn. I was offered a full ride. I went to Erasmus Hall High School in Brooklyn and we won the city championship in '44. Sid Luckman also went to Erasmus Hall, and then Columbia.'

'We didn't have a phone at home. In December '44, I'm at our football banquet, and Sid Luckman calls me there from Chicago.'

'I told him I was going to Penn and he said no, you're going to play for Lou Little at Columbia. I got no scholarship from Columbia. I was offered a full ride to Penn, but ended up at Columbia because of Sid Luckman."

Walt Bruska

While playing for Cornell, Bruska recalls knocking Chuck Bednarik down on the first play of the game, then spending the rest of the afternoon paying for it as he was on the wrong end of some devastating hits.

Walt Bruska played defensive end for Cornell University from 1947-49 and later served as an assistant coach at his alma mater. He also had a long career as an administrator at several northeastern universities. Like Chuck Bednarik, he also served in the Army Air Corp before entering college.

"I remember him well. We had just started the two-platoon system in '48 and I was the right end on offense. We played Penn and almost every play was a running play to the right and I had to block George Savitsky or Chuck Bednarik almost every play.'

'I was pint-sized compared to those guys, about 6', 175 pounds. Savitsky weighed about 250 and Bednarik, 230. They were All-Americans.'

'One of my great thrills was the first time I blocked Bednarik and knocked him on the ground. That was it; he wouldn't let a little squirt knock him down again. He caught on and he kind of pulverized me the rest of the way. I couldn't move him after that. He was one of the toughest guys I ever played against.'

'I got a couple of souvenirs from him that day. I lost a tooth and I had a knot on my right arm between the elbow and the shoulder. He was a tough character, a great football player.'

'We were not expected to do well in '48. We had lost many guys from the '46 and '47 teams; not many lettermen were back. We had a good recruiting class in '47 and with the two platoon system a lot of sophomores made major contributions.'

'Munger and Penn, they were big time. The only tougher team that we played was Army.'

'It was something of a thrill to play at Franklin Field on Thanksgiving Day in front of 75,000 people. Our stands at Cornell held about 35,000.'

'We would come down and stay at Philmont Country Club. Mr. Gimbel was a member at Philmont and we would make the arrangements and he would come in and address us at dinner.'

> **"It was something of a thrill to play at Franklin Field on Thanksgiving Day in front of 75,000 people. Our stands at Cornell held about 35,000."**

'It's amazing how football changed in a few years. In 1949 we were ranked third in the nation before we lost to Dartmouth. I think we still ended up in the Top 10.'

'The Ivy League schools ruled the roost with the NCAA in those days. These institutions were so highly regarded academically and they had good athletic programs—crew, wrestling, swimming, some of the schools with football.'

'Then, about 1952, the Ivy presidents went to the NCAA meeting with the express purpose of de-emphasizing football. You know how they de-emphasized it… no spring football.'

'The schools like Nebraska, Oklahoma, Notre Dame, Michigan thumbed their noses at the Ivys—'you guys go ahead and do it if you want.' So in '52, there was no spring football practice."

Joe Steffy

An All-American lineman at Army, Steffy recalls having his nose rearranged in various locations around his face by Chuck Bednarik.

Throughout the 1940s Army football was as powerful as any collegiate program in the country. While many of the nation's best young athletes were serving in the armed forces, Army players were matriculating at West Point, under the legendary Colonel Earl "Red" Blaik, with the knowledge that their time to serve would come after graduation. Many sturdy young men simply wanted to be part of a service academy during those turbulent years.

The most famous backfield duo in college football history, Felix "Doc" Blanchard and Glenn Davis, Mr. Inside and Mr. Outside tore away at opposing defenses.

Col. Blaik placed an emphasis on stuffing the ball up the middle and loved running power plays straight up the gut. He had a great line coach, Herman Hickman, and between them they developed mortar shell tough offensive linemen.

> **"Tell Chuck I still have my nose after he moved it all over my face. He couldn't decide where he liked it best and used to shove it from one side of my face to the other."**

The toughest and best Army lineman of all time lined up head to head with Chuck Bednarik for three straight years. This offensive guard and defensive linebacker, Joe Steffy, was almost as decorated as Bednarik during college.

The 1947 Outland Trophy winner as the nation's outstanding interior lineman, a two-time first team All-American and enshrinee of the College Football Hall of Fame in 1986, Steffy was such a crushing blocker that Blaik named a block after him and used it in training films for many years. The 'Steffy Block' was a legal blindside hit that when timed right seemed as if it might deposit the recipient in the adjacent Hudson River.

Steffy still lives near West Point. aHe is a regular visitor at practice and has not missed a home game since 1952.

"It's funny that you should ask about Bednarik, just earlier today a man asked me who was the best player I ever played with, and who was the best I played against. I told him of course, Blanchard and Davis were the best I ever played with, and the best guy I ever played against was Chuck Bednarik.'

'I went against Chuck nose-to-nose for three years and he was the best I ever played against. I was a guard and a linebacker. He played center and linebacker, so we were always on each other.'

'I went head-to-head with some great ones like George Connor of Notre Dame, but Chuck was better.'

'Those games with Penn–people today don't understand what they were like. Those games were top-notch. Penn beat us a few times in the early '40s like no one else did and Col. Blaik used that as motivation in his pep talk for the next 10 years.'

'Every year we had great games at Franklin Field. George Munger was a good coach. Col. Blaik always liked going to Philadelphia because that was where we played Navy. I don't know why we don't play Penn now.'

'We used to play Notre Dame, Penn, and Navy in that order every year. Col. Blake didn't want to play those three in a row. He wanted to play Notre Dame in October; leave Penn in November, and Navy at the end of the season.'

'I remember playing against Chuck. When you played Chuck Bednarik, it was not an easy afternoon. He was a real player, rough and tough.'

'It's been 60 years and old men forget a lot, but I don't forget Chuck Bednarik. When you see him, tell him Joe Steffy said hello.'

'He was the best. I played against Heisman winners like Johnny Lujack and Leon Hart, and guys like Bill Fischer. Out of all of them, Chuck Bednarik comes out on top.'

'Penn-Army, that was a great series, just top-notch football. That little back they had, Skip Minisi, he was so damn good.'

'Before one game, Herman Hickman said, "Joe, Minisi will reverse field—don't let him, stay outside of him all the time. Well on the third or fourth play of the game he did get around me and ran for about 25 yards.'

'Hickman also used to tell me I'd be in for a rough afternoon with Bednarik. It always was a rough afternoon.'

'Tell Chuck I still have my nose after he moved it all over my face. He couldn't decide where he liked it best and used to shove it from one side of my face to the other.'

'Those games were bigger than anything the pros put on. The pros didn't pay anything in those days and they really wanted Doc Blanchard. He went into the service because he could make more money. Amazing when you think about it."

Bernie Lemonick

All-American lineman and teammate of Chuck Bednarik at Penn.

The Munger Men of the University of Pennsylvania are one of the nations' most unique football alumni groups. The remaining athletes who played for George Munger during his 16 year reign at Penn still meet annually for a football weekend at Penn. The linchpin of the group is Bernie Lemonick. An All-American guard in 1950, Lemonick may have been the first collegiate player to bloody the face of Chuck Bednarik. Lemonick was drafted by the New York Giants and later returned to Penn as a line coach.

For many years he operated Kennebeck Camps in Maine and remains active on various boards at Penn.

'He was a guy, a leadership guy, in terms of actions on the field. He always demonstrated that he knew what football was all about. He played it as it was put on paper.'

'He had a sense of not only the game itself, but victory. He knew what he was on the field for and would do whatever was required to win games.'

'Chuck demonstrated a physical wherewithal, a skill for crushing guys at linebacker.'

'His approach included an intensity to not let anyone off the hook to not let anyone make an easy catch, an easy run.'

'I first saw him on the field in 1947 as the freshmen gathered together. I'm going out for football and I don't give a damn about anybody. I can knock anyone on the other side of the line on their ass. Chuck felt the same way too.'

'The first time I was on the field as a freshman, the varsity had just returned from two or three week of camp at Hershey. We were practicing at River Field.'

'We were only kids; we had been there for a week. Jack Welsh was the freshmen coach. He sent guys out for the first time—"you, you, you"—he picked 11 and said you're here, you're there.'

'I'm lined up on the left side of the defense; the first team is on offense. I didn't know Chuck Bednarik from Adam. All I know was that I was going to beat my guy.'

'Chuck snapped the ball and I was across the line—not offside. I was right with him when he came across the line. He came forward, my hand came up, and I wasn't going to push him; I was going to put a hole in his chest.'

'I caught him, under the lip, drew blood and he was upset. He used some good words which I won't repeat. I said to him "It's a ball game, come on." His head came up, my forearm came up, and I caught him.'

'He was initially upset, but he had a good sense about it. I was like one of those guys on the Army team that used to do this. '

'That was my first play in college. It had nothing to do with Chuck. It involved my sense of what the game was about. I was going to have intensity. If this is what it takes to get to the ball, that is what I would do.'

'I understood what the game was about, what had to be done, and Chuck was the same kind of guy. He never had a sense of being beaten. He played the game the way it was meant to be played.'

'I will never forget how he ran back down the field and headed off a receiver and dropped him before he scored. He must have ran 30 or 40 yards. His tremendous effort said, 'Hey pal, you may have caught the ball, but you are not going to score. He was pointing to the guy as he got up 'I got you pal.'

'He had a tremendous impact on all the people who watched him and he deserved all of the plaudits he got.'

'Let me tell you something, the fact that he makes an effort to be at the Munger Men reunions establish a warm feeling among everyone there. That he makes a speech; it lends the organization tremendous value.'

'He establishes himself as a Munger Man, as a guy who is exemplary in his feelings about the team, about the game, about playing at Penn.'

'One time he mentioned his father. His dad said to him, "Now listen Chuck, you recognize that man George Munger is your father while you're there. You respect him; you respect me. He is a man of great value; he can do things for you. Treat him as your father." And Chuck said "I did."

'He is a giving person and at the same time a tough guy. He has taken issue with people he didn't care about."

Bob Deuber

A star running back
and teammate of
Bednarik's at Penn,
the two have
remained long
time friends.

A fleet running back at the University of Pennsylvania, Bob Deuber was a teammate of Chuck Bednarik from 1945-48. He has remained Bednarik's most enduring friend from the college years, as the two have remained close through their common interests of polka music, the old country and golf. Deuber was in the wholesale petroleum business for 35 years and lives in Millville, NJ.

"Chuck came out of the Army Air Force during the summer of my freshman year at Penn. Summer football camp had started and Chuck was still in the service. The first time I met him was when he showed up for practice in late October of that year, 1945.'

'We had already played four games and four were left on the schedule, including Army. We were a bunch of 17-year old kids and George Savitsky when Chuck came out in the middle of the season. It was unheard of, at least I've never heard of a player matriculating in the middle of the season.'

"It was November 1, when Chuck comes on to the team. He had not practiced or played competitive football in three years. He joins the team and his football skills are a bit rusty and he didn't know the plays, but it's immediately evident that he's one heck of an athlete."

'It was November 1, when Chuck comes on to the team. He had not practiced or played competitive football in three years. He joins the team and his football skills are a bit rusty and he didn't know the plays, but it's immediately evident that he's one heck of an athlete.'

'George Munger puts him in at linebacker. Chuck is a presence; any coach that looks at him says "I want that guy." He's a little rusty, but the rest of us were green, just a bunch of kids. We did win three of our first four games, losing only to Navy. And for that game George (Munger) was in the hospital, and of course we were playing without Chuck. With George and Chuck, we probably would have won all of our games that year, except for Army.'

'That might have been the best Army team of all. Most of the guys on Army had played for another college for a year or two, and just about anyone of them could have All-American. Colonel Blaik had them motivated every game and they had an outstanding staff—Herman Hickman, Paul Dietzel, Vince Lombardi.'

'Chuck was playing linebacker and a lot was expected of him. They went out of their way to double team him every play. Chuck took a beating, but he fought back with everything in his soul.'

'Army was up 20-0 at the half and George makes up his mind that he won't get his team ruined physically. He played everyone in the second half.'

'Chuck could not carry the team on defense too much, by himself. You can't stop a flowing river. He had not played much ball coming into that game, but he handled himself well.'

'During his sophomore year, Chuck proved what he could do. The most impressive thing about him as a young man was that he worked out with weights every night at Newman Hall. He got bigger and stronger every year. We were told to stay away from weights; we didn't even have a weight room. But Chuck never got involved in fraternity life, and he worked out five nights a week to build up his strength.'

'When he got a hand on you...he was so strong that he could pull you down with one hand. And he was strong before he started lifting.'

'The fact that he got back from the war alive and well was a gift from God above. Thirty missions over German; I can't tell you how much I respect his guts.'

'We had tricky plays at Penn and he had not played center as a freshman. As a sophomore, he took over as first string offensive center, and in three years, I never took a bad snap from him. We had tricky plays, naked reverses and sometimes the snap pass from the center had to go four or five yards to the left or the right. He always put the ball on the money; without a perfect snap, the play dies.'

'Think about the pressure of snapping the ball; you have the noseguard right on your nose, smacking into you every play; it could be disconcerting. I never saw him make a bad snap, punt, extra point, anything.'

'There were so many different types of snaps in the single wing. The ball could go to the fullback, the tailback, anyone. He was absolutely the best offensive center any back could ever want to play with.'

'It was my great privilege to play with Chuck Bednarik for four years, to have known and enjoyed his company and to know how good a person he is. He is a very fine human being.'

'It was absolutely obvious from the start how good he was. It starts with personality; it's a certain thing. Bull Schweder had it; he was just as intense. Maybe it was a Bethlehem thing.'

'George Munger had a test for running backs. He would take three guys on the defense and position them ten yards apart in the middle of the field. He would have one guy on the 30, the next on the 20, and the last guy on the 10 yard line. A coach would take a football and throw an underhand lateral pass to a running back, who had to get through the three guys without any blocking.'

'If Chuck was one of the three guys, you might get through the first, maybe the second, but no one ever got by Chuck. Chuck was often the cleanup man and when he was back there no one ever got through all three guys. I know I didn't. He was so quick and he had those long arms, and then he got that 'clutch' on you.'

'He was just a top player, so great. He was the right player at the right time. He was such a good athlete, he probably could have started at any position on the Penn team. I'm lucky he wasn't a running back. I wouldn't have beaten him out.'

'I had a Spanish class with Chuck; he always had a good feel for language, but Spanish was not his thing. We both got a nice passing grade from Professor Suarez that we didn't deserve.'

"It was my great privilege to play with Chuck Bednarik for four years, to have known and enjoyed his company and to know how good a person he is. He is a very fine human being."

'I am proud to have had him as good friend for more than 60 years. Through golf, we have been able to maintain a great relationship. We've had some great golf games all over the Philadelphia area, New Jersey, Florida, Saucon Valley. I've played with him well over 100 times.'

'Chuck by his very nature, plays golf with the same intensity as he did football. He has total concentration and focus. He was about 10 handicap and he played when the chips were down. He transmitted that attitude to the other guys on his team. He is so positive. I never met anyone with a more dedicated focus.'

'The most amazing thing is that he didn't start playing golf seriously until after football. I started playing in college. It's hard to start at 35, and by 45 he was one of the better players in the Philadelphia area. Not necessarily by score, but in match play he was deadly. He might take a six on hole, but whenever he had to sink a putt, he did. You have to be mentally tough for match play; you have to have your A game. I was always amazed at how he competed in what I consider to be the toughest sport.'

'I've always made an effort to stay close to Chuck. I didn't want to lose touch with him. He has been a great asset to all of us who have known him. He taught us that life is tough and you have to get out there and fight."

Harry Gamble

Harry Gamble, who has worked at every level of football from high school to the NFL office, interacted with Chuck Bednarik during a brief tryout with the Eagles, and later as head coach at Penn and as an assistant with the Eagles.

Harry Gamble has been part of the Philadelphia-area football scene for 60 years. He has coached locally on the high school, collegiate and professional levels. He served as president of the Eagles for 10 years and worked in the NFL office in New York. He got to know Chuck Bednarik during a training camp experience with the Eagles in 1952. Later, as head coach at the University of Pennsylvania, Gamble got to better know the schools most famous football alumnus. They were reunited again when Dick Vermiel was coaching the Eagles.

"Chuck Bednarik, that's a good topic. My first experience with him was right out of college in 1952. I had gotten to know Vince McNally and I was in camp for a short time, about seven to ten days.'

'He was playing center at the time and as a young guy; I was in awe of Bednarik. I was on the offensive and defensive line; I learned a lot watching him work. He was a good guy and a hard-working professional.'

'As time went on I was signed by the Steelers and cut. I started as a high school coach at a time when there was no question that the biggest name in Philadelphia football was Chuck Bednarik.'

"He was playing center at the time and as a young guy; I was in awe of Bednarik. I was on the offensive and defensive line; I learned a lot watching him work. He was a good guy and a hard-working professional."

'You don't hear as much about him today. We get into the people of today, but there are too many people who never saw a guy like this play. There is a tendency of writers and media people to promote the guys they've seen, but Chuck Bednarik is as good as there ever was. He was a great player and a great athlete.'

'When I started at Rider in 1948, there were a lot of ex-GI's, guys like Chuck who flew in bombers, and they were real men because of the experience. You can add the military experience to the mystique of Chuck Bednarik; it made him a harder, more physical man.'

'The veterans were tougher to play against, a very special breed. They were men, separated from those who didn't have the war experience.'

'I became the head coach at Lafayette and Penn. I left Penn and joined the Eagles in '81. Dick Vermiel was coaching and Dick wanted Chuck around. It was great for both of them.'

'Vermiel gave me the opportunity to learn the pro game; he let me work with a variety of things. I spent a lot of time with Chuck on the road. I was a new coach in the league and he and I found a niche together.

To be around him, to hear his stories, it was a great experience. He was a great guy to be around.'

'Guys can disappear from the game but the people who saw him play are not going to forget. I feel that he will always be with the generation that remembers him as a player.'

'He was a great player. Within a game he did things that were not typical of other players. Out of necessity he rose to the occasion. If you have to say that modern players get more attention, I would say to you that Chuck Bednarik would be all-time at center and linebacker.'

'When I was a Penn in the 1970s he wrote a book. Bob Levy bought a copy of the book for every player on the team. As a coach it was great to have a guy like him around the current players. Absolutely; that's the way I've always felt about him.'

'He became a great speaker. I was at a dinner roast for Frank Gifford. He told the maintenance guy to dim the lights when he was introduced. When the got to the podium, they dimmed the lights and the room was dark. You heard him say, "Look familiar Frank' does this remind you of anything?"

'I don't know much about what happened between him and Leonard Tose; he just faded from the Eagles scene. There's a generation that doesn't remember him; he's someone we should all remember."

Wayne Hillman

Hillman played end for the University of Pennsylvania and remembers Chuck Bednarik as the most aggressive player on the team.

A member of the University of Pennsylvania class of 1950, Hillman played end for the Quakers and remembers Chuck Bednarik for his aggressive play on the field.

"He was the most aggressive person on the team. He knocked down everyone around him, every play.

'He was a fantastic linebacker.'

'He was a team player, always doing what he could to help the team.'

'There was no experience like those games at Franklin Field. I once calculated that during my four years at Penn, we played before one million people'

'I remember being with my wife at a game against the 49'ers when Chuck was moved back to center.'

'Leo Nomellini had been killing the quarterback and they benched the center and put Chuck in. The next day I read in the paper that Chuck was going back to playing center."

Harry Edenborn

A starting fullback for Penn before World War II, Edenborn returned after the war and was second-string for the new talent-laden squad.

When Harry Edenborn left the University of Pennsylvania for the service following the season, he was the starting fullback. When he returned to Penn after the war, the talent pool had improved so much that he rarely started again. A resident of Springfield, PA, he worked for Honeywell for 43 years before retiring.

"I wasn't a regular; there were too many All-Americans ahead of me when I came back to the team. I was the starting fullback in 1944; when I returned from the Army during the '46 season, I was third team varsity. I played for the scrub team against schools like Navy and Cornell. We were the preliminary game on River Field.'

'Oh sure, the talent improved after the war. There was a massive football build-up. I came back to a much different program.'

'Chuck Bednarik was just a great athlete and competitor. He was adamant in the huddle when things weren't going well. As far as I could tell he was most adamant.'

'I remember if we were going in the wrong direction, he would get down on one knee in the huddle telling us in very strong terms that we weren't doing well.'

'He could throw a football further than I could kick it. I was the backup punter to him and I couldn't compete. He could boom the ball.'

'Chuck was so good, Charlie Hassler the second string center didn't get to play much. When Munger tried to send Hassler in, Chuck would send him off the field. He said, "I'm not coming out; I'm staying in."

Tom Timoney

Thomas J. Timoney has been with the Fort Washington, PA based law firm, Timoney Knox, LLP., since graduating from the University of Pennsylvania law school in 1950. He was a four-year teammate of Chuck Bednarik during his undergraduate years at Penn.

"Oh man, I could talk about Chuck all day long. He entered Penn in the fall of '45, right out of the army.

It took him about two to three-weeks to get back into football shape, although he was always in shape. He looks like he could play now.'

'It became obvious to everyone on the team that he was different. Speed, toughness, instinct, he had it all he was different from everyone else.'

'I never saw anyone with his instinct; he always knew where the ball was going. He would keep his eyes on the ball carrier and knock the blockers out of the way. He could get to the ball at the same time he was beating the blocker. He always knew where the ball was.'

'I roomed in the same dorm as him, Memorial Hall. He had to work hard as a student. He worked as a student like he practiced on the field and he practiced every day like it was the fourth quarter of the Super Bowl.'

'He had to work hard as a student. He was probably a bit below average, but he did his book work every night. He hit the books every night, he and his roommate Bull Schweder had the door shut two, three hours every night studying. Bull was his best friend in college. They had gone to school in Bethlehem and they were always together their four years with the team.'

> ## "I think Chuck Bednarik is synonymous with football in Philadelphia. Four years at Penn, 14 with the Eagles, look at the record."

'On the field, all the games were the same to him – Army, Navy, Lafayette – it didn't matter. He always gave 100%. He always did it in such a casual manner, he never bragged, never acted better than anyone.'

'He was just an old-fashioned steel worker and he treated football like a job.'

'He did very little demanding of his teammates. He did his job and rarely got mad in his four years with the team.'

'The football players were big things on campus. We used to draw 70,000 to 80,000 people every game.

'The football players were big and Chuck was the best, but he never acted like it at all.'

'He was far beyond us in any sport. God, could he hit a baseball. During spring football we would watch him bat, he was on the baseball team, and he could hit the ball 360 feet. He could hit it from end zone to end zone. And he had a great arm as a catcher.'

'His arm was so good that George Munger put in a trick play for him one game. Chuck threw a pass after he centered the ball, but the other team must have spied on us in practice. They had a defender cover the center. Who covers the center?'

'I'll say one thing, he stood up to Davis, Blanchard, and the rest of the Army team better than his teammates. Chuck wasn't the biggest guy on the line, but he was tough and quick. He never folded, other guys did.'

'I think Chuck Bednarik is synonymous with football in Philadelphia. Four years at Penn, 14 with the Eagles, look at the record.'

'He is absolutely the last 60-minute man. It may sound corny, but it's true.'

'His pet name for me was 'the little read-headed son-of-a-bitch. He's consistent; he's always called me that."

All Time Penn Team 1950

PRINCETON
PENNSYLVANIA
OCTOBER 9, 1948 · 35 CENTS

A. Cornell v Penn Football program (Chuck's last game)
B. 1945 game ball from Penn vs. Columbia
C. All-Time Penn Football team
D. 1948 Princeton v Penn Football program
E. Chuck practicing punting
F. Fr. Donnelly with Chuck looking on

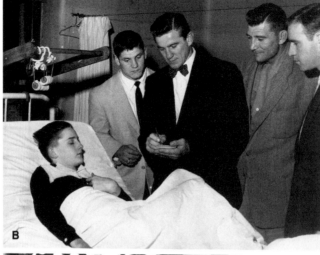

Bednarik Tops Ivy Selections

Penn Center Only Unanimous Choice

Seven of the eight schools ar
represented on the 1948 Ivy Leagu
All-Star football team selected b;
the Associated Press with the hel;
of the circuit's coaches.

Cornell's newly crowned cham
pions landed two men on the myth
ical eleven, as did Pennsylvania
Dartmouth and Columbia.

Harvard, Yale and Princeto
each earned one place, with Brow
the only team in the league to b
left off the first team.

The only unanimous choice for

Eagles Draft Chuck Bednarik

Maxwells Name Him College Star of Year

Continued from First Page

Bednarik intercepted seven passes
in 1946 and six in 1947. He has
grabbed only one enemy aerial this

day afterno
end of Bro;
of-town gues
of what's be
most every
After so n
tion finishes
seemed imp
could come
killer-diller
nerves tight
race at a fa
preceding dr
But it did.
The Arm;
was expecte
of a contest,
of the natio

A. Eagles captain Al Wistert receives gilded ball from Ralph Kelly

B. Chuck and teammates visit Children's Hospital

C. 1949 Championship celebration

D. Singing with an war buddy

E. 1949 receiving the Maxwell Award from Bert Bell, Coach Greasy Neale and former Governor John Bell witness ceremony

F. Chuck and his good friend Steve Van Buren

Chapter | **four**

The Draft and Rookie Year

The longest running football show in Philadelphia history would have exited the local stage after just four years were it not for a serendipitous draw from a hat in the fall of 1948 and an attack of old-fashioned Catholic guilt.

Despite the fact the that the Eagles would go on win the NFL championship one month later, a lucky draw from a hat gave them the right to select any collegiate player in the nation prior to the actual draft. With the same one-in-eight chance as the other seven participating teams, Eagles general manager Charlie Ewart plucked the marked piece of paper and the Birds jumped ahead of the last place Detroit Lions with something that was variously reported as the 'bonus player,' 'bonus choice,' and 'bonus selection' in the newspapers of the day.

However, even before the NFL draft for the 1949 season took place, a nervous college senior, concerned that he would not be drafted at all, was wined, dined and seduced by legendary Branch Rickey. The plot included a secret overnight train ride to a desolate town in upstate New York that culminated with a jittery young couple sitting across a desk from the crafty Mahatma.

It took 60 years to comfortably reveal, but in 2009, Chuck Bednarik admitted that he was property of the Brooklyn Dodgers of the All-America Football Conference for a brief time. The signing, though widely speculated about, was not announced nor confirmed in the press, and was quietly undone with some help from Above.

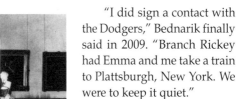

"I did sign a contact with the Dodgers," Bednarik finally said in 2009. "Branch Rickey had Emma and me take a train to Plattsburgh, New York. We were to keep it quiet."

"He put a contract in front of me, I think it was for three years, and I signed. As soon as I walked out I said "Oh, I'm in trouble."

Bednarik may not have had Vito Corleone to undo a contract like he did for Johnny Fontaine, but Chuck did have Father John Donnelly, his all-purpose adviser and dormitory boss back at Newman Hall at Penn.

"I went to see Father Donnelly and told him about the contract. I don't know who he talked to, but they got me out of it," recalled Bednarik.

"I wasn't sure I was going to be drafted and the Dodgers seemed like a good opportunity," said Bednarik.

"I wasn't thinking of pro ball. I had no idea. I was planning to be a teacher and a coach."

The relationship between Bednarik and Donnelly

constituted one of the first and certainly most unique-player-agent relationships in sports history. In and "exclusive interview" with Jack Walsh of the Washington Post late November 1948, "Father Donnelly produced a notarized pact dated May 19, 1948, in which Bednarik, 23 year (sic) old, placed himself under Father Donnelly's exclusive management regarding any professional offers."

The article went to state "...both vehemently denied a widely circulated rumor that Bednarik accepted $3,000...to play pro football for the Brooklyn Dodgers." No doubt Bednarik and Donnelly spent extra time in the confessional booth after that article.

"I was supposed to play in the East-West All-Start game after the season. Herman Hickman, the north coach in the North-South Game, told me I could build a 'big bridge' to the NFL if I played in the North-South Game instead.

"I was so unsure of getting drafted that I took Hickman's advice. Emma and I watched the Eagles '48 championship game on the beach in Florida while I was down there for the game."

The Dodgers had him in their crosshairs all along and thought they had the inside track due to the presence of one his former Penn coaches on their staff.

The Associated Press reported under the headline "DOLLAR WAR SHAPING BETWEEN PRO LEAGUES" "Spirited Bidding for Collegiate Talent Reported; Walker, Bednarik Much Sought."

The article continued, "A new dollar war is shaping up between the National Football League and the rival All-American Conference in their bid for the cream for of the 1948 college crop."

'Spirited bidding is reported already underway on such starts as Doak Walker of Southern Methodist, Stan Heath of Nevada, Johnny Rauch of Georgia and Chuck Bednarik of Pennsylvania."

Indeed head coach Greasy Neale had told reporters for several months that the Eagles would pick Bednarik given the opportunity.

Rickey, president of the Dodgers, thought one Horse Hendrickson could help deliver the Penn All-American to Brooklyn. Hendrickson,

> **"He put a contract in front of me, I think it was for three years, and I signed. As soon as I walked out I said "Oh, I'm in trouble."**

Coach Greasy Neale

the Dodger backfield coach, had been an assistant to George Munger at Penn and also coached Bednarik when he was a freshman catcher on the baseball team. (Bednarik later admitted that he couldn't stand Hendrickson while playing at Penn and walked off the baseball team during a game against Princeton when the Horse benched him his freshman year.)

Columnist Red Smith, then of The Herald Tribune, related a conversation with an assistant to Rickey as follows:

"He (Arthur Mann) said there were more ways for a coach to earn his salary than teaching guys to run and pass. He said that if Hendrickson's former connections—Horse used to help George Munger coach at Penn—enabled the Dodgers to land Bednarik and Columbia's Lou Kusserow, why that would be a coup worth two years' wages."

Rumors of the day alleged that the Dodgers did offer upfront money. While Bednarik did admit being approached by the Dodgers, for one of the few times in his life he remained evasive and told something less than the truth. When asked about the Dodgers offer, he said that the sum of their discussions amounted to whether or not he had an interest in playing pro football and his response was "I told him I did—and I hope I can."

With the help of Father Donnelly, the Dodgers faded away and Bednarik was free to be drafted by the Eagles.

(If Bednarik had honored the contract, he never would have played for the Dodgers, but may have had a long career in New York. For the final season of the AAFC in 1949, the Dodgers merged with the New York Yankees. The league folded in December of that year and the Browns, 49'ers and Baltimore Colts were merged into the NFL. Most of the Dodgers-Yankees players were assigned to the New York Giants.)

In 1947, the NFL had initiated the Bonus Lottery Pick, a gimmick to draw increased interest to the draft. Each of the league's 10 teams would select a ticket, with the stipulation once a team won it was precluded for participation for the next few years. The Chicago Bears and Washington Redskins had won the first two lotteries and were thus were both disqualified for the 1949 pick.

The Eagles, based on record, had the ninth pick in the draft that year. Without the bonus pick, Bednarik would have never dropped to them, no doubt going in the first four or five picks to the likes of the Detroit Lions, New York Giants or Green Bay Packers.

"God knows where I'd be living today if I didn't get drafted by the Eagles. It was a shock to get drafted at all, but God was taking care of me when the Eagles picked me," said Bednarik.

Chuck Bednarik puts his signature on an Eagles contract while a coterie of bosses looks on. Seated l to r: Coach Greasy Neale, Bednarik, club president James P. Clark; rear, James N. Peterson, tickets, etc., Frank McNamee, treasurer; Paul Lewis, secretary.

On November 29th, the Eagles announced that were taking Bednarik with the bonus pick. At this contract signing he told the press, "Whenever I thought of playing pro ball it was always with the Eagles."

"I signed for a $3,000 bonus and $7,000 salary and, coming out of poverty, I felt filthy rich," Bednarik recalls of his first contract.

When Bednarik reported to training camp for the 1949 season, the Eagles were the defending NFL champions and were loaded at the rookie's two positions. Vic Lindskog and Alex Wojciechowicz manned the center spot, and over on defense Wojie and Joe Muha were two of the best linebackers in the league.

From the onset, Bednarik showed the coaches and veterans that he was as good as his collegiate reputation promised. But with a loaded roster, Neale had the luxury of bringing the rookie along slowly. Bednarik got his first professional start at center in an early exhibition game against the Chicago Bears.

The game was being played in Philadelphia and when Neale was asked if he was starting the rookie as a "nice gesture" to please all of his fans from Philadelphia and Bethlehem, Neale responded, "I wouldn't start my

> **"If Bednarik had honored the contract, he never would have played for the Dodgers, but may have had a long career in New York."**

brother against those Bears unless I thought he was the best player."

This was one of the toughest veteran teams in the league, and Bednarik recalled, "Some of the guys like Pihos and Kilroy used to give me a hard time, but I was a mean, tough kid."

For all of his preseason promise, Benarik did not get any playing time the first two games of the season. These were the defending league champions and after drafting Bednarik, Neale fretted that he "might have too much talent."

Bednarik missed the season opener against the New York Bulldogs with a stomach virus. He spent the next game on the bench while the Eagles beat the Lions in Detroit, 22-14. The home opener was coming up at Shibe Park against the Chicago Cardinals the following week. On the train ride back from Detroit, Bednarik was steamed over not having played and went in to Greasy Neale's compartment to let him know his feelings.

"I was seething on the train coming back and went in and told him 'play me or trade,' recalls Bednarik. "I had never sat on the bench, and I said 'If I'm not good enough to play for this team, get rid of me.' He told me to calm down, he was just breaking me in, and I would get time when he saw fit."

His break came in the next week against the Cardinals. Neale put him in at linebacker for Wojciehowicz.

The following week he started at center for an injured Lindskog and didn't sit again for 14 years.

"I had never sat on the bench, and I said "If I'm not good enough to play for this team, get rid of me."

Linebacker was always his more natural position and playing center in the NFL required a bit of an adjustment, as he was snapping the ball in a T-formation for the first time as opposed to rifling the ball between his legs in the single wing.

'I'm sure I jammed some fingers and bruised some hands,' Bednarik recalled of his learning days.

Lindskog returned to center, Bednarik shifted back to defense, and Wojie never got his job back. The Eagles went into the championship game against the Los Angeles Rams with a record of 11-1 and Bednarik was established as a star of the defense.

In a Philadelphia Inquirer article dated December 14, Frank O'Gara reported that 'Bednarik...will learn in a few days that his burly shoulders will carry a lot of the Eagles' hopes Sunday in Los Angeles when the Philadelphians seek their second straight National Football League title." He added that Bednarik "will be entrusted with the primary job of reducing the pass-catching efficiency of the Rams' record-holder end Tom Fears."

Later the article reports, "And when Wojie gets in," remarked Neale, "he'll be so doggone mad that he'll like to tear the Rams apart." The ex-Fordham All-American is not the type to be replaced by a rookie and take the slight lying down."

The Eagles won the championship game 14-0, to punctuate Bednarik's charmed rookie season. The only disappointment was financial, a dreadful rainstorm kept the paid attendance down to about 28,000 and the gross receipts which determined the players' bonus was only $127,000. Each winning players share was $1,090.

Jim Gallagher

The ultimate go-to guy for all things Eagles, Gallagher started his long career with the team in 1949, the same year as another rookie, Chuck Bednarik.

The go-to guy for all things Eagles, Jim Gallagher served the team in just about every executive position during his tenure with the team from 1949-65. A graduate of Northeast High in Philadelphia, Gallagher's jobs with the Eagles included Personnel Director, Director of Public Relations, Director of Sales and Marketing and Traveling Secretary. A universally popular person, he was inducted into the Eagles Honor Roll in 1995.

"Chuck Bednarik was a great, great player. He and I were both rookies with Eagles in 1949, though he didn't know who I was then. I was also at Penn with him in 1948. My first job out of Pierce Business School was as a clerk in the athletic office at Penn.'

"I saw about five or six Penn games that year.. Chuck was one of the few guys to wear a facemask. He wore it to protect a busted-up nose. He snapped the ball in the single wing, played linebacker, punted, kicked off. He was super; could run, was strong, handsome.'

'I started working for the Eagles in September 1949. We were in a dinky office at 17th and Market.'

We played 12 games. Shibe Park was home, but sometimes we opened at Municipal Stadium.'

'The first time I saw Chuck was in the office and sometimes I would see him at practice at Shibe. His rookie year, we were the world champs. He blocked a punt in the championship game at the LA Coliseum. It was a messy, rainy day.'

'Vic Lindskog was the center and early in the season Chuck wasn't happy that he wasn't playing. I remember him telling me "Yeah Jimmy, I went to see Greasy. I said 'what the hell is going on here, I want to play.'" He told him that he wanted to be traded, and he started playing after that.'

'He's right up there with the best Eagles of all-time—him, Van Buren, Tommy McDonald.'

'I remember an interception he had against the Colts in 1954; ran it in for a touchdown and threw the ball into the stands. He punted a few times, kicked off.'

'It was nice what Vermeil did in bringing him back in '76. Chuck was always with us and it was good to have him around again. I don't know what happened with Chuck and Tose. I didn't get involved with Tose much. I know Chuck went in to see him when he took over the team and nothing came of it. I don't recall Tose thinking much about Chuck.'

'Chuck called Leonard looking for the GM job, the day the club changed hands – May 1, 1969. He had let Joe Kuharich go—he had a bad record and he wasn't likable. Somebody said Chuck wanted to see Leonard, and he said no.'

Bill Mackrides

Bill Mackrides played quarterback for the Eagles from 1947-1951. A second-round pick from Nevada-Reno, it was his job to help Chuck Bednarik adjust from a single wing collegiate center to a T-formation snapper in the NFL. He has remained in the area as a resident of Delaware County.

"Chuck's opinionated, so you probably have a lot of material to write about.'

'I don't think anyone had expectations when he joined us in '49. Some guys may have had doubts because he didn't play in the Southwest Conference, or another big conference. No one really spoke out against him; the attitude was more of let's see what he has.'

'He delivered.'

'Vic Lindskog was our regular center and he was about half the size of Bednarik. They got into a scuffle on the field early in camp. No one knew what started it; it could have been any little thing.'

'For the most part Bednarik wasn't treated differently. We knew he came in with a big reputation having played across the city at Penn.'

"I think Chuck became more outspoken in his later years; he resents the money. Our whole team salary in 1949 was $190,000. If you listen to him, some of what he says is true, but what drives him, I don't know."

'As a matter of fact, I was the backup quarterback and it was my job to work with him and teach him how to snap the ball in a T-formation. He had been a single wing center in college.'

'He could hit you in the hand and break a finger; it got hairy back there. I got a couple of jams, but he was an athlete and it didn't take long.'

'Though one time I pulled my hands out and he smacked himself in the rump.'

'But really it took him about one day and he was ready.'

'I'll tell you an interesting thing; I played against him in high school, when I was at West Philadelphia High.'

'We went up to Bethlehem in 1942. He was playing, but I didn't realize it until later.'

'We were both undefeated going in and it ended a 0-0 tie.'

'With the Eagles he didn't start the first few games, and he wanted to play linebacker. We had good linebackers Wojie, (Alex Wojciechowicz), Jack Meyers, and Joe Muha — he was really outstanding, he never got the credit he deserved.'

'I wanted people to see those game films; we had an outstanding defense and Muha made most of the tackles.'

'His name later became mud. After he retired, he became an official and tried to unionize all the officials. The league ran him out and you never heard much about him.'

'It's a different game today.'

'I think Chuck became more outspoken in his later years; he resents the money. Our whole team salary in 1949 was $190,000. If you listen to him, some of what he says is true, but what drives him, I don't know.'

'Basically, he's a good guy. He's been out in front of the public for so long that I think he gets the impression he's an authority on things.'

'He's a very nice person, but he gets so much publicity and I think that affects him. He's also a very sensitive person.'

'He resents things. We were just born too soon. More power to today's players. You can't take it away from guys wanting to make as much money as they can.'

'It is true that the alumni don't feel appreciated. It might be the lowest ebb with this current group. There are probably only about nine or 10 guys left from the '48 team and it would have been nice if something was done in recognition.'

'Lurie and the people who came into town with him didn't grow up in Philly."

Dan DiRenzo

Discovered on the local sandlots by Greasy Neale, DiRenzo joined the Eagles for the 1949 championship season and was a teammate of the rookie Chuck Bednarik.

Dan DiRenzo may have been the original "Invinceable" story in Eagles history. While playing sandlot ball in the semi-pro Eastern League, DiRenzo was scouted by Greasy Neale and offered a contract to join the Eagles in 1949. He was also under contract by the Boston Red Sox at the time. He parlayed his one year with the Eagles, 1949, into a successful sales and marketing career, eventually becoming head of east coast sales for Miller Brewing. He was a member of the Eagles during Chuck Bednarik's rookie season.

"The first time we saw Chuck play was actually against us when he was on the College All Star Team. The Eagles were the NFL champs, so we played the college all starts that summer. Bud Wilkinson was the coach of the all-stars, and after that game Chuck joined us.'

'Greasy personally scouted me on the sandlots. He offered me a job and I stayed the rest of the year. Greasy converted me to end. I had never played there before, but he had me lining up across from guys like Wildman Willey and Chuck Bednarik. There was not wide receiver or tight end in those days; you were just an end.'

'Those bastards used me as a tennis ball; they bounced me all over the place.'

'Chuck was a great guy; I remember those fingers. He beat the hell out of me on the field, but then he would work with you afterward and explain what I needed to do to get better.'

'Chuck was always there for me. I've met up with him at some of the alumni functions; he's one hell of a guy. He was always great with young people.'

'That '49 team had great chemistry. There were some real characters and tough guys like Bucko Kilroy and Otis Douglas.'

'It was an unbelievable experience to be part of that team. I was just a young guy. I hadn't even played high school ball, and I get a phone call one night from Greasy Neale, asking me if I wanted to join the Eagles. Next thing I'm on the field, being exposed to guys like Chuck Bednarik, Tommy Thompson, Bill Mackrides and Steve Van Buren. To me, Chuck Bednarik was THE individual star of the 1950s.'

'I had my one season with the Eagles. After the season I went in to see Vince McNally. I needed more than the $7,000 or $8,000 they were paying in those days. He asked me what I would like to do and I said I might want to get into sales.'

'I had no experience, so he told me to take a sales job with a tobacco company and come back and see him in a year.'

'I did that, came back to see him a year later, and he set me up with Fred Miller, of Miller Beer, who had been a friend of his at Notre Dame. I spent 25 years with them, becoming the head of east coast sales working out of 630 Fifth Avenue in Manhattan."

Neill Armstrong

Neill Armstrong played for the Philadelphia Eagles from 1947-1951. He was a defensive coordinator for the Minnesota Vikings during the peak of their "Purple People Eater" days and was head coach of the Chicago Bears from 1978-1981.

"I started with the Eagles in 1947 and I was there when he joined the team in '49. It clear from the start that he was a great player; he always played hard.'

'I played left end on offense and right cornerback on defense. Chuck and Wojie (Alex Wojciehowicz) were the linebackers. I remember talking to Chuck, "If you hit that guy on the line of scrimmage, you make my job easier." He had a big reach, the longest arms I've ever seen.'

'Greasy liked to turn his receivers into defensive backs. I had never played defensive back and I told Chuck and Wojie, they'd better help me out.'

'They didn't split the receivers out to much in those days, so we had Chuck and Wojie pounding on those guys as they were coming out. He had such a wingspan; it was tough for receivers to get around him.'

'He was in my mind, right up there with any linebacker I've ever seen.'

'Even in those days you paid attention to the guys coming in as high draft choices, and Chuck Bednarik went beyond what you would expect of a linebacker. Then after '51, they had him going both ways.'

"Greasy liked to turn his receivers into defensive backs. I had never played defensive back and I told Chuck and Wojie, they'd better help me out."

'One of the things I remember, he had an amazing arm. We used to watch him throw a baseball. He could stand at homeplate and throw a baseball into the outfield stands. What made it even more amazing is that I've never seen a pair of hands as beat up as his."

Al Wistert

Teammate of Chuck Bednarik and captain of Eagles when Bednarik joined the team in 1949.

A member of the NFL's All-Decade Team for the 1940s, Al Wistert was team captain when Chuck Bednarik joined the Eagles in 1949. Bednarik often credited Wistert for easing his transition to the professional game with his leadership and guidance. One of three brothers who were All-American tackles at the University of Michigan, Wistert was also named to the All-Pro team eight times during his nine year career.

When asked who he believed was the most deserving NFL player not in the Pro Football Hall of Fame, Bednarik once replied, "Without question "Ox" (Wistert) should've been in there years ago. It's a crime." Those who agree with Bednarik can go to the website "Al Wistert for Pro Football Hall of Fame" and sign the petition.

> **"Greasy Neale was our coach and he was excellent. He knew football backward and front. The only thing, he was rough around the edges. He swore a lot."**

"He's (Benarik) quite a guy. When he first came to the Eagles he made all the difference in the world. He added a lot of personality.'

'When he got here, there was a guy from Stanford in front of him, Vic Lindskog. He and Chuck got into an argument of the field. Lindskog had been a boxer and I can hear Chuck saying, "I don't care if you are a boxer, I'll fight you anyway."

'That was my first meeting with Chuck Bednarik.'

'We were in Philly and he had played at Penn, and he was well-recognized because of that. I remember watching him play at Penn, but we didn't think much of him being an outstanding player until he stepped on the field with us. He could hold his own.'

'His reputation didn't mean anything until he got on the field. He made an impression.'

'He was an outstanding player. He gave everything he could.'

'I was the team captain and I tried to be as friendly as I could to all the new guys. It helped the team.'

'Chuck was a bonus pick. There was a bidding war

going on with the AFC, and it helped everybody's paycheck. '

'Greasy Neale was our coach and he was excellent. He knew football backward and front. The only thing, he was rough around the edges. He swore a lot.'

'He cussed a blue streak and I wasn't used to that. I was raised by mother and three sisters and there was no swearing around the house.'

'At Michigan I played for Fritz Crisler, who had played for Amos Alonzo Stagg, who had been a minister. That's the kind of man he was.'

'The swearing affected my play seriously my first year. After that I got used to it. But Greasy was a fine man and he knew his football.'

'Chuck was an asset to the club the moment he stepped on the field. He wasn't playing the first few games and the told Greasy "Play me or trade me." He had words with Greasy.'

'Lindskog was the starting center and he was a good one. Greasy started playing Chuck at linebacker.'

'We had a great team and a great group of guys. Jimmy Gallagher is responsible for holding the alumni together.'

'Frankly, this organization doesn't seem to care much about the '49 team. They don't see much value in recognizing us. We feel neglected by the team.'

'It's not a case of us wanting to be around all the time, just some recognition for an outstanding job.'

'It's too bad, I always felt close to the fans in Philly. They were extra loyal. It's a good place.'

'People told me I wouldn't enjoy Philadelphia. They couldn't be more wrong.'

'They said the fans weren't enthusiastic. It was just the opposite.'

'The biggest thing I remember was going to the old Bookbinders. For every shutout, we'd get a free meal at Bookbinders.'

'If they were scoreless at halftime we'd shout, "Let's hold them and go to Bookbinders and live it up as guests of the restaurant."

'That was very much responsible for us wanting to get shutouts. It helped us a great deal.'

'Years later I went to Bookbinders and the same old doorman was out in front. He said "Mr. Wistert, what are you doing here?" It made me feel great."

Steve Van Buren

Chuck Bednarik was the second Philadelphia Eagle player to be inaugurated into the Pro Football Hall of Fame. The first was the only player Bednarik ever referred to as "my hero." Here is a heartwarming story between two former teammates and friends.

The Two Best Eagles There Ever Were got together for lunch in August 2009. Neither Chuck Bednarik, No. 60, nor Steve Van Buren, No. 15, leaves their homes much anymore, and knowing that this meeting had been set up, they were excited to see each other.

No. 60 doesn't travel well these days and he can make the driver wish that he were anywhere but in this car when heavy traffic or construction delays, slow, or suspend forward progress. (He also takes an unkind view of aggressive motorists. "Don't let that son-of-a-bitch pass you," is a frequent order if another vehicle approaches from either flank.) He gets more cranky and seems more conscious of the traffic on Route 222 as the radio signal carrying Jolly Joe Timmer's midday polka music show disintegrates into a crackle. One hates to see Jolly Joe fade away, as now Bednarik's attention will be focused on the drive.

There aren't many people that he will travel to visit and it is about a 75-minute trip from his home in the Lehigh Valley to the retirement community in Lancaster County where No. 15 resides. He is dressed and waiting near the front door when the driver arrives. It is a sunny morning and No. 60 seems more like an adolescent boy who is going to visit the best friend he hasn't seen since he moved away to another town. "So we're going to see Steve Van Buren," are his first words to the driver.

No. 60 is renowned for his impatience and usually seems to want to leave a place just about the time he gets there. In 2007, the Eagles held a ceremony at Lincoln Financial Field to honor the members of the franchise's 75th anniversary team. Of course No. 15 and No. 60 both made the cut.

The all-time Eagles team was feted on the field at halftime of the Eagles-Lions game. Not many people knew that No. 15 was present until fan attention was directed to one of the club boxes and Steve Van Buren waved to the crowd.

No. 60 bolted from the stadium shortly after the second half started. He was already riding a golf cart to his car in the parking lot when members of the Van Buren family said to a member of the Bednarik family that "Dad would love to see Chuck."

The family member was dubious, but said he would try to get word to No. 60. When he's ready to leave, he's gone. And if he was already at the car, it was unfathomable to think that he would return to the stadium for anyone.

An Eagles staff member radioed to the driver who was escorting No. 60 that Steve Van Buren asked to see him.

If there were 70,000 people in the stadium that day, No. 15 is the only one that could get a u-turn out of No. 60. In fact, No. 15 was the only person in the state of Pennsylvania and beyond who could have brought No. 60 back.

"Steve is here?" came from a background voice on the radio. A few minutes later, The Greatest Eagles There Ever Were watched most of the second half side-by-side.

It's been 60 years since they first met. In early August of 1949, the Eagles were at training camp in Grand Rapids, Michigan. No. 15 was the unquestioned star of the team, the best running back in football.

No. 60 was the touted rookie from Penn.

It is now late fall for those two boys of summer; No. 15 is 88 years old and No. 60 recently turned 84.

The retirement village No. 15 resides in has the setting, ambience and appointments of a country club. He has family members living nearby who visit often.

No. 60 is running a bit late and when he pulls up, No. 15 is waiting at the entrance to the dining hall.

The clasp hands and No. 15 starts a dialogue that is to be repeated several times during the visit.

"You were the best."

"No, you were the best."

"You were the best."

"Speak for yourself."

"No Chuck, you were the best."

"Let's leave it that you were the best runner and I was the best tackler."

As they pass through the dining hall and get seated, people start to whisper and gently point. They still recognize No. 15 and No. 60, looking past their gray hairs and shrunken frames. On this warm day in Amish Country, The Greatest Eagles There Ever Were are having lunch together.

The well-wishers and autograph seekers slowly begin coming to the table. This includes fellow residents of the village, and their visiting friends, children and grandchildren. Some have memories to share; others ask if they could have their pictures taken with the two legends. Fathers and mothers line up their kids, who have no idea who these two old guys are, for photos.

No. 15, who was born in Spanish Honduras and graduated from LSU, drops some insults and does some old-fashioned ball busting in Spanish. He tells stories that could have been inspirations for the old Jiggs and Maggie comic strip. The fastest running back in the league in his day, he claims that his speed came from having to outrun his wife while she chased him with a broomstick. He also recounts a long ago Thanksgiving when he made a hasty exit from the house, followed by a well-aimed turkey that had been thrown in the direction of his head. He pause sevarl times during his meal to state, "He was the best." No. 60 returns the insults in his family's native Slovakian tongue. The members of the two families who are present agree that it is a good day for both of them.

No. 60 talks about heaven and No. 15 says he doesn't think he is going there, but doesn't want to go to the other place because he doesn't want to run into Greasy Neale.

No. 60 was once long ago quoted as saying that No. 15 was his hero. That may have been the only time in his life No. 60 used that term on anyone, and No. 15 never let him forget hit. Over the years he would teasingly ask, "Chuck, am I still your hero?"

On this day, No. 15 is reminded of that, and he nods his head in slow affirmation.

No. 60 says, "He still is my hero."

After lunch, they do their goodbyes outside. Another round of the 'You were the best' dialogue ensues.

They squeeze hands and No. 60 takes his rosary beads out of his pocket and holds them up to the forehead of his old friend.

"I'll see you in Heaven."

Many times during the ride home, No. 60 repeats, "I can't believe that Steve Van Buren remembered me."

A. Chuck visits Grateford Prison
B. Chuck with Steve Van Buren
D. Phila Eagles basketball team
E. 1954 Emma with Chuck on the field receiving a new car

TO CHUCK
BEDNARIK
FROM HIS
ROOTERS

Chapter | **five**

The 1950s

As the 1950s unraveled, the NFL built a gradual momentum that started to bubble with the 1958 championship game between the New York Giants and Baltimore Colts, then erupted and exploded all over the national landscape in the 1960s.

For the Eagles, the 1950s hovered between mediocre and dismal. They entered the 1950 season as two-time defending NFL champs, but were smacked with a stunning loss that very first weekend, then spent the rest of the decade playing catch up.

Three teams from the upstart All-American Football Conference were merged into the NFL, led by the four-time championship squad, the Cleveland Browns. Commissioner Bert Bell, the Philadelphia native who ran the league from a center city office, arranged the schedule for the Browns and Eagles to open the season one day ahead of everyone else, with a special Saturday night game. It would be a home game for the Eagles, at Municipal Stadium, and was much anticipated as the 'World Series of Pro Football."

Widely regarded as having one of the most bruising defenses in the league, the Eagles shut out the Los Angeles Rams 14-0 to win the '49 title game. The Rams had perhaps the most sophisticated passing offense in the league, but they were completely shut down by the Eagles.

With Otto Graham calling plays drawn up by Paul

> **"Bednarik was prescient about what people remember, but fortunately for lore and legend— both his and that of the NFL- his real last season—1962, isn't the one best remembered, but fortunately, neither is 1959. Despite his words of the time, the lasting memory of Chuck Bednarik, Philadelphia Eagle, was not a loss to the Cleveland Browns that cost them second place."**

Brown, the Browns carved up the Eagles defense with a precise and sophisticated passing game that was new to the league. When the Eagles loosened up to cover the outside, Marion Motley pounded the middle. Final score was Browns 35, Eagles 10. Chuck Bednarik would be the one player who stayed with the Eagles through the entire decade, and it would be 10 years before he would get a shot at another championship.

The decade that started with the defending NFL champs losing to the Browns ended the same way. The Eagles lost to Paul Brown's squad 28-21 in the last game of the '59 season at Franklin Field, on a day in which Bednarik was to be honored on his pending retirement. He received $1,000 and a new television for 11 years of good work, and after the game told Sandy Grady of the Philadelphia Bulletin, "No, this is it," when asked if he could be tempted by a big salary to come back. The net financial gain on this day could have been greater for Bednarik, but with the loss the Eagles were denied sole possession of second place, costing each player $300.

He had been primarily a center for most of the season, and here in the finale appeared on defense for just two nondescript goal line plays. A great career was coming to an end with one championship and all sorts of recognition, but no uber legend grand finale fable for the ages.

Cub sports reporter Stan Hochman, of the Philadelphia Daily News, spent the entire day tailing Bednarik on what was widely believe, to be the last game day of his great career. Hochman arrived at the house in Abington for breakfast, tagged along for the drive to Franklin Field, and all but tucked him in after midnight. Before leaving the post game locker room, Bednarik told Hochman, "I just feel it's time to quit. I saw Steve Van Buren carried off the field with every ligament in his knee torn. I don't want to play that long. And I don't want to be cut in the middle of the season, and told I can't do the job. This is a good time to quit, because people remember the last thing you did, the last season you played."

Five National League football stats who planed to Los Angeles for the Jan 14 All-Pro game are Pete Pihos, Eagles' end, (left) and (from top to bottom) Joe Geri, Steelers' back, Walt Barnes, Eagles' guard, Emlen Tunnell, Giants' back, and Chuck Bednarik, Eagles' center.

Bednarik was prescient about what people remember, but fortunately for lore and legend—both his and that of the NFL- his real last season—1962, isn't the one best remembered, but fortunately, neither is 1959. Despite his words of the time, the lasting memory of Chuck Bednarik, Philadelphia Eagle, was not a loss to the Cleveland Browns that cost them second place.

But, as the 1950s closed, Bednarik was 34 years old and tired. He liked his job selling, what else but concrete for the Warner Company. He was sure that there was not going to be a 1960 season in his future.

Chuck Bednarik was 25 years old at the start of his sophomore season in 1950. What was there to not feel good about; he was two years married, had gotten a $500 raise; and he was the starting center for the best team in the league. The Eagles may have been a bit embarrassed when the College All-Stars beat them 17-7, to kickoff the preseason, but they recovered to win four of five remaining exhibition games.

Going into the season opener, the Browns were a curious novelty. Media people gave them about as much of a chance of beating the Eagles as the Kansas City Chiefs and Oakland Raiders would get years later in those first two Super Bowls against Green Bay. But Otto Graham would prove to be more Joe Namath than Len Dawson or Darryl Lamonica. For the Eagles, Steve Van Buren, Al Wistert and Bosh Pritchard were all hurt. Playing center, Bednarik had to deal with the best noseguard he had seen to date, in Bill Willis, and the Eagles were never in the game.

The Eagles regrouped enough to win six of their next seven, but wilted as the weather turned cold, losing their last four, without scoring more that one touchdown in any of the games. Bednarik earned his first All-Pro selection, and was named to the East squad for the inaugural Pro Bowl, but all head coach Greasy Neale got out of the 6-6 season was a telegram informing him that he was "no longer the coach of the Philadelphia Eagles."

They were only a year removed from back-to-back titles, but the distance from their last championship would only grow longer as the decade advanced. By 1951, the team barely resembled the great squad of 1949.

Greasy Neale was gone, and most of his former players would go on to call him the best coach they ever had. When Neale would be elected to the Pro Football Hall of Fame in 1969, his presenter was Chuck Bednarik.

Steve Van Buren had been slowed by a variety of injuries in 1950. The next year he ripped up his knee in a preseason game. Bednarik would say it was the worst injury he ever saw and would cite it a few years later, when he announced his first retirement, as being the type of injury he wanted to avoid.

Tommy Thompson, the one-eyed quarterback who led the Eagles to three championship games, decided to call it quits. He took with him slick ball handling skills, an efficient passing arm, and the cocky leadership traits of a championship quarterback. Two of the toughest guys on defense, Joe Muha and Hall-of-Fame bound Alex Wojciechowicz, retired.

The new head coach was Alvin 'Bo' McMillan. The season started with promise as the Eagles won the first two games, but McMillan took a medical leave of absence after the second game. He was diagnosed with cancer, and sadly passed away six months later.

Neale's firing had been most unpopular with the players, but McMillan's tough-minded approach was beginning to win their confidence. Wayne Millner, a likable assistant, took over the top job, but the team never recovered from the loss of McMillan and finished 4-8 in the franchise's first losing season since 1942. Bednarik was again named to the All-League team, and played in the Pro Bowl. He had played two-ways for most of the season.

During the offseason, Bednarik worked as a salesman for Elmo Pio Wines. His main territory was Bethlehem and the greater Lehigh Valley area. Bethlehem was loaded with pubs, and no innkeeper was about to say no when Chuck Bednarik offered to sell him a couple of cases of wine.

Since meeting Emma in 1948, Bednarik had started to develop what would become a lifelong passion for music, especially of the ethnic variety. The Pio Company, intent on cashing in on his name, created a weekly radio program for him. Bednarik loved the gig, as he got to select his own music for every show.

Millner was removed as head coach following the 1951 season and replaced by another assistant, Jim Trimble, who wanted to have Bednarik play linebacker only. The Eagles had sophomore Ken Farragut ready to take over most of the offensive center duties. A Philadelphia Inquirer article dated August 16 claimed that Bednarik was now the undisputed best center in football with the retirement of Chicago's Bulldog Turner. While playing full-time on defense, Bednarik did shift back to center as the need arose.

The Eagles finished the 1952 season 7-5, the first of three consecutive seven win seasons under Trimble.

Before the start of the 1953 season, general manager Vince McNally put the kibosh to another proposal that would have had Bednarik pulling extra duty.

Through the early '50s, Bednarik continued to play baseball with the hometown Mountaineers. McNally okayed this as long as Bednarik did not catch. However, a year or two earlier, Bednarik had also started working out with the Philadelphia A's at Shibe Park. He put on a

Bednarik told Hochman "I just feel its time to quit, I saw Steve Van Buren carried off the field with every ligament in his knee torn. I don't want to play that long. And I don't want to be cut in the middle of the season, and told I can't do the job. This is a good time to quit, because people remember the last thing you did, the last season you played."

uniform and impressed everyone in the organization with his raw home run power during batting practice. He particularly enjoyed his home run hitting contests with slugger Gus Zernial.

Bednarik later told Sandy Grady, of The Evening Bulletin, "I got to be good friends with Gus Zernial. We bet dimes for every shot we could hit for a home run. I didn't lose any money to Gus."

When starting catcher Joe Astroth was injured during the '53 season, manager Jimmy Dykes and owner Connie Mack wanted to add Bednarik as a catcher. They offered him a contract and wanted him to play a few games in the minors before joining the team. Bednarik told Grady, "I was so excited I almost started dancing," but McNally put his foot down on this one, arguing that the Eagles could not afford to lose him to a baseball-induced injury. Bednarik reluctantly agreed, but always wondered about how a career in major league baseball would have worked out.

"I was serious about giving it a try," Bednarik said in 2009. "I always loved baseball, the pay was better than football and Jimmy Dykes told me I could have a longer career with less wear on my body. I guess I just felt at the time that football was the sure thing."

His baseball career might have been nixed, but Bednarik still wanted to play two-way football. At training camp he explained, "I always played 60 minutes of football. If I didn't play I didn't feel it was going right."

While he didn't get to play baseball, Bednarik did add another job during the '53 season. He took over the punting duties after Adrian Burk was hurt. He also continued to kick off. The highlight of the 7-4-1 season was a 42-27 win against the Browns the last day of the season, which denied them an undefeated season. The Browns would lose in the championship game to the Detroit Lions for the second year in a row.

The 1954 season opened with the Eagles taking on the Browns, with the game moved to the larger Municipal Stadium instead of Connie Mack, in anticipation of great ticket demand. The teams didn't come close to filling the 100,000 capacity stadium, but the Eagles won and Bednarik was involved in an incident that would eventually lead to the most famous on-field fight of his career.

As he would throughout his career, Bednarik had the good fortune to have a future Hall of Fame member serve as his foil. This time it was a then obscure Cleveland guard named Chuck Noll. Late in the game, Bednarik was snapping on a punt and Noll whacked him with a forearm across the face. After clearing his head Bednarik's last words to Noll were, "I'll get you, you son-of-a-bitch."

The following year, in Cleveland, Bednarik and his buddy, Frank Wydo, gave Noll the old high-low double team on a kickoff, and this time it was Noll's turn to tell Bednarik, "I'll get you."

> **"Connie Mack wanted to add Bednarik as a catcher. He offered him a contract and wanted him to play a few games in the minors before joining the team. Bednarik told Grady, "I was so excited I almost started dancing," but McNally put his foot down on this one, arguing that the Eagles could not afford to lose him to a baseball-induced injury. Bednarik reluctantly agreed, but always wondered about how a career in major league baseball would have worked out."**

Bednarik waited at midfield after the game and Noll came after him, without his helmet, which broke every rule in the what-not-to-do in football brawl rule book. To this day, Bednarik recalls, "He was crazy, I still can't believe he came after me with his helmet off." Bednarik cold-cocked him and a fistfight ensued as the closing credits rolled for the televised game.

Commissioner Bert Bell summoned Bednarik to his Philadelphia office the next day and gave him the riot act for embarrassing the league on television. He also fined Bednarik $100, with the stipulation that he apologize to Noll and steer clear from any further incidents the remainder of the season. Apologies were exchanged and the two Chucks remained cordial through the years, which included many annual reunions in Canton.

After defeating the Browns in the first game of the '54 season, the Eagles won their next three and moved to 4-0. They were then upset by the Steelers 17-7, and won just three of the remaining seven games. The Eagles finished with seven wins and their third straight second-place finish to Cleveland. The Browns met the Lions in the championship game for the third straight year, but this time came out on top, winning 56-10.

Bednarik went to the Pro Bowl game in Los Angeles and put on one of the greatest performances in the history of the event. He clinched a 20-9 victory for the East when he intercepted a Bobby Layne pass and returned it for a touchdown, recovered three fumbles, and punted five times, for a 41 yard average.

He was the unanimous choice for game MVP.

The Pro Bowl performance was some vindication, as Bednarik was viewed to have had an off season by some observers. He moved back to offense when center Ken Farragut went down the first game of the season with an injured arm, and played there full-time the last four games of the season. Trimble tried to spell him on defense whenever possible, but had to use him at linebacker more than he had hoped. The Eagles coach explained to the press, "I wanted to rest him when we were on defense, but when we got into trouble; I instinctively called on him to go in there."

As training camp opened for the 1955 season, questions remained as to which would be Bednarik's primary position. Bednarik, of course volunteered to go 60 minutes, but Trimble explained to Hugh Brown of The Inquirer, "Last season, for want of an offensive center, I had to shift Chuck from his linebacker spot. Even, now, I do not know whether I am going to come up with a new offensive center so that I can send him back to linebacking."

Three years of second place stagnation came to an end in 1955, when the Eagles slipped to fourth with a 4-7-1 record, and Bednarik missed being named to the Pro Bowl for the first time. Trimble was fired after the season and took a job in the Canadien Football League with the Hamilton-Tiger Cats and tried to get his star player to join him.

At a speaking engagement in Mechanicsburg during the off season, Bednarik revealed that he had had a "row" with the Eagles front office and was "mad enough" to

> **"I always loved baseball, the pay was better than football and Jimmy Dykes told me I could have a longer career with less wear on my body. I guess I just felt at the time that football was the sure thing."**

accept any reasonable offer. His friend Bud Grant had left the Eagles for Canada following the 1952 season and doubled his salary for the effort. Bednarik knew the math and explained to the press in Mechanicsburg, "I can get more in two years up there than I can get in three with the Eagles." This tactic may or may not have contributed to a $1,000 raise in his next contract with the Eagles.

Hugh Devore was selected to replace Trimble. He proved to be one of the nicest and most well-liked coaches in Philadelphia sports history, but unfortunately

Lacing up for practice, Bednarik jokes with Norm Van Brocklin

also one of the most ineffectual. He was fired after winning seven of 24 games in 1956 and 1957.

While playing at least some offense every season since 1951, Bednarik was a full-time linebacker through 1957.

At the conclusion of the 1957 season, Bednarik initiated the first of what was to become an annual ritual of publicly contemplated retirement talk. He would be 33

At the conclusion of the 1957 season, Bednarik initiated the first of what was to become an annual ritual of publicly contemplated retirement talk.

years old at the start of the next season, the Eagles were coming off two horrid years, and he would be playing for another new coach.

Pick any year from 1957 on and it's not difficult to dig through the archives of any newspaper between Philadelphia and Bethlehem and find a handful of articles that "definitely" proclaim the football season at hand to be Bednarik's last. Retirement made more sense going into the 1958 season than most, but in quick succession only just about everything changed in the world of the Eagles—new coach, new quarterback, new/old stadium and the end the result was new center.

Veteran coach Buck Shaw took over for Devore, Norm Van Brocklin, one of the most accomplished quarterbacks in the league, was imported in a trade, the Eagles bolted Connie Mack Stadium for Franklin Field, and Chuck Bednarik gave up defense to come back and be a full-time center.

The arrival of Van Brocklin was the most important of these changes, and also the one that carried the most peril. The Dutchman had won a championship with the Rams in 1951 and held the league's single game passing record of 554 yards. He was tough, cantankerous and took charge of whatever team he was on. Bednarik had been the unquestioned leader of the Eagles since the early '50s and there were those who wondered how the two would interact. Could Concrete Charlie subjugate himself and allow another boss into the tent, especially now that he was offense, the same side of the ball as Van Brocklin?

While they never became great friends, Bednarik knew that strong leadership was needed at the quarterback position, and he never undermined or showed any public contempt for Van Brocklin. Years afterward teammates and opponents would talk about how the two had joint ownership when it came to leading the team.

The potential for discomfort was heightened by the fact that Van Brocklin had made it clear before the trade that he wanted no part of Philadelphia. He was appeased only by an apparent promise to be named head coach when Shaw retired, in a deal that was brokered by league president Bert Bell.

However unhappy he may have been with the trade to Philadelphia, Van Brocklin had too much pride to let it affect his play. As the new guy, he also went out of his way to praise Bednarik. During training camp he told a reporter for the Ohio State Journal, "Boy am I glad to have that Bednarik on my side again!" The reporter, Max Gerber, added that Van Brocklin "sounded plenty sincere." The two had been teammates on the 1949 College All Star Team.

There were few positive results to be found on the field. The team limped backward to a 2-9-1 record and Van Brocklin threw more interceptions (20) than touchdowns (15). The numbers may not have been impressive, but the Eagles were developing a reputation as a passing team. With Van Brocklin throwing the ball to them, Pete Retzlaff and Tommy McDonald were emerging into one of the best receiving tandems in the league.

Retzlaff was a converted fullback who had been picked up after being cut by the Detroit Lions in 1956; and McDonald was a reformed halfback drafted that same year. That draft also yielded the Eagles' two best running backs in Clarence Peaks and Billy Ray Barnes.

"I was used to being a star and suddenly I was just another player on just another team. At the end of the 1959 season I decided to quit."

Bednarik, playing almost exclusively at center, made another Pro Bowl, his seventh, but was not offered a raise for the 1959 season. Unhappy at not being able to break the magic $20,000 threshold and feeling every bit of 34 years old, he reported to Hershey for what was absolutely and undisputedly the last time.

In a 1961 interview, he revealed to Dick Schaap of the Saturday Evening Post, some of the motivation that was going through his mind as he stuck to the retirement story. "Then from 1957 through 1959 we didn't have particularly good teams, and the sportswriters stopped picking me (to the All-Pro team). They figured I was slowing up. So did my coach...I was used to being a star and suddenly I was just another player on just another team. At the end of the 1959 season I decided to quit."

Don Shula

The head coach with the most wins in NFL history, Shula was a defensive back for the Baltimore Colts in the 1950s.

"I first saw Chuck Bednarik when the Baltimore Colts practiced at Hershey, Pennsylvania. We would stay there for a week and we always played our first preseason game against the Eagles.'

'I still believe in old school football, and everyone admired Chuck—60 minutes; offense and defense.'

Don Shula, Dick Vermeil and Chuck at a charity function

'Everyone remembers Chuck; he loved to play the game. I spent 33 years as a head coach; a total of 43 years in the NFL. He is one of the all-time greats; he earned his spurs. He certainly could have played in any era. A later era.'

'He was a great long snapper, and those players don't ever lose their skills. Coaches always want great long snappers; you only notice them when things go wrong.'

'The middle linebackers are the quarterbacks of the defense; they move everybody around, make all the calls. All the great ones are special. I coached Joe Schmidt for three years when I was with Detroit; had Buoniconti in Miami; Mike Curtis with the Colts."

Bob Gain

An All-Pro defensive lineman for the Cleveland Browns and frequent Eagles opponent during the 1950s.

Another member of the Cleveland Browns during their great rivalry years with the Eagles during the 1950s, Bob Gain played in five Pro Bowls and made numerous All-League teams during his career as a defensive lineman (who sometimes played offense).

"Oh yeah, the Eagles-Browns games were wild. That was the dumbest thing I ever saw Chuck Noll, do—take his helmet off. That was a real jackass thing.'

'I don't remember how it started, but Al Bradley was holding Noll up when Bednarik hit him. When you walk off the field, you always leave your helmet on.'

'Keep your helmet on Buster; you never know. I learned that at Kentucky'

'I remember Bednarik being a real hard road tough guy. I got a big charge out of that hit on Gifford, a good solid hit.'

'Chuck, he was tough and he deserved what he got. He was big for a linebacker back then. Guards only weighed about 230, and tackles about 250. He was a helluva linebacker; a real tough guy who played his heart out.'

'Guys today couldn't last the whole game; they'd need oxygen. They're all overweight and pumped up.'

'Defense has changed so much. As I look back. I came into the league in '52 and you had to hold the guy down or he could get up and run again.'

'You'd get on top of him and dig your knees in. One guy crawled into the end zone and scored a touchdown on me, the son-of-a-bitch'.

'The draft system saved the NFL. In the early '50s we only had 33 players per team. You had to know the other side of the field. I had to play some offense if guys got hurt. Today you have too many players, too many coaches.'

'Football was played in black and white. We didn't have all these sophisticated movies and pictures showing where everyone lines up. The game films were sent to Chicago; the coaches would get them Sunday night, and we'd look at them Monday. You had to sweat out a bad game waiting for the film.'

'You could count the attendance while you were warming up in some stadiums. You could play in a championship game and $3,500 would be a big payday.'

'We had a first class operator with Paul Brown. If you didn't cut the mustard, you were gone. Two or three mistakes—out of here."

Sonny Jurgensen

Christian Adolph Jurgensen joined the Eagles as their fourth round selection in the 1957 draft. He won three of four starts his rookie year, taking snaps from veteran center Chuck Bednarik. Jurgensen spent most of the next three seasons on the bench, after the Eagles acquired Norm Van Brocklin. It was a useful apprenticeship. Jurgensen took over the quarterback spot in 1961 following the retirement of Van Brocklin and led the league in passing yardage and touchdowns in setting the standard for what would become a Hall of Fame career.

Without question, Chuck Bednarik was the leader of the team in everything he did. He had the respect of everyone. He was the guy who usually led in stretching and exercises. Once at Connie Mack, he stopped in the middle of a warm-up drill, said 'Hold Up', and walked over and punched a guy out. He said, if we're gonna do exercises, we're gonna do them right.

'He was a great player, great leader, a no-nonsense do it right type guy.'

'I started four games as a rookie, and we won three of four. I threw three touchdowns in a win against the Steelers, at home. We're coming off the field and as we're walking past the third base line going toward the locker room, Chuck says, "Kid, put your helmet on."

'I said, "Huh?"

'He said, "Always keep your helmet on as you're coming off the field."

'As if on cue, the fans start throwing beer cans and garbage at us. I said, "What happens when we lose?"

'He got my attention; I never took my helmet off again until I was in the locker room. They were a rough crowd.'

'He took me under his wing. Everyone around town knew Concrete Charlie. We'd go out for dinner and it seemed everyone in the place knew who he was.'

'We were playing in Cleveland, and Chuck says, "I got a guy's number, who I have to get after the game."

'We leave the field and the Browns file out in the opposite direction. The Browns always had to come on and off the field in single file. We had to go down steps into our tunnel. Chuck crosses over to their side of the field and stands near their tunnel looking for the guy whose number he had.'

'He stands there waiting as the Browns file through and when the guy he was looking for passes him, Chuck grabs him and knocks him down.'

'To show you the respect Chuck had around the league, the guy's teammates just continued to step over him as they walked past. No one tried to help him.'

> **"When Chuck yelled, "Geronimo', that was the signal to get him. Everyone went after him, that's how they took care of things in the old days."**

'In 1957, my rookie year, we're playing against Detroit in the Glass Bowl in Toledo. Chuck's the center and I'm at quarterback, the last play of the game. I call a play in the huddle to run the clock out and when we get to the line of scrimmage, Chuck yells out "Geronimo."

'I'm wondering, what does that mean? Why did they call that?'

'I take the snap and turn to hand off the ball, and no one's there. As soon as the ball was snapped the whole team went after Gil Mains. He was known as a dirty player and the must have done something during the game.'

'When Chuck yelled, "Geronimo," that was the signal to get him. Everyone went after him. That's how they took care of things in the old days. As everyone was leaving the field, his teammates left him lying on their field.'

'The Eagles had a basketball team, and Chuck took charge of that. Sometimes we played before the Warrior games. Chuck ran the basketball team like he ran things on the football field. Someone complained to him about not playing, and a fight broke out in the locker room. Chuck got that settled.'

'He was the best; having him on the team meant everything; he was the leader. He was great.'

'I have a highlight film from the 1961 season that I was looking at recently. We were playing in Pittsburgh that year and Chuck was put in on defense.'

'He was such an instinctive player. The coaches would tell him, "Move this way; take that drop; take this angle," but he did what he wanted, and he knew what the offense was doing.'

'He reached out and intercepted a pass and he's returning it near the goal line. A big offensive lineman gets in front of him. It was the biggest collision I've ever seen; you heard it all over the stadium. Chuck roared right into that guy and left him sprawled on the ground.'

'He's a great guy, with a great family. His wife Emma is a special person. You know he always wanted a boy, and I remember Emma telling me, "Sonny, please tell him to quit. It's God's will, no boys."

'As a rookie; what a great role model he was for me.

Philadelphia Eagles basketball team

He was a leader, and he did everything with honor and pride.'

'He left after '62. We had so many injuries that season and it was disappointing for him and for all of us. We never got going that year; at one point I think we had seven receivers out with broken arms.'

'Chuck had been instrumental in our winning in 1960. I took over in 1961, after Van Brocklin retired, and we had a big year on offense, and went down to the final weekend. We won a game we had to against Detroit, and we went into the locker room to listen to the Giants and the Browns. If the Browns won, we would have been in, but Ray Renfro dropped a wide-open pass in the end zone.'

'Chuck was the protector; he was the leader; he was the alpha dog."

Eagles quarterback Sonny Jurgensen on the run

Bud Grant

Named to the Pro Football Hall of Fame for his work as head coach of the Minnesota Vikings, Grant was an Eagles teammate of Bednarik in the early 1950s and the two have remained good friends.

Bud Grant has been involved with professional football since joining the Eagles in 1951. After playing defensive end and receiver for the Eagles, he became one the league's first free agents, when he played out his option and went to the Canadien Football League for more money. After a successful playing and coaching career north of the border, he took over as coach of the Minnesota Vikings in 1967 and has been involved with that franchise ever since. In 2007, the Vikings honored him with a testimonial reception honoring his 40 years of service to the team. He was elected to the Pro Football Hall of Fame in 1994.

"I lockered next to Chuck my first year with the Eagles. I had never played defensive end, but one of the defensive ends got hurt. I had a couple of sacks my first game and they left me there. I played every minute of every game.'

'That's how I got to know Chuck. I had great appreciation for him as a football player. He was a competitor, a fierce competitor. He hated to give up a yard.'

'We became good friends. I think one reason we hit it off is that we both served in World War II. He saw real action. I was in the Navy, but I saw no action.'

'Having service backgrounds we hit it off immediately. A lot of the younger guys hadn't served in the war, and the veterans tended to band together.'

'Chuck and I went pheasant hunting a few times. He took me up into his area in Pennsylvania, and we spent some time together socially.'

'Chuck was a hero not for what he did on the football field, but what he did in serving his country. I admired him as a hero and as a sports star.'

'I use this example; growing up during the time that I did, we had heroes, mine were fighter pilots and people like Jimmy Doolittle, George Patton and Douglas MacArthur, the guys who fought the wars. Old guys start wars and young guys fight them.'

'For me heroes are people who do for their country, not sports stars—guys who lay their life on the line for a cause. '

'Chuck Bednarik was a hero and a sports star all in one. Flying for hours to Germany; Berlin and back.

'Harrowing missions, counting bullet holes when they landed. And he re-enlisted.'

'This is a guy who got through 25 missions, and then he volunteered to give them more. That's heroism.'

'I don't think he has gotten enough recognition. Last year the Vikings had a testimonial for me and I really wanted Chuck to be there. He was going to come, but had some last minute health issues. I had my introduction for him prepared, "Here is a hero and a sports star rolled into one."

'I would have liked to introduce him and Emma glowingly.'

'As a star he was as good a player as there has ever been in the NFL.'

'I admired him and liked him as a person, but he was tough to play with. He demanded that you pull your weight.'

'There was a goal line play, and the other team needed one yard. Chuck was jumping in between me and the tackle and screaming "Don't let anyone inside you.'

'They scored the touchdown and from the bottom of the pile Chuck was swearing at me. He ate me out for giving up a yard.'

"Your job is to protect the inside." He really got on my case.'

'He was always giving orders in the huddle and on the field. "Don't let them do this, do that." It wasn't trash talk like today, it was strictly business.'

'He didn't like to give up one yard, let alone five or ten. He hated to give up one yard.'

'Only somebody like him could play both ways in a championship game. He was a competitor.'

'I always considered him a good friend. When he was helping out with Vermiel and I was coaching the Vikings, I always spent time with him when we played each other.'

'I don't know what happened with the Eagles, I thought he would be there forever.'

'His name should certainly go down in NFL history as one of the greatest of all time who I played or coached with and against.'

'No one reached his stature as a great football player. The great middle linebackers, Nitsche, Huff, Butkus, don't measure up to him. My definition of greatness is durability, you can't miss games. Chuck didn't miss many games.'

'Chuck measured up, played every game at a level most guys can't measure up to.'

'He was an inspiration to me.'

'Football today is better than when we played, better athletes, facilities and training. Guys are bigger, stronger, faster. Chuck is one of the few guys who could play today and be just as good as he was in his time.'

'There is no doubt Chuck could play at the same level today; he was a man among boys.'

'He enjoyed it. He was bigger, faster, stronger than everyone. He enjoyed it. He loved playing football.'

'He was playful; so strong he could throw me around like nothing. He's been a good friend my whole professional life.'

'We got along from the beginning, I'm not sure if it was because of the service. Most of the younger guys didn't have that experience. The war veterans tended to bond together. Chuck was like me, he had respect for anyone who had served their country.'

'It was a different era. It can't compare to what it is like today. It was a different camaraderie, we were all in it together, pulling together.'

'Everyone had to go to work in the off season. We couldn't live on NFL salaries. Everybody who played in our era played for love, not money.'

'I left the Eagles and went to Canada for a 40% pay increase. I was making $7,000, and they wanted to increase me to $8,000 after I made the Pro Bowl. I made $12,000 by going to Canada.'

'But it was a different era. You can't make comparisons. We used to draw 20,000 people at Shibe Park.'

'Today I have an office to go to, unlike Chuck. The Vikings have treated me well. I don't do anything, but they want me around. I have an office, they give me access to a secretary and staff. It gives me a place to come to, and have something to do. I don't know what I would do without an office to go to.'

'Today most owners come from outside football and don't think about tradition. Chuck should be an Eagle for life.'

'He was very competitive. I know the Hall of Fame thinks a lot of him. He has treated the Hall well and the Hall has treated Chuck well."

> "No one reached his stature as a great football player. The great middle linebackers, Nitsche, Huff, Butkus, don't measure up to him. My definition of greatness is durability, you can't miss games. Chuck didn't miss many games."

Marion Campbell

The "Swamp Fox" was a solid defensive lineman for the Eagles from 1953-1961 and was selected to play in two Pro Bowls. He later became a highly-regarded defensive assistant coach and succeeded Dick Vermiel as head coach of he Eagles in 1982.

"You have a team's number if you can strike fear into your opponent. You want to be a factor before the ball is snapped, and Chuck Bednarik was a factor. The other team, especially the backs, always had to know where Chuck Bednarik was.'

'He was an opportunist and a playmaker. The other team always had to be looking for him'

'I'm glad to have been part of that 1960 team when he played both ways. I was proud to be on that team, and to be on that defense with him.'

'I've always looked at it this way; when the bell rang, Chuck was there. He really loved football.'

'Those were the good old days, I liked the old rules.

I talked to Pete Rozelle once. I asked him "When are you going to bring back the axe, the clothes line and the Chuck?" He said "I don't think we'll be bringing those back."

'I said, "The fans would rather see that type of football." Chuck excelled in those days, with those rules.'

'He was a good teammate and a fine man. He was good to play with. He would always do something in a game to turn it around. The middle linebacker is a good football player in any era, they're all smart guys.'

'Chuck could take care of himself. He was a naturally great football player. He didn't have to struggle, he had the instincts.'

'I once asked him, "Chuck, what do you key?" He said, "I go to where he ball is." And that's what he did; he was smart and a playmaker on defense.'

'Chuck is proud and loyal. He's had to adjust to changes and situations, but that's the way it is.'

'I like him. The last word on Chuck is that he is a very good athlete and person."

Ernie Accorsi

Ernie Accorsi was a long time NFL executive and general manager of three teams, the Baltimore Colts, Cleveland Browns and New York Giants. His passion for football was developed while growing up in Hershey, PA, where he got to watch the Eagles and Colts who both held training camp there for much of the 1950s and 60s.

'From 1951-1967, both the Eagles and Colts trained at Hershey. That took me from the age of 10 to 26. All through the 50s and early 60s, I went to practice virtually every day. Even when I had jobs, I always managed to watch practice.'

'Hershey was a small town, only about two or three restaurants with bars. The only places to hang out were the pizzerias and we went in as kids and saw all the players. They would walk around town, and you could hear Chuck Bednarik. He was not a quiet presence. He would be walking up Chocolate Street from the community building to DeAngelis' Restaurant and you could hear him coming up, talking and laughing.'

'He personified the Eagles club as well as the game. He was huge and he had played at Penn, which was my favorite college team.'

'As I think back now, having been in his presence, and I'm sure other people have said it, he is what God had in mind when he said 'Here is a football player.''

'If I had to describe him to someone from another country, I would say "Here is what a football player is."'

'When I was with the Giants a few years ago, I told him that I would like to take him back with me to solve my middle linebacker problem. He looked like he could still play.'

'As a kid, he was everything that a football player should be, and then I realized later how great he really was.'

'In the late 90s, Gary Myers of the New York Daily News had 25 people pick the 50 best football players of

"The picture of Chuck that I remember best was from when I worked at the Philadelphia Inquirer. It was a big blowup and the tag line said 'Chuck Bednarik About to Retire." He was walking off the field, all by himself; no one else is in the picture. It was snowy, muddy, he's covered in dirt, and he's out there by himself. That picture was everything you could want in a football player."

all time, regardless of position. Most people had Johnny Unitas and Jim Brown, one or two. Out of the top 50, the 25 with the most votes made the next cut. They ran the ballots of everyone who got a vote with a story. Chuck Bednarik got one vote.'

'I called Gary and I said to him "Are you telling me that I was the only person who voted for Bednarik?"

He said, "Yes." I told him that was totally outrageous.

'The newer generation, they vote for the more recent players.'

'He was chiseled, absolutely chiseled. He played inside, outside, center. And there was a viciousness about him.'

'They played two or three pre-season games, and there was a real rivalry with the Colts. There was a viciousness in those exhibition games, in the stands as well as on the field. There was a fight that started on the field between Bucko Kilroy and Artie Donovan—they didn't like each other—and it turned into a riot in the stands. They had to get the fire hoses and turn them on the crowd to break it up.'

'Bednarik was everything you could want in a football player, even today. You can use every cliché you want, and even today it would apply.'

'The picture of Chuck that I remember best was from when I worked at the Philadelphia Inquirer. It was a big blowup and the tag line said "Chuck Bednarik About to Retire." He was walking off the field, all by himself; no one else is in the picture. It was snowy, muddy, he's covered in dirt, and he's out there by himself. That picture was everything you could want in a football player.'

'The Eagles and Colts used to play basketball exhibitions in the off season. In fact, they were the preliminary game the night Wilt scored 100 points in Hershey. I remember Timmy Brown was a great player. Chuck was a rebounder, a good inside force.'

'Those games were vicious. They built up a hostility that carried into the preseason games, and those preseason games were played like regular season games. It was a great rivalry.'

'It was a great era, and they were great story tellers.'

'I've been at a few banquets with Chuck over the years. I know he has no room or time for modern players. We were at a function in Hershey for Ara Parseghian's foundation. It was a star-studded event, so many famous people, and for some reason they had me on the dais with Chuck.'

'He looked great. He had his Eagle green blazer—the old kelly green and a yellow tie. He was sharp looking.'

'I said "Can I take you home with me to play middle linebacker? He said. 'I could still play it, too." I love his attitude, so positive.'

'I read the article about him in Sports Illustrated, and he talked about being shot at while flying missions. He said that he promised the Lord he would say his rosary every day if he landed safely.'

'I asked him, "Did you live up to your promise?" He said, "You're damn right I did."

'He's 100% authentic, that what you have to love about him. It's all authenticity; what you see is what you get. He is one of my favorites."

Gino Marchetti

A Hall of Fame defensive end for the Baltimore Colts, Marchetti remembers the wild training camp sessions when the Eagles and Colts shared facilities in Hershey during the 1950s.

Gino Marchetti played defensive end for the Baltimore Colts at a Hall of Fame level from 1953-1966. He was an army machine gunner who saw action at the Battle of the Bulge during WWII. This experience helped prepare him for the wild sessions that marked training camp when the Eagles and Colts both practiced in Hershey.

"As a player there was no doubt about his ability and toughness, and willingness to play. You can't get anyone to do today what he did. The last of the 60 minute men, it's true.'

'I first met him at a Pro Bowl in Los Angeles. He was very easy to get along with. I was astonished to find out that like me, he was a war vet. I didn't know, guys just didn't talk about it. He flew, what, 28 missions over Germany, and he lived through that. That'll make you a tough guy.'

'That had a lot to do with his ability as a football player. There was one thing you learned in the service-discipline. After going through something like that, you don't run wild on the field.'

'1953, in Philly, I think he was the first guy to throw the ball into the stands. He intercepted a pass and ran it back, 50 or 60 yards. He threw the ball into the stands; he started the trend.'

'Gifford, that was the first time I ever saw anyone do a dance on a tackle, but you have to think of the moment, it caused the fumble that secured first place.'

'I don't mind a dance at certain moments; a lineman scores a touchdown, makes a game saving play, he's happy.'

'Those exhibitions at Hershey, it got damn wild up there. I remember one in particular. We got into a heated incident on the field, Chuck was in there. Joe Campanella, a defensive tackle got into a fight, I went in there.'

'When I came off the field, I sat with a big rookie, I think named Sears. He was tackle and had been the number one or two draft choice from a Big 10 school. He had just come to camp from the College All Star game.'

'He said to me, "Is it like this all the time?"

'I said, "Hell, no. This is only an exhibition wait for the real games."

'He packed up that night and went. We never heard from him.'

'In the off season we had a basketball team. We played 42 games. We used to get standing ovations. We played the Eagles in Hershey the night Wilt scored 100. It was a rough game.'

'I remember one game we played where the ref was calling all these chintzy fouls. We only had eight guys. I told him "You keep calling them like this, we won't be able to finish." He lightened up, and the fun really started."

Bob Thomason

This former 50s Eagles quarterback once got to enjoy a cross-country drive with Chuck Bednarik and Bucko Kilroy to the Pro Bowl in Los Angeles.

Bob Thomason was an Eagles quarterback from 1952-1957. He was selected to three Pro Bowls, including one which involved a memorable cross-country drive with Chuck Bednarik and Bucko Kilroy.

"I'm a great admirer of his. I read a story about him in the newspaper or a magazine every now and then. He was the best player I ever saw.'

'I played with him six years; I came over from the Ram's in '52. It didn't take long to figure out what kind of player he was. He kept to himself, was kind of close-mouthed; he didn't travel with the guys too much.'

'When I was playing in Philadelphia, we decided to stay up there. We lived in Hatboro, then Abington. We lived close to Chuck and I played on softball and basketball teams with him in the off season. We'd travel to the airport together. I consider him a good friend, but no one got real close to him.'

'He was quite a football player; as good as they come. He was so far ahead of his time, so fast; he just got to the ball. He weighed 235, which was big for those times.'

'He's the only one I can think of who could still play today. He had no weakness, was a great athlete.'

'We both came into the league in '49. I'm 81, now. He was a little older than me when we came in because of his service time.'

> **"He was quite a football player; as good as they come. He was so far ahead of his time, so fast; he just got to the ball."**

'When I was with the Rams, I'll tell you one story. Chuck was playing center against us. He came in because Vic Lindskog was injured or something.'

'I remember the guy opposite him came to the sidelines and said "He may be a rookie, but boy is he good." He didn't play like a rookie. He was very mature; a lot of the returning servicemen were.'

'I'll tell you a story about him with the Eagles, but I won't mention any names. We're at training camp, the linemen would get in one circle for warm ups; the backs would get in another.'

'Each day a different veteran was called in the middle to lead the calisthenics. Everyone's nerves were edgy, camp was always a drag.'

'Chuck is in the middle and one guy is giving him a bad time. Chuck walked over and knocked him down—

it was like a cow going down. Chuck turned to the guy next to him, and told him "You're next."

He seldom did that, but he was out of patience that day.'

'He was an unusual guy, but he may have been the best football player I ever saw; certainly the best linebacker.'

'One year he, Bucko Kilroy and I were going to the Pro Bowl. They gave us each first class air fare to Los Angeles. Money was tight in those days, and we figured we could cash in the tickets and drive to LA from the east coast to save the airfare.'

'I'm home in Birmingham, and Chuck and Bucko drive down from Philadelphia. They get to my house about 6 or 7 in the evening and my mom gives us all dinner and we head out for Los Angeles.'

"Now there were no interstates in those days, we're driving on two and four-lane roads past houses. That was one hell of a trip. It took us three days. We took turns and never stopped driving.'

'When we get there, Chuck says he's not driving back, he's going to fly. Bucko and I drove back and picked him up in Birmingham.'

'Just imagine driving through all those states. Texas was so big, it seemed like we would never get out there.'

'We cashed in the tickets to drive, can you imagine that. We pocketed about $300 each, that's how tight money was in those days. But, I'll tell you, it was an experience I'll never forget.'

'$8,500, $9,000 was the typical salary in those days. Chuck used to get so damned mad, he was always complaining about money. We had the reserve clause, and there was nothing we could do about it.'

'Most of us played until we got a job. If someone offered you a job with a halfway decent salary, you at least considered it. But, I can't believe the players today have as much fun as we did.'

'Chuck was just an outstanding player, so far above average. We just took things for granted with him, that things were going to get done. He played hurt; he never came off the field. In the six years I played with him, I don't recall him ever coming out of a game."

Art Donovan

Hall of Fame defensive tackle, starred for Colts in 1950s.

"Fatso" Art Donovan was named All-Pro defensive tackle four times while playing for the Baltimore Colts from 1953-61. One of the best story tellers in NFL history, the native of the Bronx served as a marine in World War II. He owns and operates Valley Country Club in Baltimore.

"Bednarik, did he tell you that he was the greatest? I like him; he's a good guy, but did he give you all of the Mr. Eagle bullshit?'

'I'll tell you a funny story. We were at the Super Bowl in Phoenix—what year? Hell; I can't even tell you who played in the Super Bowl last year—it's Sunday morning and anywhere he went, Emma was with him. The three of us went to receive communion. The church was packed, a long line, Emma's in front, I'm behind him, and he starts screaming "I'm a good Catholic, I'm a good Catholic.'

'I said, 'Chuck, we're all Catholic here, what do you have to let all of Phoenix know you're Catholic."

'He was a hell of a football player, a great linebacker. As a center, I saw better, but he was as good as there was at linebacker.'

'We used to practice with them at Hershey. There was more action in the stands than on the field.

'You have Baltimore fans, Philadelphia fans and they were always fighting.'

'Oh Jesus, one time they had to train the fire hose on all the drunks. Those were wild fans.'

'There was so much going on the field in those days. You had five officials. You could hit the quarterback four or five seconds after he released the ball. The referee, he would just warn us, 'Hey you're getting close. It was an altogether different game.'

'A lot of us were World War II vets. You had to join something or be drafted. We'd be hanging out in front of Mr. Goldberg's Candy Store before going off. We'd come back and hang out like nothing happened. Nobody talked about their experience, they were just happy to see everyone.'

'I called Chuck "Mr. Bethlehem." I saw him one summer wearing a short sleeve shirt. He had all these marks and burns on his arms.'

'I said to him "What the hell happened to you?"

'He said he was sitting in his back yard and he got in a fight with a guy in a cinder truck. The guy wouldn't stop what he was doing, so they got in a fight. He got all cut up and cinders flying all over him.'

'He was a hell of a linebacker, as a center, I played against better ones. But the guy played 60 minutes, he was a tough guy. They're all tough guys from Pennsylvania.'

'The 1950s were a great experience. The Colts were something special, we all liked each other. Our 1950 team was the worst team ever, '57, '58 we were the greatest team.'

'Joe Schmidt told me he wished he had been drafted by the Colts. You guys have great camaraderie, you always have a good time."

Mike McCormack

Mike McCormack had a Hall of Fame career as an offensive tackle for the Cleveland Browns from 1952-1962. He also had a long career as a coach and administrator in the National Football League. He was head coach of the Eagles from 1973-1975.

"We had a good rivalry with the Eagles. I don't remember a lot about the fight between Bednarik and Noll, but I do recall it. We were going off the field at the end of the game and something happened. We turned around and a bunch of our guys said, if you go in the middle of the Eagles, you better keep your helmet on. Noll didn't listen.'

'Bednarik was a great player; a tough stud, started both ways."

'I don't know what happened between him and the Eagles when I was in Philadelphia. I know he didn't have a good relationship with Leonard Tose, but I don't know what precipitated it. Dick Vermiel was very smart to bring him back on board.'

'I only saw him at golf outings the three years I was with the Eagles. I don't know what his feud was all about.'

'As a player, he should be right at the top in the middle linebacker group. He was big, physical. He would hold his own with all those guys. He fit right in with the Eagles, they were a physical team that didn't make many mistakes.'

'I remember some of his collisions with Marion Motley when they were both in their prime. Marion had a lot of violence in his collisions with people. I think there was a mutual respect between those two.'

'It was a different era. If you were a two-way guy you didn't get a chance to rest; there was no place to hide.'

'It was a different game. When you tackled someone, you had to keep them down. It was not like today where you just knock out their feet. You had to keep them down, guys struggled to get up and keep running'.

'I played with Chuck in a couple of Pro Bowls. He was something special; he earned that Concrete Charlie name and he accomplished a lot."

Hugh McIlhenny

The slick running back was part of the San Francisco 49ers "Million Dollar Backfield" of the 1950s and later became a friend of Chuck Bednarik through golf outings and Hall of Fame reunions.

"He's a dirty son-of-a-bitch and a rotten football player.' (Laughter) 'I'm only kidding, he was tough but not dirty. He hit you good. What can you say, he went both ways.'

'I remember one brawl in San Francisco, he was in the middle of it, but I don't think he started it. Joe Perry had been getting beat up all day, and someone nailed Wayne Robinson with a down block. It was the wildest brawl I ever saw on the field.'

'The brawl was going on and Pete Pihos was trying to keep me out of the fight. I got a headlock on Pete, we were in the end zone at Kezar Stadium. It was the biggest brawl I've ever been in. It went on for about 20 minutes.'

'Chuck and I became good friends about 15 years ago through golf tournaments and the Hall of Fame.'

'He likes his martinis. When we go out with a group, he'll have a cocktail. And he likes his food. He wants his dinner when he wants his dinner. We may want to relax, have a few cocktails, but when its time he wants his food.'

'We had a wonderful time together when we were honored for the all-time Hula Bowl team.'

'He is a warm and caring guy, especially with football fans. He always goes out of his way to sign autographs.'

'He was the last two-way player, that's phenomenal. That's a tribute to him, the last 60 minute man.'

'He has the prettiest hands in football, I wonder why he never got those suckers straightened out.'

'If he goes to church everyday, I'll see him in heaven."

Doug Atkins

Hall of Fame defensive end for the Chicago Bears, was a teammate of another great middle linebacker of the era, Bill George

In the 1950s and early 1960s, the middle linebacker emerged as the dominant player on most National Football League defense. Some refer to the era as the "Golden Age of the Middle Linebacker." Stars such Chuck Bednarik, Ray Nitschke, Bill George, Sam Huff, Joe Schmidt and Les Richter drew national attention. Hall of Fame defensive end Doug Atkins, played with one of those linebackers, George, when both were members of the Chicago Bears.

"Bednarik was tough, both ways; I could only go one way.'

'We had Bill George during those years, he was very smart, but he didn't make the vicious tackles, he didn't hit like Bednarik.'

'They had different styles; you heard a 'thud' when Bednarik hit you.'

'Bill got some good pops, but that wasn't his game.

He played a different type of game. He knew what he was doing. He was fast; could really move. He didn't smash people, but he never missed a tackle, and ended up with the same result.'

'He was a national championship wrestler and was hard to get off his feet. He knew how to leverage himself and he always knew where the ball was.'

'He had big old long arms—he was 6'2', I'm 6'8"—and his arms were two or three inches longer than mine. He had a big span, was very smart, and knew how to anticipate.'

'Bednarik was maybe not as fast as Bill, but he had a nose for the ball and he popped people. People like to hear that pop; Bill didn't make pops.'

'It's kind of hard to compare them, but the middle linebackers were the best athletes on the team. They all had to be smart, and they all had God-given talent.'

'The defense did get away with a lot in those days. Late hits, well they weren't really late hits, but we were able to hit right after the release of the ball.'

'But the offensive line had some advantages; they could hold, hit from behind, grab, knock you down and hit you again, so it all evened out."

Ed Khayat

A country boy from Mississippi, Khayat enjoyed visiting his teammate Chuck Bednarik at home and helping out with the yard work to keep himself busy.

Born and raised in Moss Point, Mississippi, Ed Khayat, sometimes felt lost while living in a hotel in Philadelphia during his two stints with the Eagles. When boredom set in he brought this country boy energy out to suburban Abington to help his teammate Chuck Bednarik with yard work. Emma Bednarik would also make for him what he recalls was the best stuffed cabbage he's ever had. For the young Bednarik daughters, his was the first deep southern accent they had heard. At the dinner table they would ask, "Mom, why does that man talk funny."

After serving two stints as a defensive end, and sometimes offensive lineman with the Eagles, Khayat succeed Jerry Williams as head coach of the team four games into the 1971 season. He was a player in 1958-61, and again 1964-65.

"Chuck Bednarik was a great teammate, great leader and a very talented football player. Offense and defense; center and linebacker, he was also a great deep snapper. I think he even punted in the Pro Bowl one year.'

'I'm the number one Chuck Bednarik fan outside of Coopersburg. He was a hero of mine."

'There was a preseason game in Los Angeles where he walked out onto the field and kicked a 43-yard field goal without warming up.'

'What he did at age 35 was astonishing. Playing the whole game on offense and defense for five games and then the championship. You have to admire anyone, at any age, who can play the game both ways; for him to do it at 35, that was incredible.'

'If you go back through that season, even if he had to kick he could have done that. Extra points, field goals, kickoffs, he was unbelievable. He could and would do anything.'

'There were guys around the league who played some offense and some defense, like Joe Scudero and Dick James. They might play on offense one week, then help out on defense the next; but to see what a guy like Chuck did at his age...we all loved him.'

'We never doubted anything that guy could do. When Bob Pellegrini got injured, he didn't bat an eye when he was sent back in on defense. He was an unselfish guy.'

'That Giants game was one of the turning points in the season. We were down 10-0 at the half, came back to take a 17-10 lead. Then he hit Gifford and it was all over; it was a clean lick.'

'People associate him with middle linebacker, and they forget he was playing outside at that time. Chuck Weber in the middle; Maxie Baughn on the other side; a pretty good linebacking crew, wouldn't you say.'

'I'll tell you Chuck was a great guy. I lived in a hotel and missed working in the yard. I would go to Chuck's house and do yard work. Emma made the best stuffed cabbage ever."

Lenny Moore

The great Baltimore Colts running back and native of Reading, PA, was a frequent supporter of the Big 33 Football Classic, along with Chuck Bednarik.

A Hall of fame halfback for the Baltimore Colts, Lenny Moore starred during the 1950s and 60s. Like Bednarik of Bethlehem, Moore also came from a gritty old Pennsylvania industrial town, in his case Reading.

In addition to the crushing matches at Memorial Stadium, Connie Mack Stadium, and Franklin Field, the Colts and Eagles trained together at Hershey. Later, Bednarik and Moore often met at celebrity golf outings and for many years the native sons have served as honorary captains for the Pennsylvania team at the annual Big 33 football game played in Hershey.

"You know Chuck Bednarik is in a class by himself from a standpoint of stature.'

'Nobody went two-ways like he did; center on offense, one of the best middle linebackers. Nobody was tougher.'

'Especially during our time; we used to just keep banging, and banging and banging to the whistle.'

'He was the man. Nobody could do what he did. I would look out there and laugh; the offense and defense would be coming on and off the field, and he would be the only one standing on the field. The jaws

"Chuck was everything. Nitschke, all the others, they only went one way. You really can't compare him to any other middle linebacker, they got rest."

would drop on our linemen. They would be shaking their heads walking off the field, saying how is he staying out there?'

'There is no team that he could not have played for. The Eagles were very fortunate.'

'The Hall of Fame? Chuck was truly that and more. There are not enough words to categorize him.'

'Chuck was everything. Nitschke, all the others, they only went one way. You really can't com-

pare him to any other middle linebacker, they got rest.'

'Think about it, he was one of the best at each of his positions. He solidified two positions, gave his team one of the top people at two positions.'

'Especially during our time, everything was hit, hit, hit. Man, he went 58 minutes, unbelievable.'

'Everyone has such respect for him. He is so unusual, you can't help but admire his ability. What can you say. You can ask anyone about him.'

'Everybody still talks about when he took Gifford out. We know that Frank doesn't find it humorous.'

'Before I got to the pros I was a great admirer of his. To go up to Hershey and play against him…you knew who he was.'

'It is a blessing that I got to know him and see him play. I still see him at the Big 33 every year and everyone shows him respect. You just listen to people talk about him."

Mike Brown

Michael Brown, owner and president of the Cincinnati Bengals is the son of Paul Brown, legendary coach of the Cleveland Browns. Paul Brown was at the helm of Browns during the final 13 years of Chuck Bednarik's career.

The Eagles and Browns had a lively Eastern Division rivalry during that period and Bednarik got into more verbal altercations with Paul Brown, than with any other coach. Many will say that is because of the great respect they had for each other.

Bednarik and Paul Brown were both inducted into the Pro Football Hall of Fame in 1967. Bednarik still has the program from that day, and in his copy Brown inscribed, "To a wonderful guy and the best linebacker I have ever coached against."

Michael Brown was a sideline observer for most of the Browns-Eagles games during the 1950s.

"From my perspective he was one of the most highly visible players of his era, beginning with his time at Penn. He was the last great Ivy League player.'

'The Browns and Eagles had quite a rivalry. He was the most well-known of the Eagles players, and they had other good ones like Bucko Kilroy, Steve Van Buren and Pete

"There was a lot of jawing, especially with Chuck when he came near our sideline."

Pihos. They were good, but what happened to them when we joined the league, is what happened to us a few years later—the next guy comes along and knocks you off your perch. The Browns took it away from the Eagles in 1950, later the Giants took it away from the Browns.'

'They were a very good team in 1950, very solid. My father (Paul Brown) always said that first game in 1950, was the best game the Browns ever played. The teams were closely matched, and the Browns handled them easily.'

'Those old Eagles teams were respected by my father. He viewed the Eagles as the enemy. No one gave the Browns a chance to win, and no one gave credit afterward. I remember Bucko Kilroy said, "We would have won if Steve Van Buren played."

'There was a lot of talking back and forth on the field; not trash talk like today, it was more general, along the lines of "We're gonna get you, you dirty so-and-so."

'There was a lot of jawing, especially with Chuck when he came near our sideline. My dad and Chuck would be going at each other verbally. It was unusual for my father to get into it with a player, but Chuck was high on his list. It was a sign of respect. My father and his people had high regard for the Eagles, especially Chuck.'

'On the field, our guys went after Chuck, because he went after them.'

'Other guys were going both ways in those days; he just carried it on longer. He came from an era, when that was what was expected. He continued to do it when he was long in the tooth.'

'He has to be ranked at the top; no one can dispute that. He did everything a linebacker could do-he could run, he was smart, he was competitive; a great player.'

'The Browns were really ready to play that first game. We had a lot to prove, our team had been talked down, downgraded.'

'The world didn't perceive us as they saw the Eagles, as champions. We were proud of where we were. The 1950 team may not have even been our best team. The '48 Browns might have been the peak of all Browns teams.'

'The guys were special on our team, and I'm proud of them. We had a lot of nice guys, and came into the league with white hat aspirations; we wanted to be the good guys. We thought of a guy like Otto Graham, as the anti-Bednarik.'

'We had great players too; we wanted to prove that we were also champs. My dad was fond of Greasy Neale, but it was a competitive thing.'

'After the game, my dad heard Pete Pihos talking to his wife, explaining how they lost, "Honey, we just played the champions, that's all."

Ken Farragut

Took over as center and freed Bednarik to concentrate on linebacker in 1952. His injury in 1954 moved Bednarik back to center.

"He was a good player, the same as everyone else in practice. Everyone had to go all out in practice in our day. If you didn't look good in practice you were gone. I was fighting for a job every day. They made me earn my $5,000 a year.'

'I wouldn't change a thing in life, I came up at the right time. I can't stand all the celebrating. You judge a man by his humility and there's no humility on the field today. Steve Van Buren would run 50 yards and say, "Give me the ball." Today they run 20 yards and run off the field. It's all arrogance, look at me.'

'Chuck was a great player, Pete Pihos was a great player. Too bad they didn't have more humility, they could have been millionaires.'

'They had me at linebacker when I first came up, but because I had been a T-formation center at Ole Miss they moved me to center because I could get the exchange back.'

'I did everything at center, all the long snaps. Now they need five guys to do what I did. But I have no regrets, I owe everything to football. Because of football I was able to develop my roofing business. Football got me out of Mississippi and into all of the money that is available up here.'

'Football opened a lot of doors. If I had Chuck's name or Steve Van Buren's, things could have been even bigger. Those names were magic, though Steve always lost all his money at the track, but he was one of the funniest guys ever.'

'All the guys we played with stay in touch. I had Chuck and Tommy McDonald and their wives to my house for dinner last year.'

'We were like brothers, we had a bond. If practice started at 10, we'd be there at 9, playing touch football on the field.'

'I quit the year after making the Pro Bowl. I made $8,500, with three kids. I'm probably one of the few guys who retired after making Pro Bowl, but I was offered a job as sales manager, and made $23,500 my first year. I had to look out for my family.'

'When I left, Chuck began filling in at center. He and I both went to the Pro Bowl in '57."

Joe Astroth

This Philadelphia's A's catcher of the 1950s remembers when Connie Mack wanted to sign Chuck Bednarik to be his back up behind the plate.

Joe Astroth was a catcher for the Philadelphia A's from 1945, until they departed for Kansas City following the 1954 season. He was more than an interested observer when an amateur catcher named Chuck Bednarik was offered a contract to join the A's in the early 1950s.

"Oh yeah, I remember Chuck Bednarik working out with the A's. When the Eagles were off season he would come by.

'Connie Mack needed a catcher and he wanted to sign Chuck as a backup to me. He was a big man, and he could hit it into the left field seats.'

'Connie was seriously thinking about it. I was very well aware of it; I was the catcher. It was my job he wanted to get. He figured he could make a few extra dollars playing for us.'

'He would have been the backup; I would have cut his legs off if he beat me out.'

'I've played golf with him over the years and I talked about it with him.'

'He could hit; he was a big guy, athletic. Some guys can play any sport. It was nothing for him to go out and hit in batting practice. He could hit a baseball; four or five out of 10 would go into the stands.'

'Connie was always looking to improve the club. We were in last place and Connie thought another right handed bat would help us, even as a pinch hitter. Connie wanted to do it, and it wouldn't have cost too much money.'

'I considered Chuck a friend, competing for a job. If he could take my position it would make us a better ball club. We didn't mind competition; we got satisfaction from holding on to our positions.'

'It was quite a story. We used to go out and laugh when he was hitting. He'd go up all loosey-goosey and swing for the fences. He was a funny guy, I really enjoyed him.'

'He always told it like it was, and he was tough. He was a great competitor. He would have been serious if he took that offer from Connie.'

'He was competitive in golf. You could hear him say "Give me somebody who can play;" he always wanted to win. If you were good, he would tell you; if you weren't good, he would tell you that, too."

Gus Zernial

A slugging outfielder for the Philadelphia A's in the early 1950s, Zernial often had home run hitting contests during batting practice with Chuck Bednarik.

Gus Zernial, one of the best sluggers in the American League during the 1950s was traded to the Philadelphia Athletics in April, 1951. The 6'3", 220 lb. outfielder became good friends with another comparably-sized Philadelphia athlete, Chuck Bednarik.

Zernial learned of his new buddy's love of baseball and often invited him to work out with the A's and take batting practice at Shibe Park. They often had friendly home run hitting contests during batting practice.

Zernial shared a similar aggressiveness with Bednarik, twice breaking his collarbone making diving catches in the outfield. He finished his 11 year career with 237 home runs.

"I used to spend a lot of time with Chuck. Yes, he used to take batting practice with us. I would take him to the ballpark with me. He could hammer a fastball, but he didn't like the crooked stuff.'

'We used to take pride in seeing who could hit it further. I hit some long balls in Philly, and he could hit it on the roof.'

'I don't recall, but wouldn't be surprised if Connie Mack had offered him a contract.'

"He could hit those little 80 mile per hour fast balls, but he couldn't touch the curve. I used to kid him about it all the time."

'Many times he worked out with us at Connie Mack Stadium. He hit the ball a long way. One time I got behind the cage and said, "Ok Chuck, I'm gonna give you a little wrinkle. I think Les McCrabb was the batting practice pitcher and I had him throw breaking balls.'

'He could hit those little 80 mile per hour fastballs, but he couldn't touch the curve. I used to kid him about it all the time.'

'He was a neat guy. I always considered him a friend.'

'He wanted me to play for the Eagles. I was young and strong and gave it some thought; I wondered, 'maybe I could play.' I had played in high school, but I never followed through with it.'

'He was a great football player. I went to a few of his games. I always went home to California in the offseason, and one time when he came out for the Pro Bowl, he came over to my house with Dante Lavelli.'

'I had them over to the house before the game, and then Chuck got me a sideline pass for the game. I remember, he didn't like Hugh McIlhenny, and he told me before the game, "I'm going to get him, gonna nail him real good.'

'Sure enough, there was a situation right on the sideline in front of me. I'm standing there, and here comes Hugh, and here comes Chuck. Well, he put on a fake, and Chuck missed him completely, in fact, it threw him into the bench.'

'He's steaming mad, you can see the veins in his neck. Later, he gets Hugh by the shoulder pads and buggy whips him into the ground. Of course, he got a 15-yard penalty for it.'

'Hugh had put a good move on him the first time; the next time Chuck didn't go for the move.'

'When names like Butkus and Huff come up, no one was better than Chuck Bednarik. I got to know Frank Gifford and I talked to him about the famous tackle. He said it was legal. He said Chuck, "Just necktied me."

'I remember seeing Chuck on TV. He was talking about playing linebacker and always had something rough to say.'

'He was the best. He was very much a factor against the offense in the games he played.'

'I was watching TV another time, and they were talking about him being a boxing commissioner. I would have liked to have seen him in the ring.'

'He is certainly in the Philadelphia Hall of Fame of Greats. I have nothing but ultimate admiration for Chuck Bednarik as both and athlete and as a man."

Y.A. Tittle

Hall of Fame quarterback Yelberton Abraham Tittle played against Chuck Bednarik while a member of three NFL teams, the Baltimore Colts, San Francisco 49ers, and the New York Giants. Their careers spanned a similar period from the late 1940s to the early 1960s. The two were honored by the NFL at the Pro Bowl a few years ago as outstanding players of the 1950s. Tittle recalls the 50s as an era when quarterbacks got nowhere near the protection from officials that they get today.

"Well, he (Bednarik) was a great player and a great leader. His main quality was leadership. He convinced the team that they could beat anyone; that they could step up. Sam Huff had the same qualities.'

'Back in that era the middle linebackers were villainous by reputation. Bednarik, Huff, Joe Schmidt. They were headhunters. They made a living right in the middle of the field.'

'The referees, the rules; in my personal opinion they allowed the linebackers to get away with anything; elbows… they could knock your head off.'

'That era had a great reputation for great middle linebackers. They were the number one killers. In the 4-3 defense they made all the tackles.'

'They weren't dirty, but the refs made like they didn't see anything. They let them get away with everything.'

'The refs didn't throw flags. We probably had the biggest headhunter, Hardy Brown. One game in 1951, he knocked out the entire Redskins backfield.'

'I don't know what the refs were doing, I'm not picking on Bednarik or any of the other, but they all got away with murder. They must have been looking at pretty girls in the stands while they were knocking our heads off.'

'The rules were different. Today you can't touch the quarterback, in our day it was a middle linebacker's game.'

'The hitting didn't stop after the whistle half the time. It was the era of hitting, hitting and late hitting. This was the era of the linebacker and the rules were lenient.'

'The middle linebackers had reputations, wanted reputations and all wanted to be the toughest.'

'Bednarik, (Bill) George, Schmidt, Huff—they let them get away with too much. They stepped on hands, gouged eyes, all of that. They wanted to be mean. The middle linebacker was the leader of the defense.'

'They were all devastating linebackers. I'm not sure who was the best of that killer group.'

'They delighted in hitting quarterbacks, smashing them to pieces. They were the leaders of every team, no ifs, ands, or buts.'

'On our team (the 49er's) Hardy Brown knocked out 12 guys in 1951. He was a killer. He was my roommate, and I wouldn't want to play against him. They wouldn't let him scrimmage against us.'

'Bednarik and Huff were great middle linebackers, but Hardy was the most devastating hitter of all. He probably missed 50 percent of the tackles throwing himself in the air, but no one hit like him.'

'When you got up over center, you looked around. Where was Joe Schmidt, where was Bednarik? You located them, you looked.'

'They all wanted to be Billy the Kid, and they all loved what they did. Competitiveness, confidence, leadership, ability—they were the defense.'

'In the 4-3 defense, no one can get to a good middle linebacker. He moves down the line, he's free, he just pulverizes the quarterback.'

'You had to know where those guys were, you wanted to know where those guys were.'

'A middle linebacker is the fastest gun in the west. As the middle linebacker goes, so goes the defense.'

No one can get to the good ones. They're gone before the center can get to them. They can have a heyday, picking whatever hole they want to go to.'

'This was the era of the great middle linebackers, and Chuck was one of the best. He believed he was the best, he was very confident. He loved the name "middle linebacker."

Walt Michaels

Walt Michaels played outside linebacker for the Cleveland Browns from 1952-61. The son of a miner, he and his brother Lou grew up in the Pennsylvania coal country town of Swoyersville.

Current day Philadelphia fans may not understand the connection, but during the 1950s the Eagles-Browns match-ups carried a special zing. This rivalry was traced to the first game of the 1950 season, pitting the defending NFL champs, the Eagles, against the Browns, newly admitted to the NFL after dominating the defunct All-America Football Conference through the late 40s.

The favored Eagles were crushed by the upstart Browns, 35-10 at Municipal Stadium.

Michaels was not present for that game, but he got caught up in the rivalry, and was on the field for most of the other games during the decade, including one of

Bednarik's more infamous moments—a post-game fist-fight with a relatively obscure Cleveland guard named Chuck Noll. The fight played out on television as a backdrop to the game's closing credits.

"Bednarik hit him and it was over (laughter).'

'I think we were at the old Connie Mack Stadium. Noll was playing offensive guard, Bednarik was playing defense; he was actually going both ways. Bednarik was giving him a hard time all game, blitzing and rushing up on the ball and after the game Noll challenged him.

'Noll was an undersized guy, weighed about 215- 220. He would have a tough time lining up anywhere today; I really don't know where he could play. He was a low-key Catholic guy; we called him 'The Pope.' Chuck (Bednarik) was much stronger.'

'After the game, you can see them jawing, and Noll takes off his helmet and challenges him. And Chuck (Bednarik) hit him.'

'John Kissell (a Browns defensive lineman), goes to break it up, he says to Chuck Bednarik "Why are you fighting now, the game is over?"

'And Chuck (Bednarik) says "That crazy guy took his helmet off…no one takes his helmet off, what was HE doing?'

'We won that game and in the locker room Noll laughed about it.'

'We had a rowdy rivalry with the Eagles, they were good games. We always had more talent. I was looking at a team picture from '53 or '54 and we had 13 Hall of Famers—but we had good games with the Eagles in the 50s. It was a good tough rivalry; those were the games that made pro football.'

'They had Chuck, and he was good for football.'

'One year we were at the Pro Bowl, and I'm talking to Dante Lavelli. Chuck and Dante went on to become great friends after football, playing in golf tournaments and doing autograph shows together.'

'But this time Chuck looks over at Dante and says, "Why is it that every time I look at you I want to punch you in the mouth?"

'Dante looks at him and says, "I don't know Chuck, is there something wrong with you?"

Sam Huff

Sam received many honors. He was named All-NFL three times, and picked as the NFL's top linebacker in 1959.

The key middle layer of the typical NFL defense underwent a CroMagnon-like evolution in the 1950s as the down-on-all-fours middle guard developed into an agile and ferocious stand-up predator attacking the offense on two legs. Tom Landry, then the defensive coordinator of the New York Giants helped ted develop and polish the modern 4-3, in which the hulking nose guard was backed three to five yards off the ball and allowed to range as far as his lateral movement skills would permit.

This new position of middle linebacker often became home to the team's best defensive player and on-field leader. Some of the leagues first defensive legends defined this position, such as future Hall of Famers Ray Nitschke, Bill George, Joe Schmidt, Chuck Bednarik, and the guy who manned the new middle linebacker position for Landry, Sam Huff.

The middle linebacker became the public face of many of the league's defenses, and by playing out of New York, Huff became the poster boy for the position. As a star for successful Big Blue teams in the nation's media capital, Huff appeared on the cover of Time Magazine,

and was the subject of the "Violent World of Sam Huff', an episode on the Walter Cronkite CBS documentary series, "The 20th Century."

A kinship, forged of respect, emerged among the great MLB's of the era, and Huff appreciated the talents of his older Philadelphia- based rival.

"Chuck was a hellacious linebacker, a little bit different, a bit stronger, and I had great respect for him. He would have made a great coach, nobody gave Concrete Charlie backtalk. He was an individual, a tough guy.'

'We both played linebacker, I think Chuck was a jealous of all the attention I got playing in New York.'

'The Frank Gifford hit was clean. The way Chuck acted is what ticked everybody off; the fist pumping, the jumping. I thought Gifford was dead. It was unusual that Chuck did what he did. Guys didn't do that in our day'

'But it was an all out play, the greatest hit I've ever seen.'

'There was no animosity after the hit. It took a year, but Gifford came back as a receiver, he was a great athlete.'

'I had some great hits on Jim Brown, one in particular, but he always got up. One game we held him to eight carries and 13 yards.'

'Philly is Philly, a rough group, but the Giants were special.'

'New York is the sports capital of the world, and I think for anyone who doesn't play there, there is a little bit of jealousy."

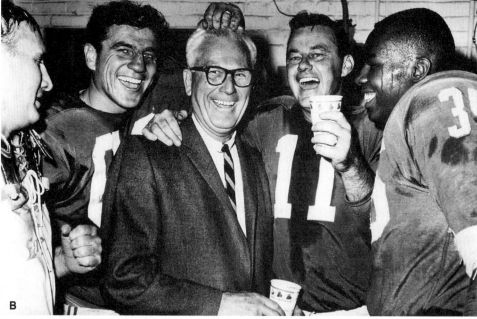

A. Jerry Williams with Chuck

B. After 1960 Championship

C. Buck Shaw with Vince Lombardi prior to 1960 Championship game

D. Iron Man from Saturday Evening Post Magazine, 1961

E. On the sidelines grasping for air

F. 1960 Hickok Belt Honorees

G. Relaxing with Frank Gifford

Chapter | six

The 1960 Season

The defining season of Chuck Bednarik's career might never have happened without the February, 1961 arrival of one Jacqueline Bednarik Chelius. Bednarik had talked retirement before, to the point of it becoming a running joke with local newspapermen. Training camp opened in Hershey as usual in the summer of 1959, and from day one Bednarik was telling anyone who would listen that this would be his last season. Hugh Brown of the Philadelphia Bulletin wrote from training camp, "This is the 11th Eagles camp for Chuck Bednarik, and as old Chief Flat Nose himself puts it, 'positively the last...you can put that it in writing.'"

He was steadfast into September, telling John Dell of The Philadelphia Inquirer, "The big reason I want to quit now is that I don't want to become a bum. I want to quit while I'm still good. I don't want to hang around so long that people get to saying 'that guy should have quit long ago."

The retirement pledge seemed official when he was honored with a Chuck Bednarik Day the last game of the year at Franklin Field. Among his gifts were $1,000 and a color television.

To this day, both Chuck and Emma Bednarik maintain that he had very real intentions that, at age 35, he was going to start living as typical and mundane a suburban lifestyle as Concrete Charlie possibly could.

"Oh, he was serious,' said Emma in 2009. 'He was tired."

A headline in the Philadelphia Bulletin the week before his scheduled last game told readers, "Bednarik Set to Call it a Career; Eagles' No. 60 Means It This Time." He told Brown in the accompanying article, "It's going to be a financial wrench as well as a sentimental tug. But I'll be 35 next year and a man has to step down."

Into the picture stepped the soon to be fifth daughter, Jackie. During the spring of 1960, Emma learned she was pregnant, and this called for a larger house. A local golfer named Bill Hyndman was selling a big house with a finished basement in Abington that seemed to meet the family's needs. Bednarik told Sandy Grady of the Phildelphia Bulletin, "I needed the house for the girls, and I needed money fast and football was the only way to get it."

He was doing reasonably well selling concrete for the Warner Company, but the expense of the new house made him nervous and he went into town to ask Eagles general manager Vince McNally if he could have his old job back. As usual, Bednarik wasn't happy with his contract—$20,000—but at least they didn't want the gifts back.

Bednarik reported to Hershey and camp opened with more team enthusiasm than he had seen in a long time. The team was coming off its first winning season since 1954. Head coach Buck Shaw and quarterback Norm Van Brocklin were both starting their third year with the team. The Giants and Browns clearly had more talented rosters, but no one on the team seemed concerned that they might u-turn back to those wretched

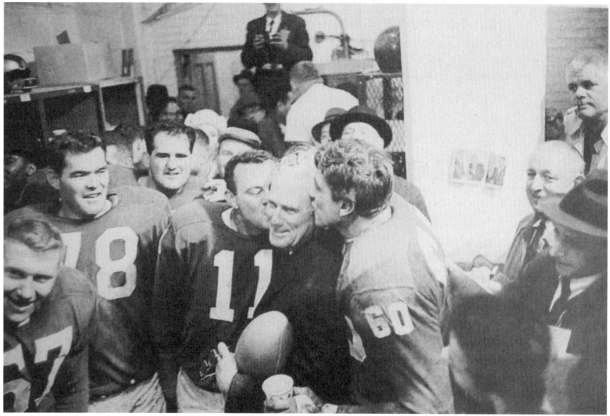

Bednarik and Van Brocklin give Coach Buck Shaw a kiss after winning the 1960 Championship.

three- and four-win seasons that dogged them just a few years prior.

The 1960 Eagles yearbook noted, "The outlook is quite bright thanks to a major overhaul that brought the team from last place to a tie for second."

The veteran Van Brocklin had taken over the offense and gave them a chance to win every week. End Pete Retzlaff and flanker Tommy McDonald had developed into two of the better receivers in the league, along with dependable veteran Bobby Walston. Billy Ray Barnes and Clarence Peaks may not have been the most spectacular running backs in the league, but neither of them would lose you a game. A pair of rookies, Tim Brown and Ted Dean, brought added speed and added depth.

> "The retirement pledge seemed official when he was honored with a Chuck Bednarik Day the last game of the year at Franklin Field. Among his gifts were $1,000, and a color television."

The offensive line was a bit problematic. Bednarik, who had concentrated almost solely on center the past two years, was the only established member of the group. The other four line spots were open for competition from a group that included J.D. Smith, Jim McCusker, John Wittenborn, Stan Campbell, Darrell Aschbacher and Gerry Huth.

The defense was nondescript at best, and coming off a season in which they had given up the third most points in the league. The only star-caliber veteran was cornerback Tom Brookshier. The rest of the defense consisted of solid, good character-type guys.

The Eagles finished the exhibition season 4-2. The opening day opponent was the Cleveland Browns, a team that had beaten the Eagles 15 of 20 times the previous 10 years. There were few signs of change that week as Cleveland won again, 41-24. A three-game winning streak followed, the last of which was against the Detroit Lions, with Bednarik getting some time on defense because of injuries. He made his first big play of the season with a late interception that helped close a 28-10 Eagles victory.

Week five found the 3-1 Eagles traveling to Cleveland for a rematch with the Browns. It was during this game that the legend of the 60 Minute Man started to take hold with an assist provided by old nemesis Paul Brown. Down 22-7 early in the third quarter, the Eagles came all the way back on a windy and icy cold day to stick the Browns with their first loss of the season. Walston nailed a 38-yard field goal with 10 seconds to play to make the final score Eagles 31, Browns 29.

Winning against the Browns under these conditions proved pivotal for the Eagles. Though it may not have been recognized as such at the time, a turning point moment occurred on the Eagles first defensive play of the game, when Bob Pellegrini injured his knee and Coach Shaw waved Bednarik in at linebacker. He also stayed in the game at center, logging 58 minutes of playing time in this critical victory.

Afterward, he called it the best game he had ever played in college or the pros, and cited Coach Brown for providing the motivation that made it all possible.

After the game, Bednarik told reporters, "He [Brown] laughed real smirkishly, as if to say, 'You dumb jerk. Why don't you quit before you get hurt? I hollered back something unprintable, but in the heat of battle, you're liable to say anything. Anyhow, his laughing annoyed me.'

'We wanted to win from the previous humiliating loss, but when he laughed that only made me want to win worse."

The play that extracted mirth from Brown and brought fury to Bednarik occurred at the Browns sideline. Bednarik stepped up to meet Bobby Mitchell on a sweep, and as he moved in for the tackle, Gert Nagler, a Browns end, wiped him out with a blind-side block. Bednarik landed flat near the Browns bench, and when he looked up, he saw Brown smiling down at him.

The season had turned in the Eagles favor and the moment could not have been more heroic for Bednarik. Here he was, at age 35, playing the first full two-way game of his career, in a game for first place, against the best backfield in the league, which included Mitchell and the incomparable Jim Brown. If those challenges weren't enough, Bednarik also revealed that he played the game with a pulled muscle in his left thigh.

Afterward he provided insight into the great internal fortitude that made a feat like this possible. He told reporters in the post game locker room, "And then there's the mental thing. No matter what we do in life, if you tell yourself you can do something, you can. I kept talking to myself saying, 'You're not tired, and I wasn't."

The Eagles were now 4-1 and the bye week could not have come at a better time, providing Bednarik an extra week to recover for the Steelers. There was some uncertainty as to whether Bednarik would be asked to repeat the iron man performance. For the veteran, just doing it once represented the culmination of a dream.

"You dumb jerk. Why don't you quit before you get hurt. I hollered back something unprintable, but in the heat of battle, you're liable to say anything."

At a midweek press conference he told reporters, "I found out what it was like and now I'm just beginning to recover. I'm hungry again, I've always wanted to play 60 minutes of a pro game, and I never thought I'd wait until I was 35, and in my 19th year of football, and against a club like the Cleveland Browns."

The Eagles won the next two games against the Steelers and Redskins, with Bednarik playing defense only. After the Steelers game, coach Buddy Parker told the Pittsburgh Press, "That guy Bednarik hadn't played defense in three years, but he moves in there at linebacker and played better than anyone on the field."

Two Giant hurdles remained in the chase for the franchise's first championship since 1949—back-to-back games with the New York Giants. The first one was to be played at Yankee Stadium, a place where the Eagles had not won since 1952. These two games would determine the Eastern Division champion.

Bednarik was scheduled to again play only linebacker in the November 20th game, but during the first half the Giant defense, perhaps the best in the league, bludgeoned quarterback Norm Van Brocklin while taking a 10-0 lead. The halftime score remained that close only because Frank Gifford was stopped at the goal line late in the second quarter.

The Giants confounded Eagle linemen with a package of blitzes, and as the Dutchman told Tex Maule of Sports Illustrated, "They came after me like I was a piece of chocolate cake in the first half." In further describing his first half pounding, he added, "Hell, one time I got the ball and [Rosey] Grier had me by one leg and [Dick] Modzelewski by the other."

A seething Van Brocklin conferred with Shaw. Two major personnel decisions were made; Bednarik would have to pull double duty and take over at center, and John Wittenborn was inserted at guard. Bednarik settled over the ball on the Eagles' first possession, and announced to Huff, "Okay, Sam, the big boys are in now."

With the presence of the veteran linemen, and play calling that emphasized short, quick passes, the Eagles neutralized the Giants' rush. When the Giants moved up to stop the short throws, McDonald slipped behind cornerback Lindon Crow for a 35-yard touchdown. A fourth quarter field goal by Walston tied the game 10-10.

The next highlight play of the 1960 season was again provided by Bednarik, when he stepped up to the line of scrimmage just as fullback Mel Triplett was plunging ahead on an inside dive. The ball popped loose from the collision and floated to the outside. Safety Jim Carr grabbed it out of the air and ran it in for a 38 yard touch-down. Walston's extra point gave the Eagles their first lead of the game, 17-10.

The Giants got the ball back and tied the score with less than two minutes left. At some point in this series, Frank Gifford's number is certain to be called as he is their best offensive player. With about a minute-and-a-half, to go, he is the primary receiver and the result is recorded in infamy.

Gifford catches a slant pass that is a little behind him as he crosses the middle of the field. He is looking for safety Don Burroughs, and does not see the outside line-backer sprinting furiously in his direction. He gathers the ball in, turns to break outside and as he does, the most ex-quisitely timed hit in the history of professional football is delivered to his open body. Bednarik drives his shoul-der and forearm to Gifford's chest region, Frank falls back and the ball bounces forward.

A year later, Bednarik described the play for Dick Schaap of the Saturday Evening Post stating, "Gifford took his eyes off me to watch Burroughs, and just at that moment I reached top speed, drove directly into him and buried my shoulder in his chest. My shoulder hooked up and caught Gifford under the chin. The ball bounced loose from his hands and one of my teammates, Chuck Weber, pounced on it. I began jumping up and down, laughing and waving my fists. 'We got it, we got it.' I shouted, 'That's the game. That's the game.' This is not quite as colorful as the words that would be inscribed on thousands of pictures over the next 50 years, but The Post was a family magazine.

Bednarik knew well in advance of the December 26 game that he would be called upon to play both ways. Unlike earlier during the regular season, when he received emergency game time summonses from Coach Shaw, Bednarik had time to prepare.

Bednarik's victory jig over the lifeless Gifford assured him an eternal spot at the top of the All Time New York Sports Enemies List. The people of Gotham booed from the bottom of their lungs, but Bednarik didn't hear them; all that mattered was that Weber had possession of the ball and the Giants didn't. While he remained deaf to the fans, the bitter words of his opponents on the field did not go unheard.

Writing for the Evening Bulletin, Sandy Grady quoted Bednarik, "The Giants screamed at me, terrible

things. I told him I was sorry. I just wanted to jolt the ball loose. Gifford never saw me. What burns me up is Chuck Conerly yelling, 'You're a cheap shot artist, Bednarik!'"

With Gifford in a New York hospital, the Giants shut-tle down to Philadelphia the following Sunday. There is talk in the New York press all week about possible retal-iatory action against Bednarik, with Conerly leading the "cheap shot" chorus. When Conerly lines up behind the center at Franklin Field, Bednarik points and tells him, "You're next."

No visible attempts at retribution are apparent on the field and the Eagles again score a comeback victory, this time recovering from a 17-0 deficit and win 31-23, with Bednarik playing 55 minutes.

Writing in the December 5 issue of Sports Illustrated, Tex Maule reported, "The Giants did not try avenge their fallen teammate." "They were rough and mean," Bed-narik said after the game. "Like always but not dirty." Once, on a punt, Sam Huff unjoined Bednarik with a whistling blindside block.

"It musta hurt," Huff said. But he didn't holler. He got up and said, "Careful Sam. You keep blocking me like that and they'll think you're picking on me."

They have now swept the Giants for the first time since 1949, and with an 8-1 record, have all but wrapped up the East.

The Eagles won the division the following week with a 20-6 victory in St. Louis. A Sunday night crowd of 10,000 greeted the team at Philadelphia International Airport. With the last two games now meaningless, they had three weeks to prepare for their first championship game ap-pearance in 11 years.

The race in the west is tight, and it is not until the last weekend of the season that the young Green Bay Packer team is established as the opposition. The Packers had started well, struggled at midseason, and finished strong, beating the Rams the last game of the season to earn the Western Division title. Both teams had finished in last place just two years ago, thus setting up one of the most surprising championship pairings in league history. "Cinderella" was liberally attached to both teams as well as the game itself.

Under Coach Lombardi, the Packers had gelled into a serious team much quicker that anyone had anticipated. Along with general manager Jack Vanisi, who had passed away suddenly just a month earlier, Lombardi built a team around young talent. The nucleus of the team included nine future Hall of Famers—Paul Hornung, Bart Starr, Jim Taylor, Ray Nitschke, Forrest Gregg, Jim Ringo, Willie Wood, Willie Davis, and Henry Jordan—all of whom had been added to the team in the past four years; and all of whom would still be with the team when they had their great championship runs later in the decade.

Lombardi was in his second year as Packers coach. In 1958, when an assistant coach with the Giants, he was the first choice for the Eagles job that eventually went to Buck Shaw. He very nearly accepted the job, but after praying for guidance at his church in Red Bank, New Jersey, and soliciting the advice of Giants owner Wellington Mara, he passed on the Eagles offer.

The Eagles were built around their two veteran leaders, Van Brocklin and Bednarik. In what was to be the last season of his playing career, Van Brocklin was named the league's Most Valuable Player. Bednarik was riding out his own mythical season.

Bednarik knew well in advance of the December 26th, game that he would be called upon to play both ways. Unlike earlier during the regular season when he received emergency game time summonses from Coach Shaw, Bednarik had time to prepare. Shaw had announced right after the season finale against the Redskins that Bednarik was starting on both offense and defense.

The advance notice was fine by Bednarik, but it was not as if he planned to do anything different. He told Jack McKinney of the Philadelphia Daily News. "It's good to have time to prepare yourself mentally, but there's not too much advance planning you can do for a ground attack like the Packers. I'm just going to stick my nose in there, try to spill something and hope for good pursuit from the boys up front."

Snow covered Philadelphia in the days leading up to the game. Though the game was being played at Franklin Field, the Packers were listed as two-to-seven point favorites. The Packers featured a strong running game with Paul Hornung and Jim Taylor. The Eagles were regarded as a passing team.

As was the standard for the 1960 Eagles season, the opponent scored first and, as usual, the damage was not as bad as it could have been. Van Brocklin's first pass of the game, intended for Billy Barnes, was intercepted by defensive end Bill Quinlan, giving the Packers the ball on the Eagles 14. Three running plays by Taylor and Hornung pushed the ball to the six-yard line. Lombardi passed up the field goal attempt and Taylor was dropped for no gain. The Packers surrender the ball on downs.

The Eagles turned the ball over again, allowing Hornung to kick a 20-yard field goal for a 3-0 lead. Twice in the first quarter, the Eagles turned the ball over inside their 25-yard line, and yet were still only down by a field goal.

A Hornung 23-yard field goal early in the second quarter doubled the score to 6-0. The Eagles gained the lead on a 35-yard touchdown pass from Van Brocklin to McDonald. This play also produced one of Philadelphia's most memorable sports moments, as McDonald runs through the end zone, slips, and is helped off the turf by

some of the overflow fans who were allowed to stand on the field.

Later in the quarter, Walston extends the Eagles lead to 10-6, with a field goal. The Packer missteps continue as Hornung flubs a short field goal on the last play of the half. The Eagles got a break on their own mistake on this play. The Eagles had jumped offside on the play, but the Packers declined the penalty because they did not want

While Hornung is in Bednarik's grip, Brookshier crashes in from cornerback and finishes him off with a full speed slam to the upper body.

to change the angle of the kick. Hornung's concentration may have been affected, as he missed the chip shot kick. The Packers had dominated the statistics in the first half, but left as many as nine points on the field, by passing up two field goal attempts, and then missing a short one.

The scoreless third quarter was marked by two memorable plays on the same drive. Midway through the period, with the ball at the Eagles 25, Hornung runs a sweep to the right behind pulling guard Fuzzy Thurston. Thurston whiffs on a block of Bednarik, who steps up, forces Hornung inside, and greets him with one of his dead sure wrestling hold tackles. While Hornung is in Bednarik's grip, Brookshier crashes in from cornerback and finishes him off with a full speed slam to the upper body. Hornung is forced from the game with a pinched nerve and numbness in his right arm. He leaves after gaining 61 yards on 11 carries. On the next play, Taylor is dropped short of the first down on fourth-and-one.

In 1961, Bednarik described the Hornung tackle for the Saturday Evening Post, stating "Then the play started and I saw Hornung sweeping toward his right—my zone. I remembered from the films how he liked to cut back. I waited for this cutback. Just as Hornung pivoted, I rammed into him. My shoulder dug into his right side under his arm. He went down like a shot. His right arm was quivering. I was really scared."

At this stage in his career, the player who many called the most instinctive linebacker of all time, revealed that it wasn't just instantaneous diagnostic reaction that made him great. Because he had studied the game films, he was as prepared as a boy scout when he stepped on the field. Earlier in the same Post article he revealed, "Studying the films, I noticed that when Paul Hornung ran around end, he often left his blockers and cut back toward the inside. I made a mental note, if he does that against us, I'll get him. Sorry about your shoulder Paul, but you never stood a chance."

A fourth-quarter pass interception by John Symnac gave the Packers the ball at their own 20, and they proceeded to take the lead on a 12-play drive, punctuated by Bart Starr's seven-yard touchdown pass to Max McGee.

What followed was another improbable play in this nearly perfect season. Ted Dean, a 22-year old rookie from nearby Radnor, PA, took the ensuing kickoff and with fellow rookie Tim Brown leading the interference, returned the ball 58 yards up the left sideline to the Packer 39.

Seven plays later, Dean finished the drive his kickoff return had started. Running a sweep from the five yard line, he followed a block by pulling guard Gerry Huth, before breaking it off inside and busting through two defenders into the end zone.

Bednarik put an end to the next Packer drive when he recovered a Max McGee fumble. Following a short Eagle possession, the Packers got the ball back again with about two minutes to play. Starting play at his own 35, quarterback Starr completed five of six passes in reaching the Eagles 23 yard line with 17 seconds left, time enough for two plays if they could execute quickly.

Chuck Bednarik had the second championship of his career. Had he remained true to his retirement pledge, he and all the other Eagles would no doubt have been sitting home on the cold December day, watching the Browns or the Giants play for this championship.

Starr drops back, but none of his primary receivers is open. The clock continues to tick as he looks around the field. His only option is a swing pass to the fullback Taylor, who catches the ball and takes off on a desperate dash for the end zone. Taylor, maneuvering with all-out determination, breaks a tackle by Maxie Baughn and makes it to the Eagles 10. Don Burroughs also misses a tackle, but cornerback Bobby Jackson slows Taylor down just enough to allow the hot in pursuit Bednarik to catch up and wrestle the Green Bay star to the ground. Bednarik remains seated on Taylor as he squirms and strains to get up. From where he sits, he is able to watch the second hand of the scoreboard clock on Weightman Hall sweep down, 5-4-3-2-1...

"Okay Taylor, you can get up now. This game is over."

Chuck Bednarik had the second championship of his career. Had he remained true to his retirement pledge, he

and all the other Eagles would no doubt have been sitting home on the cold December day watching the Browns or the Giants play for this championship.

The Packers who played in this game would be back to form one of the great dynasties in league history. Lombardi told them that their effort today was going to make them champions.

Bednarik's 58 minutes on the field yielded a team-high 12 tackles and a fumble recovery.

"Perhaps you don't realize you could have won this game. But I think that there is no doubt in your minds now. And that's why you will win it all next year. This will never happen again. You will never lose another championship," he told his team.

He let them know they had been beaten by experience. Van Brocklin was named MVP for completing passes when he had to. Old Concrete Charlie Bednarik played 58 minutes and made the game-saving tackle.

Gene Ward, covering the game for the New York Daily News recorded the effort as such:

"It was altogether fitting and proper that Bednarik, the Eagles ironman, should be the one who brought him down. It was an old Penn player saving the victory on his old college stamping grounds."

Larry Merchant, of the Philadelphia Daily News, summed up Bednarik's day by saying, "It was just another afternoon in the life of Charles P. Bednarik. Played 60 minutes of rock 'em –sock 'em football, if you don't count punt returns and kickoffs. Knocked the other team's star—Paul Hornung-out of the game with a clean shoulder tackle. Made the game-saving tackle on the last play of the National Football League championship whoopdedo. And if you noticed, said Coach Buck Shaw, they didn't run too much to his side of the field. Just another day in the life of Charles P. Bednarik."

Bednarik's 58 minutes on the field yielded a team-high 12 tackles and a fumble recovery. This was the only post-season game the immortal Lombardi would lose.

Five times during the championship season, the Eagles asked him to go both ways. Each time they won. Along the way, he made all the important stops, some against Hall of Fame opponents.

The legend would have existed without this season, but the effort this 35-year old man willed out of his body during the fall and winter of 1960 gave permanent assurance that Chuck Bednarik would always be bigger than the legend.

Bart Starr

Hall of Fame Green Bay quarterback started for the Packers in the 1960 Championship against Eagles.

When Chuck Bednarik tackled Jim Taylor to end the 1960 NFL Championship Game, it gave coach Vince Lombardi and quarterback Bart Starr the only playoff losses of their Hall of Fame careers. Together, coach and quarterback would win five NFL Championships, including the first two Super Bowls before the decade was out.

'Chuck Bednarik was one of those players who factored into your game plan. He was great, fierce and competitive; a classy player we had great respect for.'

'It was an experience to study his game films. You would get up close and could appreciate his intensity.'

'You have to have respect for him; he was one of those, who in my opinion, makes a team come to life.'

'When you are preparing for a game, you pay attention to the coach's comments about the opponent playing opposite you. Coach Lombardi was one who paid respect to people who deserved it, and he was always very complimentary of Chuck.'

'The similarities of the great linebackers of the day—Nitschke, George, Schimdt, Bednarik—were competitiveness, awareness, mental aggressiveness; they were the leaders of the defense.'

'What we remember about the 1960 championship game was the unique disappointment of losing. That was the only time we lost a championship game. It was a great lesson. After the game Coach Lombardi was upbeat.'

> **"Chuck Bednarik was one of those players who factored into your game plan. He was great, fierce and competitive; a classy player we had great respect for."**

'He said they had more experience and they deserved to win. He said there are lessons to be learned and we won't lose another one. He actually said, 'We won't lose another one. Plusses came from that game. It was the steppingstone for our championships.'

'Jim Taylor was an alternate receiver on that last play. To Chuck's credit, he stopped him. He stepped in to make several great plays that game.'

'He was a great competitor. I always think of his competitiveness; it starts with "C," the first letter in Chuck."

Dick Lucas

Lucas was a reserve wide receiver on the 1960 championship team.

Dick Lucas played wide receiver for the Eagles for four seasons beginning in 1960. He remained in the Philadelphia area and has been a longtime resident of West Chester.

'Well, Chuck Bednarik was an individual on his own. He always let you know how good he was, and he wasn't bragging; he was good.'

'He wasn't that difficult of a leader. If you were screwing up, he let you know. He was both a vocal leader, and leader by example. During calisthenics, if you were screwing around, he'd get really serious.'

'We didn't hit much in practice, I was lucky to never have to come across the field on him. The Gifford hit was clean, it caught him blind.'

'He was a great player and everyone looked up to him.'

'In 1960, the whole thing, we were a bunch of guys who had been traded from other teams. A bunch of no-names. Every week Brookie would say, "We're underdogs again." We came back a lot.'

'Against Cleveland Bobby Walston kicked a field goal to win the game. Tommy made some big catches. We came from behind a lot.'

'The first game, we got whacked by Cleveland (41-24). Jimmy Brown must have had about 200 yards, and Bobby Mitchell another 200.'

'After the game Buck Shaw said, if we score 24, we're supposed to win.'

'Green Bay, it was their first time in the championship game. We caught them at the right time. We played well; it wasn't a gift. Chuck made that tackle to end the game."

Frank Gifford

The Hit; 'nuff said.

No two opposing players in the history of the National Football League are as indelibly linked as Chuck Bednarik and Frank Gifford. A photograph by John Zimmerman that appeared in the November 25, 1960 issue of Sports Illustrated captured the play that would represent perhaps the defining moment in two great Hall of Fame careers. For almost 50 years now, barely a day evolves without either of the photo's subjects being reminded of that play.

It is probably the most famous football photograph of all time. It appears prominently in nearly every anthology of football or sports photography that has been published over the past five decades.

It remains a staple at every sports memorabilia shop and on any given day there could be two dozen offerings on E-bay. In a 1998 article Sports Illustrated reported, "Autographed photo of Chuck Bednarik standing over a knocked-out Frank Gifford ($20). Chuck Bednarik standing over a knocked-out Gifford, and Chuck has signed "Hello Frank ($60). Chuck Bednarik standing over a knocked-out Gifford, and Chuck signed 'This F — — —' Game is Over ($85).

The lone video recording, a grainy black and white clip that was taken from a single camera angle, seems prehistoric, almost a relic from the silent film era, when compared to the multi-camera, every-angle, high definition, high resolution replays that accompany every televised game today.

Yet, a few years ago, NFL Films selected it as the greatest hit of all time.

For Chuck Bednarik, it has elevated him from greatness to cult-like status. He never tires of talking about 'the hit.'

Frank Gifford is ever the gentleman; he still addresses it when asked, but leaves little doubt that he would rather be talking about almost anything else. He was a great player, who became even better known through his career in broadcasting. He still lives in the heart of Giants country, shuttling between Connecticut and New York, and people there want to know about the day he got leveled by Old Concrete Charlie.

> It is probably the most famous football photograph of all time. It appears prominently in nearly every anthology of football or sports photography that has been published over the past five decades.

Fact: One of the two subjects in Zimmerman's infamous photo was the first player in NFL history to make the Pro Bowl on defense one year, and offense the next. Hint: It isn't the guy left standing. Gifford was named to the Pro Bowl in '52 as a defensive back; the next year as halfback on offense. This is one two-way honor he beat the 60 Minute Man to.

In his 1993 autobiography, "The Whole Ten Yards," Gifford relates, "Around the time I started going with Kathie, I gave her a word of warning. "I played professional football for twelve years. I made All-Pro at three positions and Most Valuable Player once, and I'm in the Hall of Fame. But of all the things you're going to hear about me, the word you'll hear most often is 'Bednarik.'"

Kathie gave me a blank look. "Bednarik?" she said. "What's that—a pasta?"

The "pasta" comment, however lighthearted in intent, would function as a battle cry for the sometimes humorless Bednarik in later years, ("She called me a Pasta!") Maybe she should have called him the more ethnically correct "pierogie."

It might have just been another good football picture, with the shelf life of that week's Sports Illustrated, if the two protagonists hadn't been who they were. Would anyone be buying the picture if it had been two merely good players, say Chuck Weber standing over Kyle Rote?

All of the theatrics were in place to set up the play—Philadelphia-New York; Eastern Division championship on the line; Concrete Charlie; coal cracker; Bethlehem, PA vs. The Golden Boy; Southern California Steel vs. Silk.

After two seasons of generally wretched football, the Eagles show up in New York on November 20, 1960 for the first of back-to-back games with the New York Giants. The Eagles haven't played a big game in years, while the Giants won the Eastern Division each of the past two years, and three times in the last four.

The Eagles haven't lost since opening day and this year have the look of one of the better teams in the league. They go into New York with a record of 5-1-1, and this game is likely to determine the division championship.

The Eagles came back from a 10-0 halftime deficit to gain a 17-10 lead. The Giants were moving for the tying touchdown late in the game and George Shaw threw a pass over the middle to Gifford.

The best description of what happened next can be found in the pages of "A Fan's Notes" by Frederick Exley. One of the great sports novels of all-time, much of the

Eagle Chuck Weber recovers the football after Bednarik collides with Gifford

book is devoted to the hero's obsession with Frank Gifford.

"The crowd was wild. The crowd was maniacal. The crowd was his. J. was the one who noticed Chuck Bednarik, Philadelphia's — there are no adjectives to properly describe him — linebacker. 'Watch out for Bednarik,' he said. Hearing J., I turned to see Bednarik coming from behind Gifford out of his linebacking zone, pounding the turf furiously, like some fierce animal gone berserk. I watched Bednarik all the way, thinking at any second Gifford would turn back and see him whispering 'Watch it Frank, Watch it Frank.' Then, quite suddenly I knew it was going to happen; and accepting with the fatalistic horror of a man anchored by fear to curb and watching a tractor trailer bearing down on a blind man, I stood breathlessly and waited. Gifford never saw him, and Bednarik did his job well. Dropping his shoulder slightly, so that it would meet Gifford in the region of the neck and chest, he ran into him without breaking his furious stride; thwaaahhhp, taking Gifford's legs out from under him, sending the ball careening wildly into the air, and bringing him to the soft green turf with a sickening thud."

Chuck Weber recovered the ball, the game was over, and the man who was to later decry all the onfield boogying and hotdogging of later generations unleashed a victory whoop that was immortalized with click of a camera.

'This F_ _ _ _ _g Game is Over.'

Concrete Charlie took no particular thrill in waxing Gifford, but the turnover meant that the Eagles now had a clear path to the championship game. Gifford, lying prone at this feet, was an incidental prop to a spontaneous victory jig.

Few observers, Gifford included, called it a dirty hit.

Although he didn't return until 1962, he took umbrage at the "near-death" references to his condition, though immediately after the game, some confusion did fuel a brief rumor that the hit was indeed fatal.

A security guard did suffer a fatal heart attack that day. After tending to Gifford on the field' the Giants' team physician worked on the stricken guard. Attempts at reviving him failed; the guard was wheeled out of the stadium on a gurney with a sheet over his face. Whispers of "He's dead" passed through the locker room reaching, among others, the then Mrs. Gifford. The diminutive Dr. Francis Sweeney, who a few minutes earlier was seen waving his fist in Bednarik's face on the field, was left to explain that the deceased was not Gifford.

More than 100 people were contacted in connection with this book. The one person who produced the most pre-call nervousness was Frank Gifford. A Bednarik book would be incomplete with the input of Gifford. Bird and Magic; Thomson and Branca; McEnroe and Connors; Frazier and Ali — the story of either one's career is incomplete with the other.

Gifford would have been within his rights to refuse to cooperate. It was clearly understandable.

He was tired and there was nothing else to say. He was a star football player and a mega-star broadcaster, but in too many articles and discussions his life whittled down to being on the wrong end of a collision.

Bednarik had developed what almost seemed a nightclub routine around "the hit." Wherever he went, especially in New York-loathing Philadelphia, everyone wanted to hear about the time he knocked the stuffing out of Gifford. Frank Gifford had become the straight man in a story that usually brought yucks from the audience.

His wife was too often drawn into it. Someone in the audience, might yell out "I wish it was Kathie Lee on the end of that hit, and Chuck might respond with "A lot of people tell me that."

At an appearance in South Bend a few years ago, that very scenario occurred. It drew laughter from the audience and the local newspaper covered it in a humorous fashion.

A copy of the article was forwarded to Gifford, who responded with a handwritten letter to Bednarik, telling him that he hoped this was a mistake and that he didn't appreciate Chuck bringing up Kathie Lee's name.

Two phone calls were placed to Frank Gifford's office and a letter was written discussing this book and requesting his participation.

A few days later, a message is on the answering machine, with the caller identifying himself as Frank Gifford.

"This is Frank Gifford returning your call. It's four o'clock now, I'm leaving for the day. Tomorrow morning I'm speaking at my daughter's school. Call me at home in the afternoon." He leaves his home number.

The call is placed and Gifford apologizes for being difficult to reach, explaining that he has been busy, with among other things his own new book. He also wants it to be known that he will no longer discuss Chuck Bednarik.

"I'm not going there. I know what you want. I'm through discussing Chuck Bednarik. I wish he would grow up, and I'm not going to embellish his career anymore. You can quote me on that."

He could have ignored the phone calls and letter, but that would have been rude. He was gentleman enough to respond.

Some prods and probes are met with continued, increasingly exasperated "no's."

"You've got your story, you don't need me."

The caller was expecting to get a click and a dead line, but Gifford did not hang up. Neither did he request that the caller get lost and leave him alone. He just said no.

While disappointing it was understandable. He's proud, he's well-accomplished, and he's had enough of being the punchline to "the hit."

A few days later, the phone is turned on and another voicemail appears.

'This is Frank Gifford, I've had second thoughts about that Bednarik thing. I was kind of rude, I think you kind of understand some of it. Call me tomorrow.'

No Frank, you weren't rude, and yes it is understandable.

The follow-up call is placed.

"Honestly, it just kind of defined his career. I saw him at the Hall of Fame a few years ago and pointed him out to Kathy.'

'When did Chuck retire…'62? I retired in '64; outlasted him.'

'My involvement with him has stuck in people's heads. No one really understood pro football in the early '60s; the sportswriters didn't; the New York sportswriters especially didn't, as they were all baseball guys.'

'That play took on a life of its own and it has grown over the years. I've always said it was clean; it wasn't dirty.'

'The thing that bothered me is that I was never 'near death', I wasn't in a coma. I wanted to go home from the hospital the next morning.'

'I was in New York Hospital, and they didn't have CAT scans in those days. The medical treatment wasn't anywhere near what it is today. Dr. Sweeney told me to take a couple of shots of scotch every night.'

'I wanted to go home. I'd sit at the window looking out all day, and while I was in the hospital, that's when the play started to take on a life of its own.'

'About 1993, I was getting a tingling in my arm. I was given a CAT scan and a different examination. The neurosurgeon asked if I had ever been in an auto accident.'

"I thought back, and said, no, nothing major.'

'He said, well you have all the symptoms of classic whiplash.'

"I'm not sure if it came from that hit, it may not have even been associated, but I did have some numbness afterward. '

'At the time it seemed better for the game to just let it go, but Chuck made such a big thing about it.'

'It would get back to me that he said this, he said that.'

'He got used to being asked and talking about it. He turned it into a cause celebre.'

'It bothered me. He was a great player, and I said to him this should never define your career. He began to slip into the dark ages in talking about it.'

'Monday Night Football? That made it much more famous. Cosell was a big person and he would not let it die.'

"Monday Night Football brought it back. And the [Darrel] Stingley hit. It became one of the main references when they pulled out the classic hits."

'I'm over it. It bothered me more that I fumbled and we lost because of it. That's little noted but long remembered. It took some onus off my fumble in '58; no one remembers that.'

'He was a great player for Philadelphia. He became more famous because of it. Sadly, we're linked together.'

The fans in Philadelphia keep the play alive and Gifford laughs when told that the picture probably hangs in more bars, hoagie shops, basements and family rooms than the past four popes, Frank Rizzo, Frank Sinatra and Martin Luther King combined.

'And there I am lying on the ground. It's good that I don't get to Philly often.'

"I understand."

Jim Taylor

This Green Bay Packer running back is forever linked with Chuck Bednarik as the guy who was struggling to get off the ground as the clock expired in the 1960 NFL Championship game.

After the 1960 championship game, Chuck Bednarik said of Jim Taylor, "He's one-two with Jimmy Brown. I think he hits as hard as Brown. A great fullback, Taylor." Taylor, of course, spent the last few seconds of that game trying to extricate himself from the vise that was created between the ground and a happily seated Bednarik. Like Frank Gifford and Paul Hornung, Taylor was another Hall of Fame running back who contributed to the legend of Chuck Bednarik's 1960 season.

"1960, I always think of that as the 'Cinderella Bowl'. We were both 7-5 and no one expected either of us to be there.'

'We knew Chuck was multi-talented and would be on both sides of the ball. He was an unbelievable competitor. I knew I would be head-to-head with my number of carries.'

> **"I was trying to get up field, and 'BAM,' old Chucky boy hits me. I go down and I'm struggling to get up."**

'The middle linebackers of that era—Nitschke, Huff, Bednarik—they could play with any of them today.'

'They had the mechanics, the reading ability, the hitting. They were the best players on the team.'

'A thousand times? He's probably told the story about the last play of the game 700,000 times.'

'We were losing 17-13, so a field goal did us no good. Bart Starr dropped back and was looking for a receiver; he found me with an eight-yard pass. We started with about 10-12 seconds to play. I was running around looking for daylight, I had to go for the end zone. I caught it and I saw nothing but the wrong color jerseys.'

'I was trying to get up field, and 'BAM,' old Chucky boy hits me. I go down and I'm struggling to get up.

He's on top of me "5-4-3-2-1." Okay Taylor you can get up now.

'He was a great competitor; he made the saving tackle on the last play of the game.'

'That was our first playoff with Lombardi. But we knew we were building something. Kramer and Hornung came with bonus picks; in '56 we drafted Curry. I was the number two pick of the draft in '58. We drafted Nitscshke and Kramer. We stole Willie Davis in a trade with Cleveland. We were starting to build.'

'The Eagles were the more veteran team that year. But neither of us had been any good for a while.

'We were two Cinderella teams. But we were coming together and they had some good players like Van Brocklin, McDonald, Clarence Peaks and Chuck.'

'The next year they were gone, and we went 12-2. We had 10 hall-of-famers on that team, five on offense, five on defense.'

'In '60, Lombardi was setting up his system. He knew exactly what he wanted to do—he coached his players on ball possession, don't turn the ball over, maintain field position and keep the interceptions down.'

'But they beat us fair and square. We didn't make the plays down the stretch."

Jim Tunney

A long time NFL official, Tunney remembers Chuck Bednarik as one of the toughest, yet cleanest, players of his era.

"My first year in the NFL was 1960. I remember working Eagles games at Franklin Field and on the road.'

'Chuck Bednarik was typical of the linebacker of the day. He gave no quarter; he expected nothing—he gave hits and expected to be hit.'

'He wasn't dirty, just rough. He did what a linebacker did—knock 'em down.'

'He had that linebacker mentality, like Butkus. I once asked Butkus if he ever wanted to hurt anyone, and he said, "No, not unless it was a game."

'I was a field judge until '62, so I saw the play come as it came to him. He was one of the fiercest guys ever written about. Of all the linebackers of the day, he was the leader."

Leo Carlin

Longtime Eagles ticket manager Leo Carlin joined the team during the 1960 season and has been with the organization since.

'I think Chuck's problems with the Eagles started because he wanted to be more involved with the team. He wanted a job when Leonard Tose owned the team, but Leonard wasn't interested. Only Dick Vermiel responded to him.'

'Leonard could be a terrific guy; I've seen the great side of him, but he was also capable of saying anything, and I also saw him turn on people.'

'Chuck wanted to be back, and except for Vermiel, no one brought him back, and it was wonderful, what Dick did.'

'Chuck was hurt; that's just him. He probably thought there would be more recognition from the team after he retired. No one paid attention to him when the team was run by the Band of Brothers. Jerry Wolman liked having him around after he bought the team.'

'I got to know him better after his playing career ended. I've always liked him.'

'He was great, an icon as a player. What he did as a player, it's hard to put into words. He's the greatest football player to come out of Philadelphia.'

'Why that didn't translate off the field, I don't know. Chuck was never known to be diplomatic, and that has been a problem for some people. There's a group out there that probably got tired of him.'

'There was one linebacker, years ago, who criticized Chuck's coaching. He said Chuck wasn't up to running modern drills, but so much of what Chuck did on the field was a result of his great instinct. He was not much on technique.'

'I was a huge Penn fan as a kid. Ed Lawless was one of their stars, and growing up in North Philly he was like an older brother to me. He used to take me into the locker room and that's where I first met Chuck.'

'Chuck used to come and visit when we were at the Vet. He always asked for me; he'd go up to one of the young girls in the window and ask "Is Leo there?" The girl would ask,"Who should I say is calling?"

Chuck would point to the wall and say "Look at that picture, that's who it is."

'I have nothing but the best to say about Chuck. I'm glad he's calmed down in recent years. Diplomacy was never his forte, but he backed up everything he said on the field."

Forrest Gregg

Hall of Fame Packers lineman was on the field for the 1960 championship game.

In his book "Run to Daylight," Vince Lombardi called Forrest Gregg, "The finest player I ever coached." A second round draft choice in 1956, Gregg was one of the young members of the 1960 team, and stayed with the Packers until 1970. He was named All-NFL eight times during the 1960s and was picked for the league's 75th Anniversary All-Time Team.

"The main thing I know about Chuck Bednarik is that amazing story of 1960; going both ways, just an outstanding feat. To play linebacker, and all the energy it took to play that position; then play center, just totally unique.'

'Everyone who knew football marveled at what he did. What's amazing is that he wasn't an ordinary center, or an ordinary linebacker; he was a cut above at both positions.'

'In preparing for the championship game, Lombardi didn't have to point anything out to us; we knew who we were dealing with.'

'At that point in the league, nearly everyone ran a 4-3, or some version of the four-man line. There were several good middle linebackers. We had one in Nitschke. There was George, Schmidt, Huff, Butkus a little later. Chuck Bednarik was right there with that type of linebacker; he was outstanding.'

'I saw him at the Pro Bowl that year. The first story he told everyone was the Taylor tackle and how he sat on him until the clock ran out. Jim and I were not too happy about it, but we couldn't argue with the result.'

'Paul [Hornung] had an injury going into that game, he wasn't 100%. Bednarik tackled him and put him out of the game.'

'Going into that game, we felt we could win and were disappointed with the outcome, but it spurred us on for the next two years. That loss stayed with us, and we won the next two championships.'

'That Philly game gave us motivation. Lombardi used it as motivation and beat us to death about that game. I don't think we would have won the next two championships if we hadn't lost that game."

Maxie Baughn

As a rookie linebacker with the Eagles in 1960, Baughn was in awe of playing alongside one of his boyhood heroes, Chuck Bednarik.

Maxie Baughn joined the Eagles in 1960. Chuck Bednarik calls him the best rookie linebacker with whom he ever played. The Georgia Tech graduate played with the Eagles until 1965, when he was traded to the Los Angeles Rams. He had a brief retirement and coached at his alma mater in 1972 and '73. He was brought back to the NFL as a player-coach for George Allen's 1974 "Over The Hill Gang" team with the Washington Redskins. He was later head coach at Ivy League Cornell for six years, and often met up with Bednarik when the Big Red played the University of Pennsylvania.

"Chuck Bednarik, he was like a father figure to me. He had flown in World War II; oh yeah, I was in awe of meeting him.'

'My first game with the Eagles was in LA after the College All-Star Game. I had heard about Chuck, how he could do anything—offense, defense, snap.'

> **"Chuck Bednarik was the epitome of a football player. At his age, it startled me that anyone was still playing. But then, of course, before you knew it, I was playing at the same age."**

'I get there on Saturday. The game is that night. Chuck Bednarik walks out on the field and kicks a 43-yard field goal. I don't even think he knew what shoe he was wearing, round toe, square toe; it didn't matter to him. It was the damndest things I ever saw. I never heard that he was a kicker.'

'Fifteen years before that he was flying missions over Germany and I was six or seven years old. He was a war hero, and here I am playing with him.'

'No, oh no, no way we would have won in 1960 without Chuck. That team was centered around two people and two people only—Chuck Bednarik because of the way he played and his intense determination, and Norm Van Brocklin; he ran the offense, ran everything about it, even ran practice.'

'Without those two players we would have lost more than we won.'

'In 1960, we had two guys, Chuck Bednarik and Norm Van Brocklin. They were the backbone of the offense and defense, and, of course, Chuck was going both ways.'

'He hadn't played defense for a couple of years, and then Chuck Weber got hurt, and he went in at linebacker.'

'It's funny; he didn't worry about what defense we were in. He wanted us to help him along and tell him where he was supposed to be, but he just went to the ball.'

'He made all the plays. Huff, Schmidt, George; Chuck was the best I ever saw.'

'Being a rookie, I didn't know what to expect coming into the season. I didn't know much about the team. The only team we saw on TV down south was the Redskins. The pros just weren't that popular.'

'Chuck had his own way of doing things. With him and Van Brocklin around, there wasn't much funny stuff going on.'

'Chuck Bednarik was the epitome of a football player. At his age, it startled me that anyone was still playing. But then, of course, before you knew it, I was playing at the same age.'

'At camp in 1960, we had a lot of injuries. We had some talent on the defense, (Marion Campbell, Jess Richardson,) but the team was so fragile. Someone going both ways would not have happened if it wasn't for the injuries. We were a bunch of misfits.'

'It tells you something that Chuck Bednarik had to go both ways. We had no depth.'

'He went in at linebacker, and he was making plays. He didn't have to practice. If there ever was a natural linebacker, it was Chuck Bednarik.'

'I was playing the right side; he was playing some left, some middle. I had to tell him what to do when the defense was called, but you really didn't have to tell him anything. He knew which direction he had to fill. He simplified the game, played it like it should have been played.'

'The Gifford hit. I was right there. He was playing outside, Webber was in the middle. I turned when the ball was thrown and saw Chuck hit him. The ball flew right over my head."

'I saw the whole play develop as Frank turned into him'

'The first time I ever went to anything other than a football meeting in Philadelphia was a party at Chuck's house. Don Rickles was there and he was cutting on everybody.'

'Chuck and I, we've been friends a long time. When I was coaching at Cornell, we brought him up whenever we played Penn.'

'I would have him address the team and he was really funny. He'd stand there and hold out his hands— those fingers. He's a throwback to the good old days.'

'The era would not have made a difference for Chuck Bednarik. He is the best linebacker that ever played. Whatever changes the era called for, he would have done."

Pat Summerall

Before pairing with Tom Brookshier and later John Madden in the broadcast booth, Pat Summerall was a placekicker in the NFL, finishing up with the New York Giants from 1958-61.

Pat Summerall is best known as the sidekick partner in two of the most popular football broadcast teams of all time. He spent most of the 1970s paired with Tom Brookshier, then went on to a 22-year run with John Madden. He also enjoyed a 10-year career as a placekicker in the NFL, finishing up with the New York Giants from 1958-61.

"As a player, oh gosh, I remember how well he played and how tough he was. We always, as Giants, respected his talents.'

'He was one of those guys, like Lawrence Taylor, that when you drew up your offense, you had to know where he was at all times. He figured in the game planning. There have been very few people like that.'

'He was outstanding and tough, and from what I've heard, he still is. He was certainly one you respected as much, or more, as anyone else. Even in the era of the great middle linebacker, he was the guy; you always knew how tough he was.'

'The Gifford hit was legal. What I remember most of that day is that there was a guy in the stands who had a heart attack. They brought him into our locker room. We weren't sure if he had died.'

'Bednarik hits Gifford, and Frank is taken off the field on a stretcher into the locker room. The game is over and we go into the locker room. Frank's wife at the time, Maxine, was outside the door waiting for word about Frank.'

> **"The Gifford hit was legal. What I remember most of that day is that there was a guy in the stands who had a heart attack. They brought him into our locker room. We weren't sure if he had died."**

'The guy who had the heart attack dies, and word gets out "He died." The dead guy was wheeled out on a stretcher with a sheet over his face.'

"Maxine almost passed out herself, when she heard that he died, and she saw the stretcher get wheeled out.'

'As far as the hit itself, we as teammates thought he was gloating. He KO'd Frank, everyone has seen the picture, and our assumption was that he was gloating over the hit. No one understood at the time that he was not gloating, but as he explained later, celebrating that the game was over.'

'I can't say that there was a particular emotion the next time we played him to get revenge.'

'I know Chuck, and he's always been a talker. There's no alarm or trouble about the things he says, that's just the way he is.'

'I was always a little afraid of him, even off the field; even at banquets. He was a heck of a player and a unique person. I've talked with Brookie about him a lot over the years."

Paul Hornung

The Golden Boy claims that his career was never quite the same after he suffered a pinched nerve in his shoulder from being tackled by Chuck Bednarik in the 1960 Championship Game.

Paul Hornung is the second Hall of Fame running back whose career was never quite the same after absorbing a Chuck Bednarik hit in 1960. The Green Bay halfback suffered a pinched nerve and numbness in his right arm when Bednarik tackled him in the second half of the 1960 NFL Championship game.

"About the time we start talking about football players, Chuck Bednarik may have been the greatest player of all time.'

'He was a monster, so big for that time, and for what he did. He was the biggest linebacker of that era, and he was so physical, so fast.'

'The Gifford business was bullshit and blown out of proportion because it was New York. The hit was legal, and what Chuck did was a little demonstration of happiness because they won the game.'

'Bednarik may have been the best player of his time, maybe the best of all time. To play center and middle linebacker, not many guys could have gone both ways. Probably Butkus could have done it, but the list is short.'

> **"Bednarik may have been the best player of his time, maybe the best of all time. To play center and middle linebacker, not many guys could have gone both ways. Probably Butkus could have done it, but the list is short."**

'Going into the championship game, the guy we were concerned about was Van Brocklin. He may have had the best arm of all time. He was sensational; he was ahead of his time. Marino, Elway; they had the rep in later years, but Van Brocklin was every bit the quarterback they were. He made the plays when he had to.'

'I was hurt going into that game. I had hurt my neck and shoulder, but I played. Our team doctor was Lombardi, if you could walk, talk, chew gum you played.'

'The play that I was hurt in that game, Brookie stood me up and Chuck finished me. The hit extended my neck; it was a very dangerous type of injury; I was very lucky. My right side was numb and I couldn't squeeze my hand to grip a football.'

'That was the play that started my downfall. I should not have played that game I could have been paralyzed.'

'How could a doctor okay me? The doctor was Dr. Lombardi.'

'Bednarik and Butkus delivered hits, they didn't get hit. That's why those guys didn't get hurt. You don't get hurt when you're doing the hitting.'

'Taylor was never meant to be the primary receiver that last play of the game. If Bart threw to Taylor, it's only because everyone else was covered.'

'After the game, Lombardi said that Chuck had a great game and was a super player, but he also told us that it was the last time we would lose a playoff game. He told us that we would learn from this game. That game was the steppingstone for our championships.'

'We just got beat by experience—Bednarik, Van Brocklin those guys were the best. Van Brocklin's numbers weren't great, but he made the plays when he had to.'

'And that kickoff return by Ted Dean killed us. You can't let that happen after you go ahead.'

'Yeah, I remember that picture of Chuck walking off the field with Taylor and me. He was congratulating us…he was a hell of a lot happier than we were."

Tommy McDonald

Tommy McDonald was the perhaps the antithesis to the stoic, no-nonsense Chuck Bednarik in the Eagles locker room and on the sideline, but no one disputes that he matched #60 in pound-for-pound toughness and desire.

'1960 really didn't seem different from other years when the season started. It had taken a while to get the material together to win. Van Brocklin pulled things together: he wanted you to give everything. And we had Sonny Jurgensen behind him.'

'Van Brocklin and Bednarik, those two guys were our coaches on the field. We listened to them; if you made a mistake, they let you know about it. They were the captains of the ship on offense and defense.'

'We were confident going into the championship game. We believed that if we played the way we were capable of playing, we would win.'

'My touchdown was the most exciting play of my career. The stadium was oversold, people were on the ground. After I scored, some fans helped me off the ground, I said, "I want you on my team."'

'Then old number 60, sitting on Taylor at the end of the game, I was so proud of him.'

'I'd like to see the Eagles win another championship. I want it to stay in Philadelphia.'

'With Chuck, I don't go on either side when he's having his disputes. Chuck is a guy who has had a lot of hard feelings. I don't pay attention to the people who try to downgrade him. I know him as a player and a man, and he is very good at both.'

'As far as middle linebackers go, they could make a film on how the position was meant to be played, and Chuck would be the example. Coaches would pay to watch Chuck play the position. He was so good, it's not funny.'

'NFL Films could put together a clinical film on him. He got separation, he had instinct, great instinct. He always knew what the other player was going to do, and he gave an absolute 200%, like me.'

'He was absolutely the best. There were a lot of great linebackers, but I'll always take Chuck Bednarik first.'

'Chuck wanted to do it his way. God gave him talent to go with his motivation and instinct. They don't make linebackers like him anymore.'

'We never scrimmaged, they were afraid of someone getting hurt.'

'The Gifford hit, yeah it was the turning point of the season. It won the game for us, and it helped us that the Giants wouldn't have him anymore. He was one fantastic ballplayer.'

'I always loved to play against the Giants. When we came up to Yankee Stadium that afternoon, they knew we came to play.'

'God knew what he was doing when he made Chuck Bednarik. That's how you build a football player."

Tony Veteri

Tony Veteri was an official in the AFL and NFL for 26 years.

'He was an aggressive player, loved the game, played hard and had fun. He was as good a linebacker as you could find. In my book, he's right up there in the top three, with Dick Butkus and Willie Lanier, no question.'

'Guys on offense did not want to go by him; when he hit you, you were hit. He was a perfect gentleman on the field. He loved the game. He was one of those old school guys who always gave 100%.'

'Oh yeah, he was a clean player; even the Gifford hit was clean. He hit everyone hard, bingo, like Ronnie Lott. You couldn't beat him. You didn't have to watch the old timers too closely, they played clean.'

'He was one of the best. I would like to have him on my team if I was coach. He's on the all-time, All-Veteri Team.'

'All I know is, he was always on top of the pile. A lot of people mentioned Sam Huff, but he was much better than Huff.'

'Huff played in New York and the newspapers can do a lot in the plus or minus department for a player.'

'Chuck may not have gotten the press of some of the others, but this guy was a tough s.o.b."

Pete Retzlaff

"The Baron" was a receiver with the Eagles during the latter part of Chuck Bednarik's career, and he remembers Chuck Bednarik as the best middle linebacker to ever play the position.

After being cut by the Detroit Lions, Pete Retzlaff was claimed by the Philadelphia Eagles. He was named to five Pro Bowl teams as a receiver after switching over from fullback. "The Baron" blossomed when Norm Van Brocklin was brought in as quarterback, and along with Tommy McDonald formed one of the best receiving tandems in the league. He later moved to tight end, and immediately became one of the best at that position.

"It's hard to say that Chuck is alone in how he feels about today's players. A lot of old guys get disturbed by the exorbitant salaries. The talent pool is really diluted from what it was 25-30 years ago. You had about 400 players in the league then; now you have upwards of 1500. Many of today's guys couldn't make it through training camp.'

'Chuck Bednarik is the best middle linebacker who ever played the game. He was, whether designated or not, the team captain. Chuck just assumed the leadership role.'

'Every time we warmed up before practice, Chuck jumped into the middle of the circle and lined people up. He was used to being a leader. He had flown bombing missions. Most of us would not have known that. He had a maturity in him that most guys out of college didn't have.'

"He didn't talk about the military; someone asked him if it was true that he had flown 20 some missions, and he just said 'yeah.' A lot of the World War II guys were like that.'

'People don't realize that the best college football of the 20th century was played right after World War II. It was a real man's game with all of those vets coming back.'

'Back then, I was in high school and they used to show "Movietone News" for about 10 minutes. They always had something about the start of the college football season. I always thought the guy who did those features must have been a Penn grad, because they always featured the University of Pennsylvania, the Quakers.'

'The interaction between Chuck and Norm Van Brocklin was good. Chuck had been the leader of the team. Van Brocklin came over in '58, and he had a relationship with Buck Shaw, and the Dutchman assumed a leadership role even though he had just come in.'

'Whenever we were in a meeting and new plays or formations were put it, Shaw always turned to Van Brocklin for approval. He'd say "Dutch, is that right?"'

'Chuck was a hard linebacker. In 1960, no one gave it a second thought when he moved back to linebacker. He was a unique individual who would do anything he was asked to do. He was one of the strongest guys physically I have ever seen.'

'We had a lot of good people on that team. Other people may not have thought so. The New York Giants and Detroit Lions probably didn't think so.'

'If Van Brocklin had returned in '61, we probably would have won another one. Even without him, we came within a half game; if Cleveland would have won that last game.'

'We were listening to the Browns-Giants game in the locker room. They had Lou Groza, the best field goal kicker in the league. Cleveland could have tied, and we would have finished ahead of the Giants. But Brown didn't kick, he went for it.'

'After the game, someone asked Brown why he didn't go for three, and you know what, he said "I don't owe the Philadelphia Eagles anything." That's all he said.'

'There was not a linebacker as good as Chuck—Schmidt, Huff, Nitschke—he took a second seat to no one.'

'He saw things develop like any other linebacker sees the play, but he had uncanny strength. The guy assigned to take him out, couldn't get the job done.'

'There was a play in Cleveland. Chuck made a tackle and pushed, I think it was Jimmy Brown, out of bounds near the Cleveland bench. Paul Brown said something to Chuck, and Chuck took a swing at him. He missed, but he took a swing. How things have changed.'

'There were two things that separated him from the rest—one; his physical strength; and two; his maturity.'

'Gifford?, Frank probably doesn't remember that hit. It's unfortunate that it happened, but it was legal.'

'I've talked to Frank, and as far as I know, there's no animosity. It was in the open field, and with Chuck around you had better stay clear.'

> **"Chuck Bednarik is the best middle linebacker who ever played the game. He was, whether designated or not, the team captain. Chuck just assumed the leadership role."**

Bednarik stands on the sideline of an Eagles game while owner Leonard Tose looks on.

'Chuck wasn't trying to belittle anybody in that famous picture. He was celebrating the end of the game.'

'There are teams that take care of their outstanding franchise players. I think of Larry Wilson with the Cardinals. Since Larry retired, he's been with the Cardinals and he does a good job.'

'Dick Vermiel understood that. One of the first things, he got hold of Chuck and put him on the sidelines to motivate the team.'

'It was an opportunity for Chuck to fit in. After Vermiel moved on there was a change in administration and ownership. Since then, there has been a lack of communication with former players in the surrounding area.'

'We felt the organization could do more. When Jeff Lurie bought the team, he asked several of the alumni to dinner. He told us that he wanted us to feel part of the family and organization. That's the last we've heard from him.'

'I can't speak for all the veterans, but some organizations really seem to know how to do things the right way. The Patriots and Packers have veterans' days every year. The Eagles try, but all we get from them is a parking pass.'

'Some teams have golf tournaments, dinners. They spend money and turn it into a three-day event. The players think it would be great if we could get together.'

'I know some of the vets feel somewhat disenfranchised from the team. This doesn't help the alumni organize events. If we had strength in the organization, we would have more people attend meetings.'

'There are a varying number of guys that show up for meetings now. All you end up discussing is, 'What's up with the players association?'

'The Eagles have a way of doing things. They don't realize that's part of keeping tradition alive. You can't have Philadelphia Eagles' tradition without Chuck Bednarik.'

'I'm not aware of any problems or issues between him and Leonard Tose. Everything was very amiable when I was there. No one felt that he shouldn't be part of the group.'

'Dick Vermiel reached out to him, but other guys may not have been aware of Chuck wanting to be around. Something happened that contributed to Chuck's estrangement from the team, but I don't know what it was.'

'Things worked out well with the Eagles until he offered Bill Bergey advice. Bergey didn't take well to advice, though Chuck's advice should be welcomed. No one knew more about middle linebacker than Chuck Bednarik.'

'I know he's gotten in some hot water because of his first book. I'll tell you a story about that first book. I was with him at Franklin Field one day. He said, "Did you ever get a copy of my book?" I told him that I hadn't. He said, "I'll go out to my car and get you one." He comes back and says, "That'll be $16.50." I thought he was giving it to me.'

'It's a shame, we were all born 20 years too soon. Chuck, today his salary would be $2.5-$3.0 million. He'd probably have a $10 million guarantee over three years.'

'The same with broadcasting. In those days it was all how you looked, how you dressed. You couldn't even wear a turtleneck without getting permission.'

'I remember Chuck doing a good job. It's not easy to sit in front of a camera and report the news.'

'But today he would have been a personality, not just a guy reading a teleprompter. If he was asked to give an opinion, he sure would say a few things that would create controversy.'

'I listen to things, and I'm not sure what the circumstances were that caused him to be bitter with the Eagles. I think he expected more of the team. And he should have been a lifetime Eagle.'

'But a lot of the guys are disappointed in their treatment by the team."

Tom Brookshier

A generation or two of pro football fans may remember Tom Brookshier best as a colorful announcer who teamed with Pat Summerall before the latter was paired with John Madden' but there are still a lot of old time football people around Philadelphia who remember "Brookie" as the toughest defensive back who ever played for the Eagles. He made the move from playing field to broadcast booth following a devastating leg injury during the 1961 season.

'Well, the thing about him, he was made to play football. His arms hung below his knees when he walked; he had great reach and he was massive for his day. There were plays when he would take the wrong key, back into it and still make the play. His natural recovery was the best I've ever seen.'

'I was a rookie in '53, and once he found out that I was a hitter, he acknowledged me. He wouldn't have bothered if he didn't recognize me as a serious player.'

'He took everything seriously on the field. Jesse Richardson was fooling around during calisthenics one day. Chuck was in the center, and when he was leading, you had better do everything '1-2-3'. Jesse was talking and fooling around, and Chuck told him to knock it off. Jesse walked into the center of the ring toward Chuck and told him "I don't like the way you're talking to me.'

> **"He was the leader in the huddle. He would step into the huddle, stick his hand out and say "Okay, yous guys…", and with those broken fingers it seemed like he was pointing at everyone."**

Jesse was about 270 pounds and came right into Chuck like a gladiator, and Chuck dropped him to the ground with one shot.'

'He was the leader in the huddle. He would step into the huddle, stick his hand out and say "Okay, yous guys…," and with those broken fingers it seemed like he was pointing at everyone.'

'He was the standard in football, he was meant to be a football player. I remember one game against Pittsburgh, the ball goes one way while he's going the other and he just sticks his hand out and intercepts it; the ball just sticks in his hand. He knocks over this big tackle on his way into the end zone and runs it in for a touchdown.'

'It was the most unusual play you ever saw, and he came over to the sideline and acted like it was nothing.'

'I was down at a practice not long ago and one of the tight ends asked me what Chuck would be like today. I told him, with today's training, he'd be about 6'7, 265 pounds and he'd be playing linebacker.

'With those long arms, he ranged beyond tackle-to-tackle. He was the most amazing player I've ever seen.'

'The guys around the league all respected him. In those days, whether you were going into Yankee Stadium or elsewhere, after the game you would go out for dinner with guys from the other team. Chuck was right there in on that. I still see him at a lot of functions; Emma takes good care to see that he gets out.'

'He got along well with guys, but he was a guy who didn't mind not being liked. It was his way or the highway. After World War II and the places he's been, he played it straight with people. He could be very gruff, like a commander. He had a sternness about him, but if he liked you, he appreciated you.'

'Tommy McDonald drove him nuts. Some of the stuff he did would leave Chuck shaking his head. He is Mr. Football.'

'As soon as he looked at a rookie or a new player, he could decide if he was a hitter. He knew Maxie Baughn was a player as soon as he saw him. He'd look at a player, and if he was a fancy or a cute guy, Chuck didn't want anything to do with him.'

'We had an unusual group of guys on the '60 team. Eddie Khayat became a coach; Pete Retzleff was a general manager; Norm Van Brocklin was coach; Marion Campbell was a coach; even Billy Ray Barnes was an assistant coach. Everyone knew football. Chuck corralled us; he took a lot of strong personalities and pulled us together.'

'He didn't talk over people; he'd let other guys have their say, then say "Okay, let's go kill those s.o.b's."

It was funny; he would lead us in a team prayer, then finish with the epithet, "Let's go out and kill those guys." We would be laughing as we ran out onto the field.'

'The Browns hated Chuck. He stood up for himself, just like they did. They were a good team, and they thought they were tough. The fans really hated the Eagles; when we played in Cleveland they'd throw bricks, beer cans, anything at us.'

'The night before we played them in Cleveland in 1960, we went out to a bar for a few drinks. Chuck was with us. We look out the window and we see Paul Brown taking the whole team into a theater across the street. He wanted to make sure he knew where they all were the night before the game.'

'We walked out onto the sidewalk, held up our drinks and toasted them. They didn't like that.'

'Chuck and Paul Brown used to get into it on the field jawing back and forth, but that was a sign that Paul respected Chuck.'

'One thing I remember, Chuck didn't waste time practicing, he was just so natural. Billy Ray Barnes would run a pattern in practice, and Chuck would just point at him and say "I got you."

'Barnes would be yelling to him, "Cover me, cover me."

'Chuck would just bark back, "Every step I take in practice is one I won't be able to take in a game; I don't want to waste it out here." He didn't do any extra running; he said, "It's one step I won't be able to take in a game."

'You think about it, it made sense. How many years did he last, 14?'

'He must have retired two or three times. He almost retired after the '57 season and they gave him a Chrysler, but he found out it had a three-year payment plan, so he came into camp.'

'He announced his retirement several times after that. After '62, the team was having trouble, they had settled in losing ways with Kuharich.'

'I left eight games into '61. When I broke my leg, Chuck came over and said, "It's over, Brookie." Everyone else was wailing, but Chuck just looked at me and said "It's over."

'He did everything so naturally in football. Subconsciously he could search down the ball carrier. And there was nothing like Chuck in the huddle; he made it clear you did it his way. He was always Chuck.'

'I know he liked being around Vermiel, and it was a great thing that Dick did in bringing him back. I don't know what happened with Tose, but if Chuck says Leonard told him that the Eagles didn't owe him anything, well that sounds like something Leonard , as a new owner, might have said.'

'I heard about Lurie's group not buying his book. They had a chance to buy a few books, and they wouldn't pick them up and give them out. They wouldn't honor him and give him a few dollars?'

Jim Brown

The great Cleveland Browns running back recalls Chuck Bednarik as one of the toughest linebackers he ever faced.

The great Cleveland Browns running back, Jim Brown, held virtually all National Football League rushing and touchdown records when he retired following the 1965 season. He retired as both the single season and career rushing leader, and held records for most rushing touchdowns and total touchdowns.

"I appreciated Chuck Bednarik for his diligence on the football field. He went two ways; was a great linebacker and a great tackler. I have nothing but good things to say about him.'

'He was a physical person, but always very nice, and direct in his conversation.'

'He was one of the best, very physical. I have the greatest respect and appreciation for this ability. I don't get into ranking guys, or saying who was better or best, but he was one of the best. He was as great as any linebacker who ever played."

Dick Butkus

Another famed middle linebacker, Butkus is often cited as the player who would have been best equipped to continue the tradition of the two-way player in the NFL.

Dick Butkus is the middle linebacker who became the defensive face of the National Football League while playing for the Chicago Bears in the 1970s. His style of play has often been compared with Chuck Bednarik. He played two ways in college, and is the player most frequently mentioned who could have continued the two-way tradition.

"I didn't get to see him play much. Our careers didn't overlap, and in those days television didn't carry the NFL like it does today.'

'I got to know him through the Hall of Fame. I sat with him a few times and I could see by talking to him the way he believes in the game. He believes in the game, he loves the game and that's the only way he could have played the way he did.'

'I would quiz him and you could tell he was into it."

'In later years he got more conservative, more old school. He would gripe about how the attitudes of the players had changed, they were more into being celebrities. He couldn't stand the dancing and posturing.'

'I looked up to him. I probably could have gone both ways if I was asked. Gibron asked me if I wanted to play center, but that would have been to continue my career; not while I was playing linebacker."

Tom Kelleher

Tom Kelleher grew up in Philadelphia and served as a back judge in the National Football League from 1960-1987. He graduated from Northeast Catholic High School and Holy Cross College. He also played on several softball teams with Chuck Bednarik while were both living in the Philadelphia area.

"Big Chuck, oh yeah, he was a great one. He was very hard, tough and rough, but fair and honest. I liked Chuck very much, he had all of the attributes that great players have.'

'He never thought about anything other than stopping the play. He wasn't out there looking to hurt guys.

Invariably he stopped them, but he did it clean. No one should have ever had a bone to pick with him.'

'I played in some Philadelphia softball leagues with Chuck when he was living in Willow Grove. Things were never uncomfortable because he was a player and I was an official. He could hit the nuts off the ball. He hit it as far as anyone I've ever seen.'

'Chuck was one of the great ones in the league. Sure he hit guys hard, but he was never one of the guys you had to keep your eye on. At no time did he ever try to hurt anyone. He was one of the guys I could kid with about plays.'

'There was no one I would rather honor than my big boy. If you've ever been around Chuck Bednarik, you remember being around him. He was pro football; he played pro football the way it was supposed to be played.'

'My grandson C.J. Myers is the center for the Houston Texans, and I tell him that he plays just like Chuck."

"Chuck was one of the great ones in the league. Sure he hit guys hard, but he was never one of the guys you had to keep your eye on. At no time did he ever try to hurt anyone. He was one of the guys I could kid with about plays."

Tim Brown

Tim Brown had one of the great life stories in the history of the Eagles, having grown up in an Indiana orphanage before becoming an All-American back at Ball State Teachers College. He developed into a great kickoff return man, twice leading the league in return coverage. Brown was selected to the Eagles 75th Anniversary team as the best return man in club history.

"I came over to the Eagles in '59. I had been cut by Green Bay and was placed on the taxi squad. I was well in awe of Chuck Bednarik when I got to Philadelphia. He had been around so long and had such a reputation as big, tough competitor.

'He was so respected because he played it by the book. He played the game clean, had a reputation as a clean player. He had the aura of someone who played the game the way it should be played. Old school, hard core; all those terms apply.'

'It defies sensibility that he went both ways. It was a different kind of game. Chuck could look up and call out the defenses from center. He knew the game from both sides of the ball. His knowledge of defense helped our offense.'

'We respected him; this guy could do it all. He was a leader who didn't complain about anything. He never complained about playing too much.'

'I know he retired after 1959. I think he saw me coming and decided to stay (laughs). We had a good nucleus in 1960, Theron Sapp, Bill Ray Barnes, Ted Dean, we had a lot of competition in the backfield. I had to wait in line; luckily I got my opportunity in '61.'

'It was difficult; guys like Billy Ray were popular, they all went out together. It was a close team, and no one wanted to see their friends get replaced. They tested me. You had to earn your way in there.'

'You had to gain respect on that team. I think I got it when I showed what I could do when given the opportunity. I didn't handle the ball much, but I showed flashes.'

'You had to prove yourself to Chuck Bednarik, but I think he respected me. I didn't think he liked me at first. I used to hang around with Tommy McDonald; he and I were the two little guys. It meant a lot. It was a great honor to come back for the 75th Anniversary Team with Chuck Bednarik and Tommy McDonald.'

'Chuck was old school. He was always serious about practice; there was not to be any clowning around. I grew to like him a lot.'

'It made my head swell when I knew that Chuck liked me and accepted me. At the 75th Anniversary gathering, we talked about the mutual respect we had for each other.'

'He saw what I could do in '61 and '62. After he retired I read some things he said that were very complimentary of me.'

'Years later, after I was retired, someone sent me an article where Chuck was asked if he could still play today. He answered "WHAT DO YOU THINK, AND DON'T YOU THINK TIM BROWN COULD PLAY IN ANY ERA?"

'I didn't get a lot of carries and would have had even better numbers if I handled the ball more. The more carries I got, the more I relaxed. There were times I wished I had played for Chicago or Cleveland where their backs got the ball 20 times a game.'

'Jim Brown once told me that it was unlucky that I got picked up by the Eagles, a passing team.'

'I'll tell you one thing about Chuck Bednarik, he was THE man, and a good man. He abided by the rules, and he played the game the way it should be played.'

'And he has a wonderful wife; what a twosome. He has what we all wanted, to find a woman like that.'

'There's not going to be another Chuck Bednarik, believe me. He follows his morals. The world is getting to be a funny place, but he maintains his intense beliefs.'

'He's like the Jim Thorpe story, an American hero playing America's game. He's living the American dream; a true American."

Chapter | seven

Paying Tribute

Chuck Bednarik was honored as a favorite son of Bethlehem on several occasions over the past 60 years. Many of those people who have known Chuck best took the time to commemorate him in letters that acknowledged his feats and his friendship.

Following are some of the letters that were written about Chuck from the people who knew him best in conjunction with the testimonial dinners that were organized to pay tribute to him.

BROUGHAL JUNIOR HIGH SCHOOL
Brodhead and Packer Avenues
BETHLEHEM, PENNSYLVANIA

REUBEN W. BUNGER, PRINCIPAL   9 May 1960

Dear Chuck:

It is with a great deal of pleasure and satisfaction that I write these few words in connection with my dealings with you as an outstanding athlete, a very good sport, and a person whom I've always said would help anybody, anytime ---anywhere!

Chuck, the professional football world, "the Eagles" especially, with your retirement have lost one of the best players that ever wore a pair of football shoes. A fellow who would do or die for the club that he represented.... whether it was a sandlot team, a high school team, a college team, or the professionals. Anywhere you played the same spirit prevailed, as you played with your heart, and you loved the sport. True you loved to win, who doesn't? But win or lose, you received satisfaction from knowing that you gave your all. You were that type of a guy, Chuck, because *of your love for sports.*

Chuck there is always one thing that I'll remember about you: "no matter how big you got, even as an all-American at Penn for two years, you were never too big for the local boys!" Many a night you drove up from Penn to take part in some recreational activity going on in the city. And, your being present, with your overwhelming power, your leadership, and your general characteristics of sportmanship. Especially your characteristic of being able to take the abuse that was handed to you both physically and vocally, proved that you were the man that made you an "All-American" by the applause that you received after each contest, whether it was given by friend or foe.

Chuck, there may be other All-Americans at Penn, but there'll never be another "Chuck Bednarik;" the rough, tough, and ready football player of the collegiate and professional world.

-2-

Chuck, I know, come next football season, when the pig skins are flying, and newspaper columns are telling the merits of this or that team, or the player that will bear watching; you may not be out there digging in for some defensive job.....or carrying out an offensive assignment; but spirtually you will be back of every player. No number "60" next season will run up and down the field. And, that number "60" will be missed by the Eagles." But, the other clubs will be happy, for if there was one guy who got in the opponents hair, it was Mr. Football himself, "Chuck Bednarick!" And who do you think is going to miss you more??? The little fellow who is wearing a football suit for the first time! How many times, Chuck, have I heard the expression: "when I grow up, I want to be just like Chuck Bednarick!"

Chuck, may I take this opportunity to congratulate you on being chosen for this most coveted award! God bless you, and the best of luck to you Chuck.

Sincerely,

Jack Conti, Instructor
Broughal Junior High School

JJC:fvl

Mr. Chuck Bednarick
Boys Club Fraternity
115 East Fourth Street
Bethlehem, Pennsylvania

Joe "Pickles" Perletz

Former Head Basketball Coach, Liberty High School

The name Chuck Bednarik is synonymous with fight, work-horse, loyalty, sacrifice, and inspiration. He has never forgotten the area of his boyhood, remaining fiercely loyal to his family and friends. All of these personal characteristics have mellowed with passing time and he now is a splendid example of loyalty and sacrifice and an inspiration to the youth of our community.

John Butler

Former Head Football Coach, Liberty High School

As a high school player, "Chuck" was a big tough, rough-boned kid with a lot of moxie. He was willing to play any position, and this fact made him one of the easiest players to coach I have ever worked with. His neverending determination to win created an air about him that was recognized early in his potential career, as he was mentioned as an All-State football candidate in his junior year and never achieved All-State honors because in his Senior year he entered the Armed Forces. As we all know, his record speaks for itself.

LIBERTY HIGH SCHOOL
BETHLEHEM, PENNSYLVANIA

FOOTBALL
SOCCER
BASKETBALL
WRESTLING
SWIMMING

BASEBALL
TRACK
TENNIS
GIRL'S BASKETBALL

PHONE UN 6-4971
8:15 A.M. TO 4:00 P.M.

DEPARTMENT OF ATHLETICS
PHILIP F. PHILLIPPI--DIRECTOR

May 5, 1960

Dear Charlie:

It seems like only yesterday that a tall gangling boy walked into the field house and said, "Coach Butler wants me to have a larger pair of practice pants, so that I can stoop down easier to pass that ball." "My backfield days are over, I am going to try out for the center position." So began your football career as a lineman.

You've played many a game since that season, and you've become a credit to the game, to your schools, to your family, and to all who know you.

I sat in the stands at Pennsylvania University when the crowd around me had their field glasses focused on "Chuck" the Clutch. In a very short time you captivated the sports loving people throughout the nation -- you gave the fans a thrill each time you played -- you gave your best effort all the time, the only way to achieve greatness.

My heartiest congratulations to you, B.H.S. #38, U. of P., and Eagles #60, for a job very well done. May your future bring you and yours prosperity, health, and happiness.

Most sincerely,

George "Shadow" Resetco

George "Shadow" Resetco

P.S.: I have enclosed a few momentos which you may treasure.

---

728 Delaware Avenue
Bethlehem, Pennsylvania
September 2, 1969

Mr. Mark Belletti
517 E. Saucon Street
Hellertown, Pennsylvania

Dear Mark:

It was a pleasure to hear from you and to learn that the citizens of Bethlehem are going to honor Chuck Bednarik before he is officially taken into the football hall of fame.

As a high school player, Chuck was a big, tough, rough-boned kid, with lots of moxie. He was willing to play any position, and this fact made him one of the easiest players to coach I have ever worked with. His never-ending determination to win created an air about him that was recognized early in his potential career, as he was mentioned as an all-state football candidate in his junior year and never achieved all-state honors because in his senior year of school he entered the armed forces.

As we all know, his record as an athlete speaks for itself and I am really sorry that I will not be able to attend the banquet honoring Chuck because for the first time in my life I will be on Sabatical leave and will be in Europe on the day you are honoring him.

Thank you for the invitation and congratulations to all concerned and in particular to the guest of honor, Chuck Bednarik.

Cordially yours,

John W Butler

John W. Butler

JWB: DCB

Dear Chuck & Emma -

As I have always said - you are the last of a great Era - and dully recognized as the best the past decade.

You have often said that football has been good to you and your family. There is little doubt of that but don't lose sight of the fact that you have been good to the great game of football. No man has done more as a player to enhance and elevate the game. You have been a true "Champion." In our association - a great privilege has been mine. Sincerely, Nick Skorich

Paul Troxell

Former Coach, Broughal Jr. High

Outstanding prospect on the squad. Tall and rangy. Good shot and natural ability and instinct for basketball. Chuck had good basketball sense, and liked the game. He was coachable in any sport he participated in. Chuck's achievements since he graduated from Broughal speak for itself. I am very proud of you Chuck, as is the City of Bethlehem upon whom you have heaped many honors.

BETHLEHEM RECREATION COMMISSION
713 EIGHTH AVENUE
BETHLEHEM, PA.
PHONE UN 6-0682

April 28, 1960

Mr. Charles Bednarik
c/o The Bethlehem Boys' Club
115 E. 4th Street
Bethlehem, Pennsylvania

Dear Chuck:

It was a thrill and a pleasure to hear that the Bethlehem Boys' Club Fraternity has chosen you for the coveted "Award of Honor." It just couldn't happen to a more deserving person.

It has been a very rewarding experience for me to follow your many achievements from the time I first met you as a thirteen year old player at Broughal Jr. High School in 1939; through Liberty High School; the Second World War; as an All-American at the University of Pennsylvania; and as an All Pro selection with the Eagles in the National Professional League. All this without ever being anything but an All-American person, which I think is equally important.

Best personal regards, and best wishes for continued success.

Sincerely yours,

Paul

Paul S. Troxell,
Supt. of Recreation.

BETHLEHEM RECREATION COMMISSION
CITY CENTER
10 EAST CHURCH STREET
BETHLEHEM, PA. 18018
PHONE 865-2751

October 8, 1969

Dear Chuck:

Sincerest congratulations upon being elected to the National Football Hall of Fame.

It has been a great source of pride to watch you achieve the many honors bestowed upon you since I first met you as a pupil at Broughal Junior High School.

I shall never forget the day the 14 year old boy reported for football practice and simply stated " I would like to play football", and how you played football—it didn't take a genius to see that outstanding achievements were to be a part of your destiny.

The desire to excell, the dedication to achieve and the courage to accomplish were quite apparent at that early age. It all added up and clearly indicated that greatness was not to be denied you.

Mrs. Troxell and I are very happy for you, and again congratulations and best wishes from us both.

Sincerely yours,

Paul

Paul S. Troxell

Jodie McLernon

Former Line Coach, Liberty High School

When "Charlie" reported for football at Bethlehem High School, he was a halfback candidate. As a defensive right halfback in the first scrimmage. He was eager to get up to the line of scrimmage, he could tackle and he had enthusiasm. After practice, he was told to report with the line as a center.

Thus began a career that culminated in being acclaimed as the greatest center in football. Throughout his football career his enthusiasm never waned. If anyone has heard any of his recent "after-meal" speeches, you will easily note that his enthusiasm is greater than ever.

"Gus" Garcsar

Former Baseball Coach, Mountaineers A.C.

If I would have had "Chuck" under my wing earlier in his career, I would have made a pitcher of him. He had a strong arm, and was a hard thrower. Not taking anything away from his football talent, but had he concentrated as much time in baseball as he did in football, "Chuck" definitely would have been major league material.

Lou "Smelly" Bukvics

Basketball Coach Mountaineers A.C.

If it weren't for the many nights we lugged Chuck back and forth from Philadelphia to help fortify our team mates, I am sure the Mountaineers would not have been the city's basketball Class A Champs for so many years. Even when Chuck hit the professional category, he was always thinking Bethlehem. We are indeed grateful to have been a part of, however small, the progression of one of the country's outstanding athletes.

LAUFER'S HARDWARE
JOHN HORVATH, PROP.
Bethlehem's Oldest Hardware-Store - Est. 1875
411 Wyandotte Street   Bethlehem, Pa.
Phone UN 6-5141

BPS PAINTS
GLASS
ELECTRICAL SUPPLIES
U. G. L. PRODUCTS
HOUSEWARES
STANLEY TOOLS
LAWN & GARDEN SUPPLIES
BURPEE'S SEEDS
SCOTT'S LAWN CARE PRODUCTS
BUILDERS HARDWARE
BLACK & DECKER POWER TOOLS
GALVANIZED WARE
CLEANING SUPPLIES
LOCKWOOD LOCKS

May 11, 1960

Mr. Charles Bednarik
The Bethlehem Boys' Club Fraternity
Bethlehem, Pennsylvania

Dear Chuck:

Congratulations "Chuck" for being chosen as the "Award of Honor" recipient. It couldn't have happened to a nicer guy.

Chuck, I have been proud over and over again on each occasion that the many honors have been bestowed upon you, just being a fan and admirer of yours. I recall your days at the University of Penn when the Mountaineers were in the Class "A" playoffs; and, especially this one night when Oscar Siftar, Ski Morinsky and I got down to Penn between 6:30 and 7:00 o'clock and the very important playoff game between the Mountaineers and King Oilers was to start at 8:00 o'clock at the Broughal gym. Remember "Chuck" it was snowing that night and we had a hard time convincing you to come back with us inasmuch as we should have been there about 5:00 o'clock. Knowing Ski and Oscar, they asked me to stop for a few drinks and that is where we got tied up for a few hours. Do you recall driving to Bethlehem in that snow and ice. We got to Quakertown at about 8:00 o'clock and you insisted on driving the rest of the way in that old 1936 Buick that I had at that time. After slipping and slidding all the way from Quakertown, we finally got to Broughal at 8:30 with the first quarter of the game completed and the Mountaineers were behind. All our fans and cheerleaders really gave out with a welcoming blast when you arrived at the scene, knowing that the Mountaineers were now sure of a victory.

"Chuck", if you are only half as successful in the business world as you have been on the athletic field and gridiron, you will make a great competitor and successful businessman.

Very sincerely yours,

John P. Horvath

To Mark F. Belletti-

I selected "Chuck" Bednarik as my prefered draft choice, and he is

the only lineman who was ever selected on the prefered choice-

He was without a doubt, was the greatest linebacker that ever played

in National Football League- He showed that 2 weeks ago when he was

on T. V. and directed the defense-

He was one of the greatest, and I was tickled to death with our

selection- Sorry I can not be there to Honor him

Earle "Greasy" Neale
Best to "Chuck" and his
family —

George A. Munger

Former Head Football Coach, University of Pennsylvania

I was in the stands to see the Allentown versus Bethlehem football game "Chuck's" senior year. Captain Numbers had the reputation as the best center in the area. Frankly, the tall lanky center from Bethlehem caught my eye, not only for skill and technique, but for his aggressive leadership on the field. How pleased I was several years later when Coach John Butler called and said Chuck's life has been a series of happy successes-school, war, college, lovely Emma and daughters, pro football and the business world. Congratulations, you earned it. Continued success to you.

The Pittsburgh Press

Pittsburgh 30, Pa.

March 25, 1960

Mr. Chuck Bednarik
Bethlehem Boys Club Fraternity
115 E. Fourth St.
Bethlehem, Penna.

Dear Chuck:

I am particularly pleased to hear that you are being honored by your home town as a native son who has achieved success in your field of endeavor.

It couldn't have happened to a finer guy!

As a sports writer, I covered your career since the day you broke into professional football and feel obliged to commend you on this occasion. You have always been a credit to the game.

You spanned an era which took pro football from the sandlots to the Ivy League. You are an ideal representative of the game, a star who combines the qualities of manhood, leadership and athletics in a product of which Bethlehem can certainly be proud.

Although I frequently cheered against you, I -- as every Pittsburgh Steeler fan did -- always regarded you as a tough and uncompromising foe, a true sportsman who played to win.

It was a spirit typical of you people who have made professional football America's real National Pastime.

Sincerely,

Pat Livingston
Pat Livingston

CC:
Pete Rozelle
Vince McNally

P.S. You're not quitting are you? Your buddy, Frank Wydo, tells me he's found the fountain of youth, a $14,000 no-cut contract and anticipates many more big years with the Boston Patriots.

MIRROR NEWS
LOS ANGELES EVENING

145 SOUTH SPRING STREET · LOS ANGELES 53, CALIFORNIA · TELEPHONE MADISON 5-2311

May 11, 1960

Mr. Charles "Chuck" Bednarik
Linebackers, Inc.
Center of the U.S.A.

Dear Chuck:

No kidding, that above address fits you very well. I've never seen a greater linebacker, and I know that as an offensive center you were, and still may be, the best in the game.

I want to congratulate you on your being chosen for this year's Award of Honor by the Bethlehem Boys' Club Fraternity.

No man deserves it more, quite probably no man (in the knowledge of the Fraternity) as much.

It has always been a personal pleasure to me to see you play because you play the game hard and clean, the way it is supposed to be played. I have always found you a very fine fellow and a very cooperative person.

Kindest personal regards,

Max
Maxwell Stiles
Sports Columnist

Call-Chronicle Newspapers, Inc.

SIXTH AND LINDEN STREETS
ALLENTOWN, PENNSYLVANIA
18105

Dear Chuck:

You've done more than your share to publicize Bethlehem. I'm delighted to see that your hometown friends haven't forgotten you.

It was a sad day for you, I'm sure, when you pulled off the green No. 60 for the last time in St. Louis way back in 1962. It was just as sad for all of us who followed your career with great interest and pride.

The rewards were many and it is pleasing to see that you have accepted them with the humility of a true champion. Congratulations on your Testimonial Night. It was a pleasure to be there to share your happy moments.

Best Personal Regards,

John Kunda
John Kunda, Sports Editor
The Morning Call
Allentown, Penna.

The Evening and Sunday Bulletin
30TH AND MARKET STREETS   PHILADELPHIA 1

May 4, 1960

Mr. Chuck Bednarik
% Boys Club Fraternity
Bethlehem, Pa.

Dear Chuck:

The job I like most of all in this business of sports writing is covering college and professional football games and I have done it every season since I was a freshman at the University of Pennsylvania in 1912. That's one way of saying I have had a lot of fun in the last 48 years.

Even before 1912, I saw a lot of college football. My brothers -- three of them -- were ahead of me at the university and each used to take his kid brother to see Penn games. I have seen all the Penn stars and those who opposed them since Vincent Stevenson and Bill Hollenback down through last fall when a fine bunch of young fellows won the Ivy League championship for the University.

What I'm getting around to Chuck is this: In my lifetime, Pennsylvania has never had a football player like you and I enjoyed every minute you were playing from the first time you played as a freshman. You recall I have written often that you were Penn's all-time greatest, and in my book you also were the all-time greatest of the Eagles.

As much as I have enjoyed you football playing career, I can say in all honesty that I have been getting almost as much of a kick out of hearing of your success as a salesman and out of hearing you talk at banquets.

After you went with the Eagles, I didn't hear you talk in public for several years. Then, you may recall, I introduced you at a Maxwell Club dinner. After you had finished I commented on how much you had improved and how the years with the Eagles were almost as good for you as another college education. I was, and I still am very proud of how much you have helped yourself in public speaking. In this, you have done an excellent job.

And now, I understand, you're doing another fine job as a salesman. Wonderful! Also, I hear you rate very high as a husband and father. Great!

Thanks Chuck, for countless thrills and to you and yours the very best of everything.

Sincerely,   *Ed Pollock*
Ed Pollock

EVERGREEN 2-7600   IN PHILADELPHIA NEARLY EVERYBODY READS THE BULLETIN

GEORGIA-PACIFIC CORPORATION
CONTAINER DIVISION—SAN FRANCISCO
P.O. BOX 2407 • SOUTH SAN FRANCISCO, CALIFORNIA 94080
TELEPHONE: 873-7800 • AREA CODE: 415

THE GROWTH COMPANY

2 May 1969

Dear Chuck:

My hearty congratulations on your appointment and subsequent admittance into the National Football Foundation's Hall of Fame.

In all my 38 years in the Chair for spinning and weav-
ing in a futile attempt to unravel the mysteries of
tripod squat, I can think of absolutely no one more deserving or worthy of such high honor.

You were truly magnificent in your performance on the
field - your superb action, your inspirational leadership, your indomitable spirit - and off the field, your
splendid example for youth. Surely, your name and your
deeds are bound forever in the benediction of all Eagle
supporters.

May I assure you that you were one of the few dependables
who kept me in the Eagle picture following my first horr-
endous and disasterous season of '58 when it really appeared that we would never get off the ground. I shall
always believe you were the stimulating and arousing
force which carried us to the top over those next two
years.

Do want you to know, Chuck, that since my first month in
Eagle camp and up to this very hour, in private and in
public, I have constantly sung paeans of praise in your
memory whenever the topic of kickball bubbles to the
surface. As I look back over my coaching years my one re-
gret, above all others, is that I was not privileged to
work with you during your brilliant collegiate career and
beyond through your long and illustrious years in professional play. What a pleasurable and rewarding experience
that would have been. I must be content with my 3 short years.

The great wheel of time brought me to mandatory retirement
with the above giant in early '64. However, I still have
my hand in their cookie jar, but barely up to the first
joint. Nevertheless, it keeps me off the streets at night,
out of the pool halls and bistros so, after all, my bit
of activity does serve a useful purpose.

WARNER COMPANY
1721 ARCH STREET
PHILADELPHIA, PENNSYLVANIA 19103

ROBERT A. FOX
PRESIDENT

October 1, 1969

Mr. John G. Gorek
919 East Sycamore Street
Allentown, Pennsylvania 18103

Dear Mr. Gorek:

It is my pleasure to write you expressing

my congratulations to Chuck Bednarik on

receiving his much-deserved selection to

All-Time Football Team.

Chuck is not only a great athlete but,

more important, a first-class human being,

and one who deserves much credit for his

accomplishments.

Sincerely,

Robert A. Fox

RAF/bpm

GEORGIA-PACIFIC CORPORATION
CONTAINER DIVISION—SAN FRANCISCO
P.O. BOX 2407 • SOUTH SAN FRANCISCO, CALIFORNIA 94080
TELEPHONE: 873-7800 • AREA CODE: 415

THE GROWTH COMPANY

- 2 -

Do remember me with a note one day when you find
a moment of freedom and bring me up to date on
the present activities of your good self together
with a report on the financially distressed Eagles.

Warm personal remembrances and choice greetings
to your family. Once again, lusty cheers on your
entry into the vaunted pantheon of kickballers.

Cordially,

L. T. "Buck" Shaw

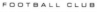

PHILADELPHIA EAGLES
FOOTBALL CLUB
THIRTIETH AND MARKET STREETS · PHILADELPHIA, PA. 19104 · 215 EVERGREEN 2-5000

October 1, 1969

Mr. Chuck Bednarik
1812 Canterbury Lane
Abington, Pa.

Dear Chuck:

People often ask "Where have all the players gone?"....... in your case it's right to the top.

To be picked as the greatest center ever to play professional football and to be inducted into both College and Professional Hall of Fame is an achievement second to none.

Congratulations on your honors tonight from your friends in Bethlehem and from your friends here at the Eagles.

Sincerely,

PHILADELPHIA EAGLES FOOTBALL CLUB

Pete Retzlaff
General Manager

PR/lh

Earle "Greasy" Neale

Former Head Coach, Philadelphia Eagles

selected "Chuck" Bednarik as my preferred draft choice, and he is the only lineman who was ever selected as the preferred choice. He was without a doubt the greatest linebacker that ever played in the National Football League. He showed that a month ago when he was on T.V. and directed the defense. He was one of the greatest, and I was tickled to death with our selection.

L.T. "Buck" Shaw

Former Head Coach, Philadelphia Eagles

My hearty congratulations on your appointment and subsequent admittance into the National Collegiate Hall of Fame. In all my 38 years of coaching, I can think of absolutely no one more deserving or worthy of such a high honor. You were truly magnificent in your performance on the field. Your superb action, your inspirational leadership, your indomitable spirit, on and off the field, your splendid example for youth. Surely your name and your deeds are bound forever in the benediction of all Eagle supporters. Whenever the topic of kickball bubbles to the surface, I have constantly sung paeons of praise in your memory.

OFFICE OF THE COMMISSIONER
410 Park Avenue
New York, New York 10022
PLaza 8-1500

AMERICAN FOOTBALL LEAGUE / NATIONAL FOOTBALL LEAGUE

September 2, 1969

Mr. Chuck Bednarik
1812 Canterbury Road
Abington, Pennsylvania

Dear Chuck:

As you may know, to celebrate the National Football League's 50th Anniversary Season the NFL is publishing a book entitled "The First Fifty Years."

One section of it is devoted to a series of all-time teams--with selections made by the Board of Selectors of the Pro Football Hall of Fame. There are teams for the 1920s, the 1930s, 40s, 50s and 60s and this is capped by 16 men who were chosen as the overall best at their positions in National Football League history.

These teams have been released to the news media over the past 10 days and the all-time team will be announced in Sunday papers of September 7.

This is to inform you that you are included on the team as the all-time center. An original drawing of you in action commemorates your selection in the book and will be presented to the Hall of Fame in an exhibit later this fall.

Our congratulations to you on your selection and continued best wishes.

Sincerely,

Don Weiss
Director of Public Relations

DW:lv
cc: Jim Gallagher

EARL E. SCHAFFER, Mayor
DIRECTOR OF PUBLIC AFFAIRS

BETHLEHEM, PA. April 14, 1960.

Mr. Charles Bednarik,
c/o Bethlehem Boys' Club Fraternity,
Bethlehem, Pa.

Dear "Chuck":

The Bethlehem Boys' Club Fraternity has advised me that you are to be the recipient of their "Award of Honor" at the annual Banquet of Champions to be held on Saturday, May 14, 1960.

While I will be unable to be present at this affair, I am delighted to join in this tribute with the Boys' Club Fraternity and your legion of friends in the City of Bethlehem. This I do, both personally and officially.

Having known you and your family for many years, and having followed your career from your boyhood at Bethlehem High School, through the University of Pennsylvania, and all during your professional football career with the Philadelphia Eagles, I know that your outstanding performance and your high sense of sportsmanship and fair play have been a living example for the youth of our city and elsewhere. Your fine record has reflected much credit to the City of Bethlehem.

I extend to you the greetings and felicitations of the people of the City of Bethlehem, together with our warmest regards and best wishes for health, happiness and continued success.

Sincerely,

Mayor.

EES/rrg.

---

522 Eighth Avenue
Bethlehem, Pennsylvania
May 14, 1960

Dear Chuck,

This is a night for recalling some of the happy days and events of your stellar athletic career. It was a privilege and happy duty to coach you when you were a member of the Mountaineers basketball squad.

You were at that time, a student at Pennsylvania, but we wanted you - and you wanted to play - with the Mountaineers so we had a car pick you up in Philly before the game and also return you the same night. Remember the one night you came in late because of the snow. We were losing and all because of one man, Louie Lange, a star at Lehigh that year. During the second half of that ball game Lange had but one field goal. It was your cool defensive play which turned the tide for MAC that night and we went on to win the City Championship in Class A competition.

Remember the game when Mr. Frank Broad invited the folks of the Blind Association to "watch" you play; later you went and talked to all these good people.

Even as a "pro" you expressed your fond desire to play basketball with your old buddies. Once the red-tape was over and done with, you never missed a game. Of this part of your career, the events of the last game and the last championship for the Mountaineers is significant. We were playing the Lehigh Tavern quintet which boasted such names as: Pete Carril, Toner, Gallo, Downing, Rogers, Gerencser and Scipio. This was a good pressing team. At the half you yelled to me: "Coach, we have them!" In the last quarter with three minutes left to play you took the ball out. In this situation, the Mountaineers used a pick-off play and Hips Pecsek was designated to take the ball out at all times. Pete Carril came up fast, stole the ball and made an easy basket; this was bad enough, but the same thing happened three times in the closing moments of the game. After a time out, you cooled off and we won the game and the championship. After the game, at the club and during the post-mortem, Hips wanted to know why you took the ball out in the first place. Your answer to that question, perhaps can be the keynote of this evening's celebration for you said: "We are having such a good time, let's remember the pleasant things not the unpleasant ones".

Yes, Chuck, let's remember the happy days with the Mountaineers, and may your future days be filled with blessings and happiness.

Your old coach and friend,

Louis Bukvics

COMMONWEALTH OF PENNSYLVANIA
GOVERNOR'S OFFICE
HARRISBURG

THE GOVERNOR

November 3, 1969

Mr. Charles P. Bednarik
1812 Canterbury Road
Abington, Pennsylvania 19001

Dear "Chuck":

Congratulations and best wishes as you are being honored tonight by your many friends in the Bethlehem area.

We in Pennsylvania are fortunate to have you as a member of our State Athletic Commission. Your knowledge and understanding of the world of sports, gained through your fourteen years as a professional football player during which you were named All Pro nine times and elected to Pro Football's Hall of Fame, have been fine assets to the Commission and our Commonwealth.

I sincerely hope that your dinner will be a most enjoyable and memorable one and that you will enjoy the blessings of health and happiness in the years to come.

Kindest regards.

Sincerely,

RAYMOND P. SHAFER

The Philadelphia Eagles, Inc.
FOOTBALL CLUB

WORLD CHAMPIONS, 1948—1949   EASTERN DIVISION CHAMPIONS, 1947, 1948, 1949

S. E. CORNER 15th AND LOCUST STREETS   •   PHILADELPHIA 2, PA.   •   PEnnypacker 5-4014

JAMES P. CLARK
Chairman of the Board
FRANK L. McNAMEE
President
JOSEPH A. DONOGHUE
Exec. V. P. & Secretary
HARRY S. SYLK
Treasurer
VINCENT A. McNALLY
General Manager
LAWRENCE T. "BUCK" SHAW
Head Coach
EDWARD S. HOGAN
Publicity Director

April 12, 1960

Mr. Chuck Bednarik
c/o Bethlehem Boys' Club Fraternity
115 East Fourth Street
Bethlehem, Pennsylvania

Dear Chuck:

We are quite happy that the Boys' Club Fraternity of Bethlehem has seen fit to honor one of the greatest football players in college or in the pro ranks. You richly deserve the "Award of Honor" given to a former Bethlehemite who has attained success in his field of endeavor beyond the boundaries of Bethlehem.

Your years of examplary service with the Eagles afforded all of us many thrills but particularly impressive was your good sportsmanship and high ideals of manhood. It is one thing to be a great athlete which you are but of infinitely more importance is the ability to "keep your head". And if you hadn't, you wouldn't be so honored.

So, Chuck Bednarik, accept the sincere congratulations and best wishes of all of THE EAGLES. You well merit them.

All our best,

Sincerely,

Frank L. McNamee, President
Joseph A. Donoghue, Vice-President
Vincent A. McNally, General Manager

MEMBER NATIONAL FOOTBALL LEAGUE

Chapter eight

Music

The Bednariks of the south side of Bethlehem were not a musical family in any sense. No one can recall an instrument of any type ever being part of their household, but the family enjoyed listening to Eastern European ethnic music. Their eldest son, Charles, was hanging out at the Croatian Hall in Bethlehem when he became enthralled with a young tamburica player named Emma Margetich.

The Margetich family played at clubs, affairs and picnics around the Lehigh Valley, sometimes billing themselves as the Bethlehem Tamburitazans. While Bednarik clearly had a crush on Emma, he was enamored by musical talents of the family. Through the Margetichs he developed a lifelong passion for music, and eventually came to play the accordion and harmonica. While the accordion does not get much play these days, he still whips out the harmonica with little or no encouragement.

"My father made all of his kids learn how to play musical instruments," recalls Emma. "He said music kept us off the streets. We all had to play in the family band; we got $2 apiece'

'I played the prim tamburica, which was the soprano. My father Steve played tenor; my brother Willie was bass. Uncle John could play anything and Uncle Roy played the cello. My sister played piano.'

'Charlie learned accordion and harmonica, and he would join in at family parties."

Chuck Bednarik and his accordion became semi-regulars at the Austrian Village in Rockledge, Pa. For many years it was not uncommon for Saturday evening diners to find that their entertainment for the evening was in part provided by the most famously mangled fingers in America, dancing their way across an accordion keyboard.

Over the years he has ingratiated himself with some of the most popular polka and ethnic musicians in the business, including Jimmy Sturr, Jolly Joe Timmer and Al Meixner.

Roy Klenovich, John Hugitz, Bill Margetich, Emma Margetich and Stephen Margetich

Joe Timmer

Chuck Bednarik is a frequent caller to the request line for Timmer's daily radio polka show.

Jimmy Sturr may be America's unofficial Polka King, but the native of Bethlehem holds court over a smaller fiefdom and is recognized as Pennsylvania's Polk King. Joe Timmer is considered royalty in the world of Pennsylvania polka, and can be found on the local airwaves six days a week. He claims to be the only performer in America who has appeared live on the radio for 60 years and says that his Thursday night polka show is the longest running cable show in America, broadcasting into northeastern Pennsylvania homes for 36 years and counting.

A hall-of-famer in his own right (inducted into the Polka Hall of Fame), "Jolly" Joe's most devoted request caller and occasional studio guest (sometimes unexpected) is one Charles Philip Bednarik.

"Well, he does sometimes come in here during a show. He loves his Slovak music, and Emma loves Croatian music. Sometimes he brings a CD and says you have to play this. He's an ardent polka fan and loves to show everybody his favorite music.'

'Sometimes he calls in requests for birthdays or other special events. He requests all the Slovak music.'

'Sometimes he sits in the studio and takes phone calls. People love talking to him.'

'There's two things he does everyday, go to church and listen to me.'

'I've heard him play his harmonica (laughs)…as a harmonica player…he's…oh,…not like he played football."

Chuck standing in front of Jolly Joe Timmer's store located in the Southside of Bethlehem.

Al Meixner

A longtime friend of the Bednarik family, a musician specializing in polka and ethnic music.

The official musician of the Bednarik family, Al Meixner has been invited by Chuck to play at numerous weddings, anniversaries, and birthday celebrations. An accomplished musician who specializes in polka music, Meixner is a member of the Ironworld International Polka Hall of Fame, located in Chisholm, Minnesota. He has had the pleasure of having Chuck Bednarik grab a harmonica or accordion and jam with him on more than one occasion. He presides over Al Meixner Music and River's Bend Recording in Laury's Station, Pennsylvania.

"Chuck got me a gig at the Austrian Village. I played there for his and Emma's 30th anniversary. It was a big blowout; all of their friends were there.'

'Bill Bergey was there, and he was a real hardass guy at that time. He gets up to give a toast and talks about the first time he met Chuck.'

'Bergey says "The first time I met Chuck Bednarik, I went up and told him 'Mr. Bednarik, I've always admired you.'

"He tells me "Well, I'll have you know I was All-Pro 11 times, and we were tough, we ate nails."

'I replied, well Mr. Bednarik, I think I'm pretty tough."

> **"Chuck has been an outspoken hero. He comes with a big picture, he's bigger than life. He speaks in an 'expletives-deleted' way, but all the time with his hands on his rosary beads. He's confessing as he's cursing."**

'Chuck replies, "Well Mr. Bergey, when I played I was the Heisman runner, I was this, I was that.'

'Well Mr. Bednarik, I was All-Pro three times, and I always try my hardest.'

'Well, Mr. Bergey, the last year I played I made $30,000."

'Bergey, replies, "Sit down, Charlie."

'Chuck has been an outspoken hero. He comes with a big picture; he's bigger than life. He speaks in an 'expletives-deleted' way, but all the time with his hands on his rosary beads. He's confessing as he's cursing.'

'He made my family and me part of his family. I remember Christmas Days at Emma's family's house on Stefco Boulevard. Everyone would pick up the instruments in the basement and play music. Then, in later years, Christmas Day shifted to Chuck and Emma's house.'

'There were all of these ethnic pockets in Bethlehem. Chuck's family was Slovak, Emma's Croatian. The Southside was home to the Windish people, who came from Slovenia for the jobs at the mills.'

'We're part of his family. Of course he didn't have a son, and he would wrestle with my son. My kid would go around telling people, "I pinned Chuck Bednarik."

'Emma always said, "I'm glad we didn't have a boy; it would have been tough living in his shadow."

'My son is a musician, but he's somebody else's kid. Chuck's son would have had to have been an athlete.'

'Chuck's music ability? Oh, God knows... technically he's a musician. He's competitive at everything he does, including the accordion and harmonica.'

'I wrote out some simple accordion tunes for him. He would go over the same song, over and over and over again. When he liked a song, he liked a song; and when he likes something he let's everyone know. He goes out of his way to let people know. If he doesn't like something, you can't change his mind.'

'He took us to a gigantic party in South Jersey at Bob Deuber's house. Chuck is playing his accordion along with my son and me. He plays "Have I Told You Lately That I Love You" twice. Then he says, "Al, you play it now,' and he pulls out his harmonica. We finish, and he says "Hey Al, let's play it again."

'What I also remember about that day was the trip there. We drove from Coopersburg, and he was impatient the whole way. We got caught in a traffic jam on the

Schuylkill Expressway, and he got out of the car and was directing traffic.'

'He was a superstar in Philadelphia and in the NFL. He was at the highest echelon in that particular era. It was a great time; you could go to picnics and parties and Chuck's house and there would be people like Stan Lopata, Andy Seminick, basketball players, other athletes.'

'You would see athletes from all the sports when Chuck was at the Austrian Village. I met Dick Vermiel at the Austrian Village. We were playing one night and he came over and said, "When, not if, we get to the Super Bowl, you guys are playing there." His intentions were always great. He got them to the Super Bowl, that was always impressive to me.'

'My group played at Chuck and Emma's 50th anniversary. The band was seated with the guests. My drummer was from upstate New York. We're talking to the guests, and the drummer is chatting with the guy sitting next to him.'

'He turns to me and mumbles, 'Who the hell walks around with a name like Yogi? There's only one person I know named…oh, my God."

'He turns back to the guy, "You're Yogi Berra, right? Yogi tells him, 'Yeah, and you guys are my favorite polka band."

'You know about Chuck's grotto, right? He used to have a shrine to the Blessed Mary, at the dead end at the top of this block. The guy across the street was a Polish accordion player. He would go up there every morning and pray. He'd keep the area clean around the shrine. Now I know he's moved it to his yard."

Jimmy Sturr

The Polka King has a frequent groupie in Chuck Bednarik when he performs in the Lehigh Valley region.

If there are two divine forces in the life of Chuck Bednarik, they are his love for his wife Emma and a passion for his Catholic religion. Now that he doesn't play much golf, those are the interests that occupy most his time and attention. When he is not at church or keeping company with Emma, he is probably listening to ethnic music, likely Polka variety. In earlier years, he might have played along with his accordion, but these days most of his music making is done with a harmonica.

Fortunately there is enough polka music played on the television and radio airwaves of the Lehigh Valley for Bednarik to get his daily fix. He also does not have to travel too far from home to catch the occasional live performance.

All of the local broadcast hosts know Bednarik as a devoted listener, and he and Emma have also become friendly with many of the artists who have appeared live in the region.

A multiple Grammy Award winner, host of an RFD TV show, and the nation's reigning king of polka, Jimmy Sturr makes regular stops in northeastern Pennsylvania, and often sees his friends, the Bednariks.

"The first time he shook my hand he almost broke it.'

'We were playing at the State Theater in Easton. Someone came up to me and asked, "Have you ever heard of Chuck Bednarik?"

'I was thrilled. I said bring him back after the show, I'd love to meet him.'

'He grabbed my hand and pain shot through my arm. I'm serious about that.'

'I still see him from time to time and I have his picture on the wall in my office.'

'I know he loves Polka music. He listens to all the shows. He calls them up and you'll hear the host say this song was requested by Chuck Bednarik.'

'I called him up on the stage one time at the Bethlehem Musikfest. He played a couple of tunes with us on his harmonica.'

'How was he as a musician? Let's just say he was a much better football player. I whispered in his ear, "Don't give up your day job."

Chapter | nine

Boxing

I n 1969, the, governor of Pennsylvania, Raymond P. Shafer, appointed the person he thought was the toughest guy in the Commonwealth to the position of regional boxing commissioner for the Pennsylvania State Athletic Commission. In the spring of 2009, Governor Ed Rendell reappointed Chuck Bednarik to the same position that he has now held for 40 years.

Chuck being sworn in to the Pennsylvania State Athletic Commission by Governor Schafer

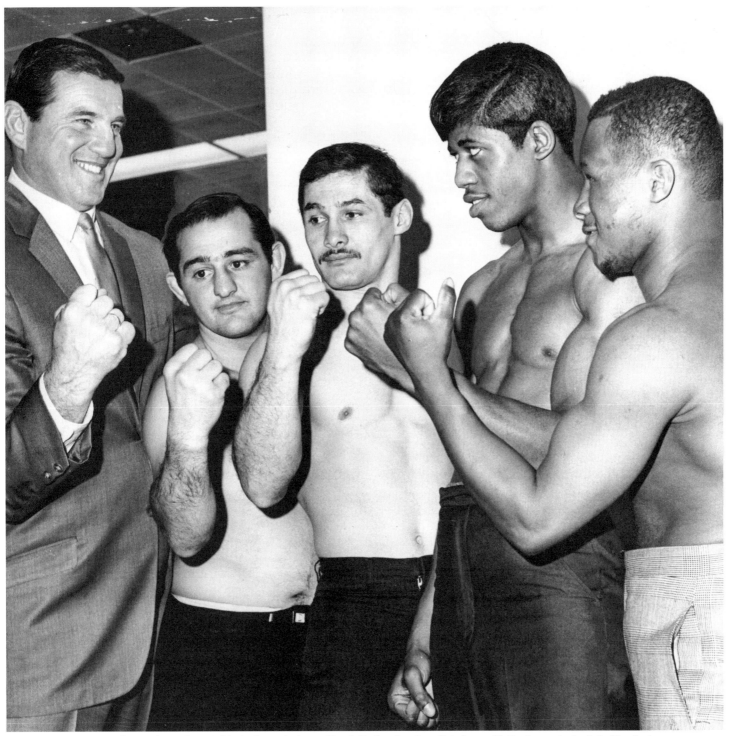

Putting Up Their Dukes - State Athletic Commissioner Chuck Bednarik raises fist along with the four principals in Monday's Doubleheader windup boxing show at the Arena. From left: Dick DiVeronica, Miguel Barreto, Al Massey, Roger Evan. (February 1968)

Bednarik has primarily been responsible for overseeing fight-related activities in the northeast portion of the state. He has occasionally been involved in decisions outside of that district, most notably when he was asked to cast the deciding vote on allowing a suspended Muhammad Ali to fight Joe Frazier in a bout that would be sanctioned by the state athletic commission. His verdict was of little surprise to anyone.

A well-known boxing writer, Ali's business manager, and some locally-based fight promoters and managers are among those devotees of the sweet science who remember him well.

Bert Randolph Sugar

With his massive cigar and wide-brimmed fedora, Bert Randolph Sugar is one of the most recognized figures in boxing. A member of the Boxing Hall of Fame, he is a well-regarded historian of all sports.

Bert Sugar was a college roommate of the guy whose injury in 1960 forced Chuck Bednarik to step in at linebacker and create the lasting legend of The 60 Minute Man.

"I saw him [Bednarik] a few times at fights at the Spectrum. He wasn't around Philly that much. He was based out of Scranton for this job with the Boxing Commission. It was his business to make sure all of the medical forms were correct, and he oversaw that paperwork with an iron hand. '

'Gene Kilroy was the point man when they were trying to get a license for an Ali comeback fight in 1969 or '70. They had to go through Chuck in Pennsylvania, and he said "No". He took a hardhat approach to boxing, but his response was not really unique for the era.'

'Bednarik was a tough son-of-a-bitch. I remember as a kid, watching the Penn-Cornell game on Thanksgiving Day. That was a big deal in the '40s—Skip Minisi, Reds Bagnell; Chuck Bednarik; that was a big f'ing game.'

'I have a minor confession. It was my honeymoon weekend the day the Eagles played the Giants in 1960, and he knocked out Frank Gifford.'

> **"Bednarik was a tough son-of-a-bitch. I remember as a kid, watching the Penn-Cornell game on Thanksgiving Day. That was a big deal in the '40s; Skip Minisi, Reds Bagnell; Chuck Bednarik; that was a big f'ing game."**

'Howard Cosell kept that play alive. I was at a banquet one time, and I was in a changing room getting into my tux, and Gifford was changing into his tux. I started talking about Cosell and Gifford was upset and got up. I was fumbling around with my tux, and mentioned that Cosell always said he invented the name "Giffer." Frank walked over to me, took off his shirt and pointed to a tattoo that said "Giffer."

'He said, "I don't know what the hell Howard is talking about, I've had this tattoo since high school."

'Cosell made it part of the currency. He did as much to destroy football as he did boxing.'

'My roommate in college at the University of Maryland was Bob Pellegrini, the guy who replaced Bednarik at linebacker. He was a tough son-of-a-bitch. He and Eddie Khayat were always together.'

'Pellegrini was big fan of Bednarik. I don't know if Bednarik was his mentor, but he was his senior.

Chuck Bednarik was his idol; I got that straight from Pelly.'

'As tough as Pelly was on the field, he was a real sweetheart, a pussycat off of it, though I loved to piss him off.'

'Bednarik was a real throwback, an anachronism, not just because he was The 60 Minute Man. He epitomized toughness in life. We won't see the likes of him again.'

'Those veterans of World War II, they came back and said, "What am I gonna be afraid of, some kid who is a stranger to a razor?" They took their GI Bill and changed college football. They were tough guys like Bednarik and Artie Donovan. Donvoan once said, "Calisthenics? My calisthenics is picking up beer."

'Bednarik was tough and fair. Sam Huff used to get all the media hype because he played in New York. Imagine if Bednarik had played in New York. There was no media in Philly; he didn't get the press. Same with Tommy McDonald; he was one of the best receivers ever. He was a little guy, with his flapping sleeves, but he could run and get open.'

'Huff used to just get on the pile. He was made by that "Violent World of Sam Huff," television show.

'He wasn't even supposed to be the subject of that show; it was supposed to be Jim Katcavage or Dick Modzelewski, but somebody said their names were too "ethnic sounding." They said, "Let's take Sam Huff; he has a nice, simple American name."

Andy DePaul

Former Pittsburgh-based boxer has served on the PA Athletic Commission with Bednarik for many years.

Andy "Kid" DePaul, lifelong resident of Pittsburgh, has served with Chuck Bednarik on the Pennsylvania State Athletic Commission since 1990. A 1947 Golden Gloves boxing champ in both Pittsburgh and New York at 135 lbs., DePaul won 82 of 92 amateur bouts. In 1950, he was the ninth-ranked middleweight in the world.

A lifelong boxing guy, DePaul was not a big football fan, but got to know Bednarik and understand his place in Pennsylvania and Philadelphia athletic lore.

The State Athletic Commission meets four times a year, and one member is usually the catalyst to keep things moving.

"Chuck always wants to get the meeting done quickly. He's not big on a lot of unnecessary talking. We had a lawyer on the committee for a while who really liked to talk. Chuck didn't like him very much.'

'He's a helluva nice guy, no BS, straight shooter, doesn't like characters.'

'What drives him crazy these days is MMA (mixed martial arts); he doesn't like it at all. He says those kids will all look like fighters in a few years. Their faces take a beating with those four ounce gloves.'

'It's terrible to hit a person when he's down. It goes against everything we were ever taught. Chuck thinks it barbaric.'

'I didn't realize how big Chuck really was until we went to a fight in Philly. It was Mike Tyson's first fight after jail; he KO'd the guy in five or six rounds.'

'I can tell you when they did the pre-fight introductions, the people in Philly acknowledged Chuck more than any of the fighters. There were five or six champions, other big name boxers, but the place roared when they introduced Chuck. All the fight fans know Chuck Bednarik.'

'During our meetings he pays attention and knows what's going on. He's no-nonsense. We'll get something like a guy who wants to fight at 45 years old, and Chuck will say, "Get him the hell out of here."

Gene Kilroy

The business manager for Muhammad Ali was given a direct and blunt "No" when he approached boxing commissioner Chuck Bednarik about licensing an Ali-Frazier fight in 1970.

Gene Kilroy gained fame as an insider in the entourage of Muhammad Ali, dating back to the Cassius Clay days. He first met Chuck Bednarik while working in the promotions department of the Eagles when Jerry Wolman owned the team. His friendship and familiarity with Bednarik did not gain him any favors when he approached Pennsylvania State Boxing Commissioner Chuck Bednarik about granting a license for an Ali-Joe Frazier match, when Ali was under suspension for draft evasion.

Kilroy and Bednarik remained friends through the ordeal.

"Chuck's a good guy. I remember one time he said, "I finally got a guy in the house; we got ourselves a dog." It turned out the dog—Tippy or Dippy—was a female, so he still had a house full of women.'

'I had to deal with him when I was trying to get an Ali-Frazier fight licensed in Pennsylvania. There were three commissioners I had to get approvals from. The first one, I think his name was Widener, said okay. I go to see the second guy out in Pittsburgh, and he says ok.'

'Then I went to see the third commissioner, Chuck Bednarik, and he barks back, "That draft dodger, what are you out of your mind? I wouldn't give him a license for anything. That put an end to that fight."

'I have a lot of respect for Chuck. He's such a good guy and sticks by his principles, but I never mentioned the licensing thing again; he scared the shit out of me.'

'Chuck is the real deal. I liked what he said about Deion Sanders, that he couldn't tackle Emma. That's the way you want to deal with people, not ass-kissers. You want them straight. He's such a good guy, I love him.'

'Jerry Wolman loved him too. I was the promotions director for the Eagles and Chuck used to come around. Jerry always said to take care of Chuck.'

'Chuck would come around and say, "Where's my sideline pass?" and we always took care of him.'

'If there are two guys that Philadelphia should put up statues for, it's Joe Frazier and Chuck Bednarik. They were the real things.

'Sylvester Stallone is a jerk, and you can quote me on that. He's a jerk and fake who never did anything and they put up a statue for him.'

Joe Frazier and Chuck Bednarik are the real symbols of Philadelphia, and why the city doesn't honor them, I don't know."

Leo Turley

A veteran of more than 50 years managing hotels and resorts, including Split Rock Lodge in the Poconos, Leo Turley has been a long-time friend of Chuck and Emma Bednarik. He has hosted them at several of the properties he managed and enjoyed going to fights with boxing commissioner Bednarik. Turley lives near Lake George, in upstate New York.

"He is a magnificent person and they are a magnificent couple. He's very strong, was a fierce player and remains today, a fine guy. He stopped here on his way to a Catholic shrine in Montreal, the Shrine of St. Anne De Beaupre. A lot of people don't know that side of him, how religious he is.'

'I was with him when he was enshrined in the College Football Hall of Fame. President Nixon was there. He looked at Chuck and said, "Big number 60." Chuck was thrilled; what a thing it was for him that the President knew his number.'

'I used to go to the fights with him while he was boxing commissioner. One time, we're in Scranton, and two supposed gangsters are arguing in the corridor. There's some difficulty going on between the two of them, and Chuck looks and tells them, "You're talking like that in front of me! I'm the commissioner."

'They're yelling and cursing at each other, and Chuck grabs them on each arm and pulls them apart and tells them, "You don't talk like that."

'I thought we were going to be shot, but the two guys realized who he was, and they were beaming; they were proud to be manhandled by Chuck Bednarik.'

'Another time, we were watching Bob Foster fight before one of the Frazier-Ali fights. Foster knocked out the guy in the third round, and Tony Galento leans forward and tell Chuck and me, "Now you know how good Frazier is", because Frazier had knocked out Foster.'

'Chuck is unique, as solid as the Rock of Gibraltar. He has great integrity, does everything right. He has manners and a goodness about him; he's never late for anything. He has inherent good manners that you wouldn't associate with such a tough guy.'

'Did you ever see that NFL Films piece where he talks about playing linebacker? We showed it to the guests at one of our hotels, and they loved it. They said he should be the next John Wayne.'

'He's an old-fashioned guy in the greatest way. He's genuine, no airs about him, but he has a commanding presence.'

'I've been astonished in the places that I've been with him, how people relate to him. He's a man's man, a special person. He and Emma, they're just a great couple.'

'Let me tell you my Sam Huff story. I was with Sam when he was trying to buy a hotel for Marriott. I grabbed a postcard and addressed it to Chuck. I wrote on the back, "Leo Turley and Sam Huff are better men than you." I signed it and asked Sam to sign it. He didn't want to do it. He said, "I don't want to get that rattlesnake mad at me." He eventually signed, and I sent it to Chuck."

Jim Williams

A Philadelphia boxing manager, Williams recalls dodging beer bottles and waiting out a riot alongside Chuck Bednarik underneath a boxing ring following a disputed bout.

Jim Williams has been a Philadelphia-based boxing manager for 40 years. He trains at the Joe Hand Gym, and among his current fighters is Mike Jones, a leading welterweight contender. The scariest night of his boxing career was spent hiding under a ring with Chuck Bednarik, seven cub scouts, and unknown attractive woman during a riot at the old Philadelphia Arena.

"There was a riot at the Arena. I don't even remember who the fighters were, but I'm sitting in the front row next to Chuck Bednarik, there was an unpopular decision and a bottle comes bouncing under us. I see that and I'm getting under the ring.'

'We get under the ring and we're holding the apron down me, Chuck Bednarik, a pretty girl and seven cub scouts. We're holding the apron down, and it sounded like World War III. It seemed like it lasted forever—bottles, chairs, garbage, you name it, is flying down at the ring.'

'I remember looking at Chuck, and he's staring out with this disgusted look on his face. He's shaking his head; he can't believe this is happening in Philadelphia.'

'It was so loud, you couldn't hear anything. The little cub scouts were petrified. We thought the ring was going to come down on us, so we shoot for the exits. Everyone was laughing at us and throwing stuff.'

'The picture was in the Bulletin the next day of us ducking under the ring. The worst part for me was my wife wanted to know who the pretty girl was. I had to explain to her that I have no idea who she was; she just jumped under the ring with us.'

'That was my closest interaction with Chuck. He was a nice guy, but completely disgusted with the whole situation."

Russell Peltz

As a young boxing promoter, Peltz was sent home by boxing commissioner Chuck Bednarik to retrieve his press area seating list prior to the fight card at the Spectrum.

Russell Peltz has been the leading boxing promoter in Philadelphia for the past 40 years. He was also the boxing director at the Spectrum from 1973-1980. Peltz was inducted into the International Boxing Hall of Fame in 2004.

"My one main run-in with Chuck Bednarik came in 1971. He primarily ran the Scranton end of boxing in the state, but he was usually around when there was a big fight in Philadelphia. This was my first big show at the Spectrum, and we brought the fighters in for weigh-ins and pre-fight publicity.'

'Frank Wilderman was in charge of Philadelphia, but Chuck showed up for the weigh-ins at the commissioner's office in the state building. He insisted on seeing all of the seating in the press section. He wanted to know who was sitting where, and how many seats he could get for the fights.'

'I was 23 or 24 years old, and he was very intimidating. I figured I could put him off for a few hours by telling him that the list was at my house in Germantown.'

'He said, "I want to see them now". I got in my car and went home to get them. When I got back, he wanted to know everything, "Who is this guy?" "Why is this guy seated there?" He got what he wanted.'

'He was in Scranton, and all the action was in Philly. I remember the story about him nixing the Frazier-Ali fight; he REALLY nixed it.'

'I love to hear him talk. I agree with everything the guy says, whether he's talking about Deion Sanders or all the dancing and celebrating. I wish there were more guys around like him.'

My favorite Bednarik quote came during the 1962 season. The Eagles had lost their first two games and they played Cleveland at home and won 35-7. In the locker room one of the reporters asked him if this had been a "must win" game for the Eagles. Chuck answered, "No last week was a must win; this week was mustier."

Greg Sirb

The current executive director has been with the PA State Athletic Commission since 1989.

Chuck Bednarik has served as chairman of the Pennsylvania State Athletic Commission for more than 25 years. He is the longest serving commissioner in the history of the SAC. The SAC licenses and regulates sporting events and competitions throughout the state, including boxing, wrestling, kickboxing and mixed martial arts. In addition to attending quarterly meetings, Bednarik has been in attendance at a number of fights and matches during his tenure.

"Chuck is definitely an amazing guy. Wherever we are in the state, anyone over 40 years old knows who he is and to many of them he is God.'

'He is a walking legend. There have been a number of times where people don't care about the main event, but they ask, "Where is Chuck?" He has overshadowed many of the matches, no question.'

'One time we were at a pro wrestling match at the CYC Center in Scranton. I believe it was the early 90s. One of the promoters had an issue and wouldn't stop complaining. He was a tough-looking guy; I think he was from New York. He wanted his wrestler to be able to do certain things, and we wouldn't let him. I was the guy on the front line.'

Pictured are Greg Sirb, Chuck, and comedian Bill Cosby

'He kept screaming that he wanted to go over my head and see the commissioner. He said he would like to get the commissioner in the ring.'

'Well the commissioner was there that night, and he wasn't in a good mood. He was upset about some other issues that happened earlier in the night'

'That commissioner was Chuck Bednarik and I called him over. The promoter's jaw dropped when he saw Chuck.'

'He recognized him immediately and said he was taking his issue off the table. Chuck scared the bejeebees out of him. I said I guess you don't want to get in the ring with him'.

'Chuck can be very intimidating when he is not in a good mood."

A. Chuck at Whitemarsh Valley Country Club
B. Having fun with Arnold Palmer
C. Chuck takes time out to greet some military guests
D. Chuck with a golf buddy
E. 1967 Philadelphia Golf Classic

Chapter **ten**

Golf

Chuck Bednarik has often said that, for all of his great athletic accomplishments, winning the club championship at Whitemarsh Country Club was his favorite personal achievement. The golfer he defeated, Bill Robertson, had won the club championship a number of times. Bednarik likes to recall, "He [Robertson] was so pissed off he didn't even shake my hand."

Bednarik did not start playing golf seriously until after he retired from the Eagles in 1962. Within a few years he was one of the best amateur golfers in the Philadelphia area and was a popular guest at many golf outings all over the nation. He was just as competitive and as focused on the links as he was on the football field. While he was expected to crush the ball great distances, what surprised many teammates and observers was his soft touch around the green and a complete absence of the "yips" when he had to make a pressure putt.

He held his own in foursomes with the likes of Arnold Palmer and Lee Trevino, and in various tournaments players angled to get Bednarik as a teammate because they knew he was out to win.

A round of golf with Chuck Bednarik was always memorable. Several of his golf companions recall their experiences.

Hogan

Hole-In-One Award

This Certificate Is Presented To

Chuck Bednarik

In recognition of one of golf's most outstanding achievements.
Your accomplishment took place on the __11th__ hole
at

Saucon Valley C.C.

The Ben Hogan Company congratulates you and is proud to be part
of your achievement.

Ben Hogan

Chairman, Ben Hogan Company

Bobby Shantz

This Philadelphia A's pitcher and area resident has played basketball and golf with Bednarik over the years.

A native of Pottstown, PA, Bobby Shantz pitched for the Philadelphia A's from 1949 until they left for Kansas City after the 1954 season. He was named Most Valuable Player in the American League for winning 24 games for the A's in 1952. A longtime resident of Ambler, PA, Shantz has been a regular player on the local charity golf tournament circuit for many years.

"I didn't see it, but I heard that he did take batting practice with the A's. They said he hit the hell out of the ball. He was a big strong son-of-a-bitch; they say he hit quite a few out of the park.'

'They said he used to have home run contests with Gus Zernial. He was probably stronger than Gus. I've played in a few golf outings with him; he talked about it quite a bit. If he swears to it, it probably happened.'

'He was a pretty darned good golfer. I know he won the championship at Whitemarsh. We used to play in an outing in the Poconos. We'd ride up together; I would pick him up and bring him back. When he played golf, he hit the ball. Everybody wanted to be in his group; he usually won.'

'He's a hell of a nice guy, I always enjoy being around him. Does he still play his accordion and harmonica?'

'We used to go to the Austrian Village and he would bring his accordion. He always drew a good crowd when he started playing. He was pretty good.'

'I picked him up one morning to go to the golf tournament in the Poconos. He picks up the newspaper in his driveway, and next thing he's bitching and angry,'

'I said to him "What the hell's the matter with you?"

'He shows me the headline. It's about this guy Deion Sanders who is going to be the new Chuck Bednarik, a two-way player.'

'He's steaming, "He couldn't tackle my wife Emma."

'He was talking about that the whole ride to the Poconos. He was really mad. We get there, and he's showing the article to everyone.'

"I've seen him play basketball. He played a few games with us. We had a team, Robin Roberts, Curt Simmons, Richie Ashburn, Stan Lopata, Bobby Wine, Paul Arizin. We had a good team; we didn't lose much, had a good time. Chuck would get under the basket and clear the boards; he knocked the shit out of guys."

Andy Russell

The former Steelers linebacker has hosted charity golf tournament that Bednarik played in many times.

Andy Russell was named to the Pro Bowl seven times during his 12-year career with the Pittsburgh Steelers. He is also well-known in the Pittsburgh area for the community service work performed by his Andy Russell Charitable Foundation. For the past 33 years, he has raised funds for the foundation through a celebrity golf tournament. Chuck Bednarik was one of the earliest and most consistent supporters of the golf outing.

"I was fortunate to meet him many years later at some NFL event and we even played a round of golf together. What impressed me greatly was that he played golf with the same passion, intensity and concentration that he played football with. I think he told me that he started playing at a club after his retirement and that he became very serious about the game, working hard on his techniques, and ultimately becoming his club champ. It was clear to me then that he was a very driven person, one who makes no excuses, seeks perfection and, (this is probably most important) works himself to exhaustion.

Chuck helped me get our golf tournament started here in Pittsburgh many years ago and I am forever indebted."

Ed McKeon

Ed McKeon is the longtime publisher of Construction Equipment Guide, the Fort Washington, PA-based trade publication that covers the construction industry. An avid golfer, he has played several times with Chuck Bednarik, some of which were quite memorable.

"Chuck and golf…he is proud of his golf ability. You know he was the club champ at Whitemarsh around '75. In his biggest match he beat Bill Robertson, who had been the champ for several years; Chuck knocked him off his peg.'

'We had some experiences. I used to publish a local golf magazine. For one issue, about 1962, I put together a foursome for a round in Warrington. We had a fellow named Sussman, who I believe was owner of the club; Tim Early, who worked for the magazine; Chuck; and Skee Riegel.'

'Riegel was a pro, one of the best golfers from this area. He won the U.S. Amateur (in 1947) and almost won the Masters one year (1951). Finished second to Ben Hogan.'

'Chuck could hit the ball, but around the second or third hole, you could see he was getting upset. He wasn't the longest hitter in the group. Riegel was out-driving him.'

'Next tee, Chuck sets up and really winds up; he crushes the ball. Riegel is wondering, "What the hell is going on here?" and he hits it past Chuck.'

'They had a competition going on all day. One hole Skee hits it past Chuck, the next hole Chuck outdrives him. Sussman and Early realized they were out of the match. They couldn't get over watching Skee and Chuck hammer the ball.'

'Riegel won, but it was a very good match. Chuck was on his tail the whole day. He was dead serious.'

'There was another day, about 1995 up at Saucon Valley. There was a fellow named Tom Gargen. He had played quarterback and kicker at Cornell. I think it was 1948, Penn played Cornell and turned into a real kicking game. Gargan was the punter for Cornell and Chuck was the punter for Penn.'

'There was a dinner before the Penn-Cornell game some years later, and I remember George Munger introducing Chuck and Gargan, saying we have the two kickers from that great '48 game here tonight.'

'Gargan calls me one day and says, "Let's play some golf. You get someone and I'll get someone." He gets Frank Fischl, who had played running back at Army and was later the Mayor of Allentown. I got Chuck.'

'On the third hole, Gargan says to Chuck, "You know I outkicked you in that '48 game."

'Chuck looks at Gargan and says 'you beat me at kicking?'

'Then Fischl jumps in and says, "I played against you when I was at Army in 1948."

'Chuck says, I remember you guys won at the last second. Somebody caught a pass to win the game.' (The player was John Trent.)

'Fischl says, "You know he [Trent] was killed in Korea.'

'Chuck says,"I remember that so well, I pray for him often."

'Chuck is quiet for a moment, and he realizes that he never won a game against either of these guys. He was disappointed. The rest of the day he kept shaking his head, saying, "I can't believe I didn't beat either of you guys."

Bob Feller

This Hall of Fame baseball pitcher, like Bednarik, is a veteran of World War II, and the two became friendly on the celebrity golf circuit.

Bob Feller, the great Cleveland Indian fireball pitcher, was also a veteran of World War II. He and Chuck Bednarik became friendly at celebrity golf outings and memorabilia shows.

"I've played golf with him in a few celebrity classics. He's a great football player and a great American—one of the best.'

'He flew over Germany and helped win a war we had to win. He's a good American and a great person.'

'I was at a golf tournament in Pennsylvania with him and Joe DiMaggio. We had a good time."

Stan Lopata, Chuck, and Yogi Berra at the 1958 Philadelphia Sportswriters Dinner.

Yogi Berra

huck Bednarik and Yogi Berra became good friends on the celebrity golf circuit. Born 11 days apart in 1925, they were often paired together. It was not uncommon for Bednarik, a serious competitive golfer, to gripe about having Yogi in his group, "I love the guy, but I can't win anything with him as a partner."

Bednarik has played in Berra's annual tournament in New Jersey many times, and the two have attended various family functions that the other hosted.

"We became good friends; he's a very good golfer and a very strong guy. We played a lot together at different outings. He can get mad on the course. We finished second a few times, and he'd always say, "Aah, we should have won". He's a good guy, though.'

'In golf, he is competitive. I laugh at those crooked fingers, but he could hit a ball.'

'I was usually the bad golfer in the group and he'd give me hell. It was always serious with him, but we had a lot of fun.'

'He and I played at Saucon Valley with Sam Snead in a charity outing.'

'He talks about when they didn't use face masks. He talks about all the money today. A lot of guys in baseball wish we were playing now. You gotta blame the owners.'

'He's come up to my golf outing a lot. The New York fans love him; they love to talk about the Gifford hit. I saw him play against the Giants after the hit. It was a grudge match."

Chapter | eleven

Post Playing Days

No one is quite sure what Chuck Bednarik expected from the Eagles when he walked off the playing field for the last time in December, 1962. Whatever it was, in his eyes, he rarely found it. There is little doubt that the Dick Vermiel era was the high point of Bednarik's post playing association with the Eagles and, since taking over as head coach, Andy Reid has warmly reached out to make Bednarik feel welcomed and appreciated by the organization.

If the franchise had one primary set of owners through the years, such as the situation is with the Pittsburgh Steelers, Chicago Bears, New York Giants or Kansas City Chiefs, Bednarik would have been welcomed back annually as an iconic legend, entrenched in the tradition of the organization.

The Eagles have changed hands four times since he retired. Bednarik's best chance of having a lasting position with the team would have come if Jerry Wolman had been able to hold on to the ownership. Bednarik was less than 10 years removed from the playing field, and contracts had not yet soared into the six-figure plus range. In other words, he could still somewhat identify with the players on the field.

Wolman and his chief lieutenant, Ed Snider, both had the greatest respect and appreciation for No. 60, and were prepared to make him a meaningful part of the organization. Wolman's outside financial problems forced him to relinquish the team, and Bednarik never got along with the next owner, Leonard Tose.

Bednarik volunteered himself for the position of general manager when Tose took over the team during the spring of 1969. For many years to come, Bednarik relayed the sting he felt when, in his words, Tose told him,

> **Bednarik volunteered himself for the position of general manager when Tose took over the team during the spring of 1969. For many years to come, Bednarik relayed the sting he felt, when, in his words, Tose told him, "The Eagles don't owe you anything."**

"The Eagles don't owe you anything." A former Bednarik teammate, Pete Retzlaff, got the job.

The first coach of the Tose era was Mike McCormack, who recalls that during his three years with the Eagles he never saw Bednarik even once around the team. Next up on the Eagles sideline was Vermiel.

While Tose did not invite Bednarik into his front office, he did agree to let Vermiel bring him back to the organization with the nebulous title of "honorary coach." Bednarik's primary responsibility under Vermiel was to remind the current players of what the Eagles once represented; he was a pivotal player on the franchise's last two championship teams.

Bednarik was present for the entire Vermiel tenure. Most of the players enjoyed having him around; others saw him as rustic, negative, and contemptuous of modern players. During those years, Bednarik always assigned his loyalty to Vermiel, not the franchise he played for. When Vermiel left in 1982, so did Concrete Charlie, never to be seen around the team again with any degree of frequency.

The next owner to follow Tose was Leonard Braman. Though Braman was a Philly Guy, at least by birth, and claimed that owning the Eagles was the fulfillment of a

Vice President Ed Snider (left) and coach Joe Kuharich (right) welcome Chuck holding his retired #60 jersey back
to the Eagles as a special representative for the team.

lifetime dream, he never really embraced the team's tradition. Braman made little effort to reach out to any of the alumni, and Bednarik's relationship with him was at best neutral. Bednarik and Buddy Ryan, the coach for most of the Braman years, did understandably like one another, and Ryan made a couple of trips to Bethlehem to attend local functions with Bednarik.

Jeffrey Lurie bought the Eagles from Braman in 1994, and it was his second coach, Andy Reid, who became the first team representative since Vermiel to personally call Bednarik and invite him to be around the team. Coming from Green Bay, which does as good a job as any franchise in remembering the past, Reid understood what it meant to have the old legends around.

Under Reid's direction, Bednarik has an open invitation to any game or team function, and needless to say, Reid is his favorite coach since Vermiel. Each year Reid invites Bednarik to the team's training camp at Lehigh, and Bednarik usually makes the 15 minute ride from his house at least once every summer.

As owner, Lurie inadvertently played a part in Bednarik's most vocal and publicized estrangement from the organization. The two had a cordial relationship, so much so that Bednarik felt emboldened enough to ask

Lurie to buy about 100 copies of his book, "The Last of the 60-Minute Men," to distribute to players and others in the organization.

Lurie politely declined, citing a league rule that prohibited him from giving gifts to the players.

Bednarik found himself unable to get past the "No" part of the response. For several years he made sure that any reporter, fan or other party, interested or disinterested, was made aware that the Eagles were "cheap," and he went so far as to wish them defeat when asked who he was rooting for before the 2005 Super Bowl. These were not his finest moments.

It would have been unpleasant for a number of long-time Eagles fans to see the team's greatest legend close out his days on such bitter terms with the franchise he helped build. But it looks like the story will have a positive ending, as Bednarik has found repentance and the Eagles have been magnanimous.

It's been a sometimes tortured ride for Chuck Bednarik and the Eagles the past 45 years, and while the faces may have changed, most of them have made an effort to understand the man many people think of as Mr. Eagle.

Dick Vermiel

One of Vermeil's first official acts upon taking over as Eagles head coach in 1976 was to appoint Chuck Bednarik an honorary coach with the team.

It is well-documented that Dick Vermiel helped put an end to Chuck Bednarik's first estrangement from the Eagles organization shortly after being named head coach in 1976. Vermiel recognized that the tradition of the team was not being recognized and sought to remedy that situation.

One of Vermiel's first official acts was to add Bednarik as an honorary coach. In this capacity, Bednarik helped out at training camp, traveled with the team, and was a sideline presence at games. Bednarik departed from the Eagles when Vermiel resigned following the 1982 season. The two have remained close friends.

"In '76, I had just gotten hired by the Eagles and was doing a speaking engagement downtown. Chuck was there and I overheard him say to someone that he had nothing to do with the Eagles.'

> ## "He is one of the very few players in the Hall of Fame that if he were playing today, he would still be a Hall of Fame player."

'I went over and asked him to dinner. We met at Bookbinders, we had some wine, and I asked him why he was so bitter. He said he was totally ignored by the organization and felt nothing but bitter.'

'This organization had been losing for a long time. Chuck Bednarik was the only winning symbol the organization had, so I made him an honorary coach and he was with me over seven years.'

'I had to give him something to do on the sidelines, he was always yelling and cursing, so I had him chart plays to keep out of trouble. Some of the players enjoyed him,

some were irritated by him, but overall it was a positive experience.'

'Leonard Tose didn't understand that Chuck is a very sensitive guy. Sometimes he brings on his own problems, but a lot of that is caused by his insecurity.'

'I'll tell you a funny story. He traveled with the team and one game he is late for the flight. We had a policy that we wait for no one.'

'The plane is ready to pull out, and we look out the window and see Chuck running like mad. He runs on to the plane and he's a mess, really disheveled.'

"Chuck, what happened?"

'He said I got in a fight on the way here. I was driving along and some kid flipped me the bird. I caught up to him at a traffic light and made him get out. I grabbed the guy, two others get out of the car, and I'm fighting three guys. One of them says "Oh, my God that's Mr. Bednarik, let's stop.'

'I was doing okay until they stopped.'

'He's very prideful, very respectful. I enjoyed him. He made a real contribution, sometimes people forget.'

'We went to play Green Bay in '78 or '79. Chuck and I walk out early and people start applauding. I look up and wave, and someone yells, "Not you, him."

'He is one of the very few players in the Hall of Fame that, if he were playing today, he would still be a Hall of Fame player.'

'I used to go to the Bethlehem Club with him. One year they made me an honorary member. We would get to Bethlehem and first we would visit his mom and dad.'

'His mother wouldn't let his dad drink without company, so he was happy to see us. We would go to the basement, he would give each of us a shot glass, we'd clink them and say, "Nostrobia!

'Next we would go over to Emma's family. We would do the same thing; her father would pour a shot of Slivovitz, we'd clink glasses, Nostrobia."

'Then we'd head over to Hips Pescek's bar and have shots and beers with all the steel mill guys who had just gotten off work.'

'Then we'd go to the Bethlehem Club, and by God, that was quite an evening. Needless to say I always stayed over.'

'In his personality he wants people to be aggressive in developing relationships. The new guys came into town–Braman, Lurie– and he felt disrespected, left out. Sometimes owners from out of town don't understand tradition.'

'In Kansas City they do a great job with the alumni. Two guys travel with the team every game. They have a spring reception. Before every home game they have a big tent next to the stadium for the alumni.'

'Lamar Hunt planted a redwood tree for each hall of famer outside the stadium. That's the way it is.'

'Chuck is a great guy, integrity and character throughout. He is an unbelievably loyal American, old school and whatever is on his mind, he feels compelled to say it."

Buddy Ryan

This former Eagles head coach found a kindred spirit in Chuck Bednarik as neither of them ever hesitated in offering an unvarnished honest opinion.

The two Eagles coaches that Chuck Bednarik has been closest with over the past 40 years have been Dick Vermiel and Andy Reid. If there was one coach who Bednarik might have best matched up with in personality and temperament, it was Buddy Ryan, who was head coach of the Eagles from 1986 to 1990.

Ryan was famously unfiltered in dishing out thoughts and opinions. The two did develop a friendship, with Ryan visiting Bednarik at home several times.

"I'd go to his house and he'd play his squeezebox. We had a lot of fun. I know he's had an off and on relationship with the team, but he was always welcome when I was there. He's my kind of guy.'

'We had something in common; he didn't like the owner either. He was fun to have around. I think he always felt welcome with me.'

'He could have played on my defense any time. He was great."

"We had something in common; he didn't like the owner either. He was fun to have around. I think he always felt welcome with me."

Bill Bergey

Middle linebacker for Eagles when Bednarik was honorary coach, assisting Dick Vermiel.

When Bill Bergey was traded from the Cincinnati Bengals in 1974, it represented one of the most significant acquisitions in Eagles history. Bergey's role as an All-Pro middle linebacker solidified the 'Gang Green' defense and helped lead the Eagles to three playoff appearances and a trip to the 1980 Super Bowl.

Chuck Bednarik served as a special assistant to Dick Vermiel during most of Bergey's career with the Eagles and the two strong-willed middle linebackers sometimes clashed.

"He was nothing really special when he was with us. We were veterans and into doing our own thing.'

'I just can't give him a ringing endorsement. I resented some of the things he said. He'd run in on the sidelines bitching about guys.'

'I yelled at him on the sideline, "Damnit Chuck, can't you say anything positive."

'He called me at home that night and reamed me out. I just said, "OK Chuck, if that's how you want it."

"He's always been opinionated and today he doesn't endear himself to the team he helped create. I would say to him, "Why don't you join us and be part of us." I wish he could endear himself more to the Eagles fans than he does.'

'He resents modern athletes. He's too old school. I resented it when it he said he hoped the Eagles would lose the Super Bowl in Jacksonville.'

'It was ridiculous that he got upset with Jeffrey Lurie when he wouldn't buy his books.'

'There's no rhyme or reason, It's just him being him. If that's the way he wants to be, fine."

"He's always been opinionated and today he doesn't endear himself to the team he helped create. I would say to him, "Why don't you join us and be part of us." I wish he could endear himself more to the Eagles fans than he does."

Andy Reid

The current Eagles head coach is the first coach since Dick Vermiel to openly welcome Bednarik back into the Eagles family.

The most meaningful phone call Chuck Bednarik receives every summer comes from Andy Reid, head coach of the Philadelphia Eagles since 1999, and executive vice president of football operations since 2001. The Eagles summer training camp is held at Lehigh University in Bednarik's hometown of Bethlehem, and Chuck still lives about 15 minutes from campus.

In calling Bednarik and inviting him to visit camp and speak with the players, Reid is the first Eagles coach since Dick Vermiel to make him feel like a meaningful part of the organization.

"He's awesome. He was a tough guy, and he's still a tough guy. If he says he could still play today, I wouldn't put it past him.'

'He's so strong and honest. I love talking to him about football, having him sum up his memories, telling his stories. He has great insights.'

'My first year here, he talked to the team for about 40 minutes. I think it does mean a lot to have him around the team. The guys think he's awesome; they talk to him as they come off the field. Jeremiah Trotter liked talking to him; they had a mutual respect. The players like having him feel part of the team.'

'He's the last 60-minute man, and very proud of it.

He's quite a story, from World War II, to Penn, to being the first pick in the draft, to All-Pro player, to the Hall of Fame. For as big as he did things, all the stories tell us that he is an all-timer.'

'I have a pretty funny story. He invites Harold Carmichael and me, sometime either in my first, second or third year with the team, to visit his house.'

'He's taking us to the house in his big Cadillac and he has polka music playing in the car. He loves his music.'

'He's taking us on these tiny, windy roads up where he lives, doing about 150 miles an hour. He's bopping and humming to the polka music. He has no concept of speed or what's around the next corner.'

'I look back at Harold, and his arms are gripping the seats; he's holding on for dear life. He's deathly scared, and I'm scared too, and Chuck is just happily listening to his polka music. It was hilarious, really funny.'

'His wife is a sweetheart. He's from that era, people don't understand him today. If you get to know him, you won't see the angry guy. You can tell he loves God, loves his wife, and loves his family. He always mentions his wife and God.'

'He made two positions—center and linebacker—on the Eagles All-Time 75th Anniversary Team; it was well-deserved.'

"I try to get the call into him to come to camp just before the veterans come in, so that they can see him. I have his picture in my office. He's the man.'

'He's from the Archie Bunker era. He talks big, but really likes everybody. He doesn't dislike anyone. He's a good man."

Jerry Wolman

I f not for a problem with concrete of all things, Chuck Bednarik's post-playing career with the Eagles might be much more rancor-free.

Chuck Bednarik's relationship with the various Eagles ownership regimes has been contentious at times. Bednarik's sensitive nature has been triggered at times by a perceived lack of appreciation from some of the team owners over the years. Sometimes the team did not reach out and Concrete Charlie would feel estranged from the Eagles family. Bednarik's disappointment started when he was denied a management position by Leonard Tose.

Things may have been much different if Jerry Wolman had been able to hang on to the team.

Wolman bought the team in December 1963, a year after Bednarik retired. While Wolman had a great sense of the Eagles history, he and Bednarik never worked together in an official capacity. Chuck was, however, around the team quite a bit and helped out as an extra training camp assistant.

Ironically, defective concrete played a major role in the path to financial distress that forced Wolman to sell the team in 1969. At a time when Bednarik was earning the nickname Concrete Charlie, while selling for Warner Company, concrete problems on a new office building in Chicago caused construction delays, cost Wolman $20 million, pushed him into bankruptcy, and led to the sale of the Eagles.

Wolman revealed that, if not for his financial problems, Bednarik would have had a major role in Eagles management.

"Chuck was gone when I got the team, but I had grown up in Shenadoah, PA and Chuck Bednarik was my hero. Very few people played the game like he did.'

'He was Mr. Eagle to me and he should have been Mr. Eagle to everyone, forever.'

"He was Mr. Eagle to me and he should have been Mr. Eagle to everyone, forever."

'If I didn't have my problems, I would have made sure that he got the recognition he deserved. I was going to take him on board.'

'I'm sorry that I was never able to do that. I have always had respect for both him and Emma. I respect Chuck as a man and a player.'

'I came from Shenadoah, had a similar upbringing to Chuck, and that helped me appreciate him. I never would have had the opportunities that I did without Chuck; he was an inspiration.'

'I'm an old coal cracker, and to an extent Chuck is too. We came from a different breed. We know the meaning of hard work, always give 100%.'

'The game wouldn't be where it is today without people like Chuck and Art Rooney, old school guys who helped build the league.'

'If I had not run into trouble, it was my intention to have Chuck join the team in a significant authoritative capacity. Joe Kuharich felt the same way.'

'Everything changed after I ran into problems with that building in Chicago. Chuck knew how I felt.'

'I knew of him going back to his high school days. I think, as far as the Eagles are concerned, he should always be the face of the franchise.'

'Memories of Chuck...I'll give you memory, he came to 80th birthday party and he broke a rib hugging me so hard. I remember that very well."

Frank LeMaster

A linebacker with the Eagles during the Vermiel years, LeMaster became close with Chuck Bednarik, who frequently brought him to his home for dinner and family functions.

Frank LeMaster joined the Eagles as a fourth round draft pick out of Kentucky in 1974. As a linebacker, he worked closely with Chuck Bednarik when the latter served as an honorary coach under Dick Vermiel.

LeMaster spent a great deal of time off the field with the Bednarik family, and appreciated the home-away-from-home atmosphere that was provided.

"I guess the first time I met Chuck Bednarik was during Dick Vermiel's first year here. Dick was doing everything he could to bridge the gap between the new staff and the team's history.'

'He put particular emphasis on the championship teams, Philadelphia's great teams. Dick wanted to continue the tradition and help the current players understand the Eagles franchise. He told the team that Chuck Bednarik is the epitome of the Philadelphia Eagles, and he represents what we want to strive for. He made sure that we knew that he was a championship player, an all-time great, and the last guy to play both ways. I was from Kentucky and I didn't know anything about the Philadelphia Eagles.'

'Dick brought him to games and prac-tices. Chuck would give out bits of advice, particularly to the offensive line and the linebackers.'

'I was a linebacker, and I enjoyed talking to him; he was informative about playing the position. He would give advice, talk about the past team's tradition. He gave us something to strive for. I didn't know anything about the tradition, didn't really know who he was.'

'I will say this: when I came to Philadelphia, Chuck Bednarik was the first person to reach out to me. He brought me to his home for dinner; had me meet his family; played golf—he was a friend. It meant a lot to me.'

'I think that sometimes Chuck got caught up in the excitement of the games. A competitor like he was; Chuck got fired up during the heat of a game.'

'Vermiel had to tone him down a few times. I understood both their positions; Chuck was excited and wanted to keep the team fired up, and Dick needed to maintain discipline and calm.'

'He was very engaging. He had a great family and used to take me to his favorite German restaurant. He was one of the people who reached out to me; he opened his home, he was a generous man.'

'I remember his twins the first time I came to dinner. They were gorgeous girls. Being away from home at 21, 22, it was very special to me."

Marv Levy

In 1969, Dick Vermiel was hired by George Allen of the Los Angeles Rams to be the league's first special teams coach. That same year, Marv Levy became the second special teams coach in the NFL, when he was hired for that job by Jerry Williams of the Eagles.

Chuck Bednarik was a special training camp assistant for the Eagles that summer, helping out with the linebackers and long snappers.

Levy went on to become a Hall of Fame coach, leading the Buffalo Bills to four consecutive Super Bowls. He resides in the Chicago area.

"I was in awe meeting Chuck Bednarik when I joined the Eagles. It was great having a guy around who everyone respected. I got to know him that summer, and have spoken with him at the Hall of Fame over the years.'

'I was the special teams coach. There were only two of us at the time, Dick Vermiel and me; and Chuck would jump in with the long snappers and whip the ball back. He didn't do a lot of posturing, but everyone knew of him.'

'He'd just step in and show them how to do it. He could do so many things on the football field."

Vince Papale

As a special teams player for the Eagles during the Dick Vermiel era, Papale's Philadelphia background and appreciation for local sports lore gave him the insight and understanding of Chuck Bednarik that eluded some of his teammates.

'What happened in the 1970s? There seemed to a wedge between the alumni and the Eagles. There was no participation among the retired players. There was an emotional passage when Dick Vermiel and his staff came on board.'

'Dick came in and said the future is shaped by the past. He thought it was both great and important to have guys from the championship teams around.'

'I was excited; I was the biggest Eagles fan in the world. The 1960 champs were my idols; it was exciting to me to have Chuck Bednarik, Tommy McDonald and Pete Retzlaff around.'

> ## "I remember Chuck walking into a meeting room; he had such a presence, he dominated a room. I don't remember what he said, but he had the team's attention."

'I remember Chuck walking into a meeting room; he had such a presence, he dominated a room. I don't remember what he said, but he had the team's attention.'

'I think with a guy like Chuck, some guys got him, some didn't, when Dick made him an associate coach.'

'A guy like me, I got him.'

'Some guys didn't like it when Chuck would get upset if he didn't like the way they were playing. They would be like, "You're not my coach, coach."'

'Some guys didn't want to hear what he had to say, didn't want him around; that was them, I was me.'

'He was in a position of influence on the sideline, and I thought he was needed. I was just trying to make the goddamn team, and I was happy to be in the presence of Chuck Bednarik, Tommy McDonald, Tim Brown and Steve Van Buren. If Tommy McDonald came up and told me I should do something, I did it.'

'They made him associate coach because he was the face of the Philadelphia Eagles. Chuck takes it to the next level, and he can rub some people the wrong way.'

'To me, as a local guy, he'll always be the Last of the 60 Minute Men. He was a rock, a warrior. As a special teamer, I had to be a warrior, and he's a guy you want to emulate.'

'At the 75th anniversary celebration, it was amazing to be in their company; to be a peer, to be on the same team with Chuck Bednarik, Tommy McDonald, Steve Van Buren, Tim Brown.'

'When I was a kid, I would not have slept for a week if someone told me I would be on the same team, be part of that tradition.'

'One of the things that always amazed me about Chuck was how great a golfer he was. He was a tense competitor on the golf course; he could hit a dinky 5 wood 250 yards, but the most impressive thing was his touch around the green.'

'He was great, he used to win every goddarned tournament; everyone wanted to be on his team.'

"One thing that was funny, he wouldn't let me date any of his daughters. He said, "Don't even think about dating them.""

'I was single when I made the team, and Chuck had a motor home he brought to every game. We used to hang out, tailgate there after the game.'

'It was so different then. The whole team used to hang out and tailgate with the fans. Then we'd go out together later; someone always had a party at their house.'

'I grew up a passionate fan of Chuck Bednarik, his ferocity, his willingness to play both ways.'

'I wish he was remembered more for being the last guy to get to Jim Taylor, than for his hit on Gifford. That said it all about Chuck—how he had the energy to run him down and make that tackle. The enduring memory should be him sitting on Taylor."

Chapter | **twelve**

Hall of Fame Induction

In August, 1967, Chuck Bednarik became the second former Philadelphia Eagle to be inducted into the Pro Football Hall of Fame. Steve Van Buren, the player that Bednarik called "my hero," entered the Hall in 1965.

The Class of '67 was only the fifth enshrinement group. This was Bednarik's first year of eligibility and he was joined by Charles Bidwill, Sr., Paul Brown, Bobby Layne, Dan Reeves, Ken Strong, Joe Stydahar, and Emlen Tunnell.

Bednarik proudly finishes most of his autographs with the notation, "HOF '67," and he has been the last remaining member of that class since Brown passed away in 1991.

Bednarik was presented by his first professional coach, Greasy Neale. Bednarik returned the honor when Neale was inducted two years later.

Neale was distressed, feeling that he did not give Bednarik a deserving introduction to the Hall. A few weeks after the induction, the old coach sent a letter to Bednarik that read in part:

"I considered it a great honor to introduce you at the National Pro Hall of Fame, yet I was more than disappointed what I said about you.

'First, I want to say that I considered you the best linebacker, especially middle linebacker, that I ever saw in pro football. Your range from your position on defense was simply something beyond belief.

'...Your range was something I had not seen previously on a football field. And I doubt if I ever will see it again. Your ability was exceptional, almost abnormal.'

'I could have said all this because it was on my mind when I introduced you—about your ability, your range and your great desire to win and your 60-minute games—but people told me to make my speech short since so many had to speak. I was unlucky I came first of I would've definitely made it longer.

'But if I had it to do over again, I would give you as great a sendoff as the others received. You deserve anything I could have said about you, Chuck. You were the greatest."

COACH
NEALE

HALL
OF FAME
1967

WESTERN UNION

CLASS OF SERVICE	WESTERN UNION	SYMBOLS
This is a fast message unless by deferred character is indicated by the proper symbol.	W. P. MARSHALL CHAIRMAN OF THE BOARD — TELEGRAM — R. W. McFALL PRESIDENT JM	DL=Day Letter NL=Night Letter LT=International Letter Telegram

The filing time shown in the date line on domestic telegrams is LOCAL TIME at point of origin. Time of receipt is LOCAL ... (22)

PA193 CTD350   1967 JAN 4 PM 2 46

CT CAB016 DL PD=CANTON OHIO 4 207P EST=

CHUCK BEDNARIK (REPORT DELIVERY DONT FONE =DLR CK US CHGS)

= 1812 CANTERBURY RD ABINGTON PENN=

IT IS MY PRIVILEGED DUTY TO ADVISE THAT THE NATIONAL
BOARD OF SELECTORS HAVE UNANIMOUSLY ELECTED YOU TO PRO
FOOTBALLS HALL OF FAME. THIS IS THE HIGHEST OF ALL HONORS
IN THE GAME YOU HAVE SERVED WITH SUCH DISTINCTION. GUARD
THIS INFORMATION AT THIS TIME WITH CLOSEST CONFIDENCE
UNTIL NATIONAL PUBLICITY MEDIA IS COORDINATED. WE WILL
ADVISE OF OFFICIAL ANNOUNCEMENT DATES AND OTHER DETAILS.
HEARTIEST CONGRATULATIONS=

     DICK MCCANN DIRECTOR PRO FOOTBALL HALL OF FAME=

THE COMPANY WILL APPRECIATE SUGGESTIONS FROM ITS PATRONS CONCERNING ITS SERVICE

A. The Official Enshrinement photograph of the Class of 1966.
Front row (l to r): Bobby Layne, Ken Strong, Paul Brown, Dan Reeves
Back row: Chuck Bednarik, Emlen Tunnell, Joe Stydahar

B. Standing in front of his display
C. Wearing his HOF jacket proudly
D. Handing over his uniform after last game to be sent to the HOF in Canton.
E. His license plate - what else?
F. Friends joining him at induction ceremony

Chapter | **thirteen**

Post-Football Jobs

I f the order of employment had been reversed, Chuck Bednarik might have been known as "Cardboard Charlie," rather than the deliciously perfect moniker "Concrete Charlie." While still playing for the Eagles, Bednarik started selling concrete for the Warner Company, and Hugh Brown of the Philadelphia Inquirer seized the perfect opening, and tagged Bednarik with the "Concrete Charlie" nickname.

Bednarik stayed with Warner until the company was sold, and then moved on to sell pierogies for Mrs. Paul's. He remained in this position until the company was sold to Campbell's in 1982. He stayed close to the pierogies, as he did some promotional work for Mrs. T's.

Bednarik closed out his working years as a salesman for Regal Corrugated Cardboard before retiring in 1995.

Whatever product he was selling, very few prospective customers refused to take calls from one Charles Bednarik, as several of his former bosses and customers remember.

Domonic Toscani

Toscani became both a golfing buddy and major customer of Chuck Bednarik, when the latter was employed by Regal Corrugated Cardboard.

Paris Business Products, based in Burlington, NJ, became one of the largest accounts for Chuck Bednarik when he was a sales rep for Regal Corrugated Cardboard. Paris CEO Domonic Toscani rarely accepted cold calls from outside salespeople and had his administrative staff rigorously filter and deflect such inquiries. He bent the rules one day in the early 1980s and it later led to a call for him to receive last rites.

"Chuck phoned me one day…I used to tell my girls to say that I was busy; I avoided most sales calls.'

'One of the girls comes back and tells me that the guy on the other end said, "You tell him it's Chuck Bednarik on the phone." I said I had better take that call.'

'I've always been a frustrated football player, I love the game. I had to give him an appointment.'

'I agreed to see him, and said, "When do you want to get together? He said, "How about this afternoon?"'

'He came in that afternoon. I brought my sons and daughter in. We talked football and had him snap the ball to us. We had a great time.'

'Because of him we became a million dollar account for Regal. Chuck always did a great job; he followed-up, he was good with people, we never had to call him. It wasn't the same after Chuck retired. We eventually terminated them. He was a good man.'

'One time he came into the office and it was just me and him. He was talking about World War II. I wish I had a tape recorder that day; he was very interesting.'

'Later, we got socially acquainted. To his great horror, he had to play golf with me a few times. He didn't have a lot of patience with bad golfers; he put up with me. He also served on our board of directors.'

'He was always gracious and helped out whenever he could. One year he brought Dick Vermeil to the Union League to speak at a dinner for my family's foundation, Caritas. He gave the introduction; he was a good speaker.'

'I had two brothers who were Augustinian Priests. They became close with Chuck. I used to bring them to some of the meetings. You know how Chuck is with religion and saying the rosary.'

'One time he asked one of my brothers to hear his confession. He said the last time he was at confession was on the sideline of an Eagles game. He asked my brother to hear his confession right there. We got up and left and he gave his confession in my office.'

'He's a big golfer. I was involved with many outings for things like Villanova and Jerry Sandusky and the Second Mile. Jerry was the defensive coordinator at Penn State and he started the Second Mile.'

'I was with Chuck and Jerry at one of the Villanova outings. The three of us were talking and the Gifford hit came up. Someone said, "Let's re-enact the Gifford hit; Dom, you're Gifford."'

'A group gathers and Chuck said, "You come across the field, and I'll give you a forearm shiver". One of my brothers was there.'

'I came across the field imitating Gifford and Chuck nails me with a forearm across the chest. I don't come up. I'm lying on the ground and Chuck yells out, "You better bring Father Pete up, he needs last rites."'

'The funny thing is that he got a scratch on him, and he says, "Look at that Dom, you drew blood.'

'The next June we are at the Second Mile tournament at Penn State. I'm with Chuck and Jerry again, and there are a lot of ex-Penn State players. Someone says "Let's re-enact the Gifford hit."'

'I'm Gifford again, and I come across the field. He belts me hard…he really hit me. This time I'm down on the ground even longer.'

'I asked him, "Why did you hit me so hard?"'

'He says "You asked for it."'

'One year I brought him to the Villanova-Holy Cross game. Holy Cross was one of the best teams in the country and they were getting a lot of attention because they had a player going both ways, Gordy Lockbaum.'

'There were articles in the newspaper, and Chuck was interviewed, and he said things like, "He's not a real two-way player; he plays only a little on one side of the ball." He was always proud of being the last two-way player.'

'I set it up with coach [Andy] Talley to bring Chuck into the locker room. He gave a pre-game speech and hung on the sidelines during the game. It was a big deal because of the tie-in with Lockbaum.'

'Villanova lost, but we gave them a real good game.'

'I've met many sports celebrities and Chuck is unusual. He's a very down-to-earth tough guy. He backs up what he says, and he's a very plain-spoken person. He has no guile at all."

Bob Fox

Bob Fox, chairman and CEO of Philadelphia-based RAF Industries, was the top executive at Warner Concrete during the latter part of Chuck Bednarik's tenure with the company. It was as a sales rep at Warner that Bednarik picked up the lasting and simply perfect nickname, "Concrete Charlie." Prior to employing Bednarik, Fox had the pleasure of playing head-to-head against him college.

"There are two things I remember best about Chuck; first, he was a pussycat when it came to closing deals.'

'If he had any doubts at all about closing the deal, he'd say. "You have to come with me". He's a tough guy, but not so tough that he could stand rejection, not that any of us can. If it was a tough deal he would take me with him.'

'Second, he was a great door opener. I had hired other athletes, but he was by far the best door opener in the business. If he called to set up an appointment, well everyone wanted to meet Chuck Bednarik. And he was a great salesman; he produced some big results for us.'

"He was a great door opener. I had hired other athletes, but he was by far the best door opener in the business. If he called to set up an appointment, well everyone wanted to meet Chuck Bednarik. And he was a great salesman; he produced some big results for us."

'He just didn't like rejection.'

'He helped land a lot of big deals, and opened a lot of doors. One of the big ones was the M.H. McCloskey Company.'

'One time Chuck and I were going to a golf outing in New Jersey organized by Bob Levy. The phone rings and we get a message the Mr. McCloskey wants to see Chuck right away.'

'We turn around and go to his office. Mc-Closkey starts in, "You guys are doing a lousy job, blah, blah, blah." But it was really nothing; he just liked to see Chuck and pull his chain.'

'Chuck made contact with all the out-of-town contractors. They all knew who he was and loved to meet him.'

'Chuck invited me when he was inducted into the College Hall of Fame in 1969. He said to me, "Bob, you have to come up to the dinner," so I went with him to the Waldorf Astoria in New York.'

'It was a great affair, and after dinner Chuck said, "Let's go up to the ABC suite on the fourth floor." Monday Night Football was relatively new, and it seemed that every week Howard Cosell would tease Frank Gifford about Chuck's hit.'

'We go up to the suite, open the door, and who comes walking out, absolutely bombed, but Howard Cosell. Cosell is drunk, and Chuck walks up to him and sticks his bent finger in Cosell's face and says,

"I hit him fair and square."

'Cosell stares at him and says "Get your finger out of my proboscis"

'Cosell walks away and Chuck says to me, "What the hell is a proboscis?"

The next Monday night, Cosell mentioned running into Chuck, and I got a chuckle.'

'My on-field football memory of Chuck occurred my sophomore year at Dartmouth. We were playing at Franklin Field in front of 63,000 people. Stu Young, our starting defensive center, gets hurt and I was second string.'

'The coach, Johnny Dell' Isola, grabs me, "Foxie, you go in and submarine Bednarik." I do it, and first play he lands on me. "Bang." I have 235 pounds on top of me.'

'We're watching the movies on Monday, and the coach says "Hey Foxie, you took him out."

'I just shot the gap and submarined him all afternoon and learned what it was like to have 235 lying on top of you."

Tim Twardzik

Pierogies are a classic staple of most Slovac family kitchens. Similar to ravioli or a dumpling, these small castanets of dough can be stuffed with meat, potatoes, onions, or nearly any other refrigerator remnant.

The first big mass producer of pierogies, Mrs. T's emanated in northeast Pennsylvania, and when a certain corrugated box salesman by the name of Bednarik cold-called on them, the makings were in place for a deep working relationship. That salesman happened to be Philadelphia's most prominent Slovac athlete. Chuck and Emma Bednarik started making public appearances and doing product samplings for Mrs. T's all around the Delaware Valley.

There really was a Mrs. T, and when Mary Twardzik's son Tim graduated from college, he set out to introduce the world to those delicacies that his mother Mary produced in her kitchen and Chuck Bednarik was just the product spokesman he needed.

> **"Chuck was a classic guy, one of a kind. He was always good to Mom and Dad and our business."**

"Chuck was a classic guy, one of a kind. He was always good to Mom and Dad and our business.'

'We first met when he sold us corrugated packaging. We used to tell him, "You're not Concrete Charlie any more, your're Cardboard Charlie.'

'After one of the early sales calls, we had lunch with Chuck. Our favorite part of having Chuck come up to our place came after sales calls. We weren't very fancy when it came to wining and dining.'

'He wanted to take us out, and we said we want to take you to a restaurant. We took him to Joseph Romanelli's in Shenadoah. It was nothing fancy; he made 120 sandwiches everyday, and when he ran out, that was it, he closed up shop for the day. You walk in grab one of his sandwiches and a soda and sit down.'

'Chuck loved the place, and Joe Romanelli was a big sports nut. He could talk to Chuck for hours.

Chuck asked, "Where am I?" This place had one table and three chairs.'

'Romanelli couldn't get over that "'the greatest football player in the world is here in my hoagie shop" and he knew all about Chuck's career and was talking about all his games with the Eagles.'

'Chuck comes up the next week, and we go back to Romanelli's, and now Joe is talking to him about all of his Penn games.'

'A few weeks later, Chuck says that he has to bring his wife Emma up to visit Romanelli's. We go in, and now he's talking about Chuck's high school stories. He knew all about Chuck from high school to the pros.'

'Emma came to work for us doing food shows, trade show demonstrations and store samplings. Chuck would attend a lot of the events with her, and of course that always attracted a crowd.'

'We knew Chuck loved golf, and we wanted to work with him with golf somehow. We had a big yellow bag made for him with our name on it; I feel bad for any caddy who had to carry it. And we wanted to have a set of clubs made for him.'

'We talked to a local club maker and he told us to bring Chuck in. We bring Chuck in and he says, "I want graphite shafts." The pro told him, "No, you're too strong, you swing the club like a 45-year old man, you need steel shafts."

'Chuck was about 70 at the time, and he was glowing and all proud when the pro told him that.'

'Once he brought Dick Vermiel to our pierogie plant. We put Chuck and Vermiel on the line packing pierogies. The employees got a great kick out of that.'

'They weren't as quick or efficient and the women on the line. You could say they "failed their tryout."

George Piszek

The eldest son of the founder of Mrs. Paul's, George Piszek had a memorable motorhome ride with Chuck Bednarik when they drove to New York to promote the company's line of pierogies.

The eldest son of Mrs. Paul's founder, Edward Piszek, George Piszek was in charge of sales and marketing for the company. He worked with Chuck Bednarik when the company hired him to help promote their new line of frozen pierogies.

"Chuck Bednarik, the football player is one thing, but he's a good man and a good American."

'When Mrs. Paul's was getting away from all fish and into pierogies, Dad brought Chuck in to help with sales of that and other products.'

'He was looking for extra work; he was an ethnic guy, a big name, and was perfect for promoting pierogies. He'd do food shows and demonstrations for us.'

> **"He was working with the Eagles as an honorary coach—it's wonderful what Dick Vermiel did in bringing him back. Whenever Chuck was on the road with the Eagles we would send him to see customers."**

'He had a relationship with my father Ed. Chuck was Slovak, my father Polish. They were good acquaintances and had a nice respect for each other.'

'They were both good men. They both worked themselves up from nothing, were good Christians, church-going people. They might throw out a few curses, but they never missed mass.'

'He was working with the Eagles as an honorary coach—it's wonderful what Dick Vermiel did in bringing him back. Whenever Chuck was on the road with the Eagles we would send him to see customers.'

'He was an ambassador for Mrs. Pauls. All the buyers knew who he was and they loved to reminisce. He was revered, one of a kind. The 60 minutes, the championship, the big plays, look at those achievements.'

'He did a good job for us.'

'He'd do his own thing. He might be down in Dallas; he'd meet the local sales guy and take him out.'

'He had them eating out of his hand. He might give them a copy of his book. He was smart enough not to ruffle the home team.'

'Even in those days he might lament about players'

salaries. Now he has even more to bitch about–that was 20, 30 years ago.'

'We would play in golf outings; he hit the ball a mile, with a beautiful soft, smooth swing. He had a swing like a 150 pounder. He was a great golfer.'

'I headed up sales and marketing. I remember a funny story. We were putting on a new broker to rep our lines in New York. We were going to the Rye Hilton for a big dog and pony show. There were about six or seven of us. This was New York Giant country.'

'Chuck says, "Lets go up in my Winnebago, I'll drive." We said "Oh, fine."

"All the way up we're listening to his Oom Pah music. That's all he played the whole way. We get into the parking lot at the Rye Hilton, and for some reason you couldn't open the door from the inside or out.'

'We're stuck in the parking lot with Oom Pah music playing. We have a bunch of business guys in suits backing out of a small window, with this music playing–very unprofessional. A crowd is gathering to watch us, and of course everyone knew who he was when he came through the window.'

'In our day he was probably a bit more mellowed. He was in his element with Vermiel. Everyone liked him when he was with Mrs. Pauls.'

'He sponsored me at Whitemarsh Country Club. There was some kind of NFL Alumni Golf Outing and some ex-player came over to Chuck and told him that it looked like he had put on weight.'

'The next eight holes, he kept saying to me, "George, does it look like I put on weight?" He was bent out of shape all afternoon, because someone told him he looked out of shape.'

'He's a great guy, a lot of fun, and he was perfect for the job. He's still the number one Eagle.'

'I was always impressed with how tough he was, a real Pennsylvania guy.'

'He used to tell me how scared and frightened he was on that bomber crew in World War II, going out on every mission, not knowing what he faced.'

'I always asked Chuck football questions, and I always remember two things that he said.' First, I remember him remarking that the big linemen in his day were big, fat guys. Today the big linemen are strong and fast. He said he would have a tough time because the game had changed so much."

'Second, I asked him who was the best player he played against. He said, "Jim Brown, that guy, it hurt to take him down."

'Vermiel was a wonderful guy; he made Chuck feel like a million dollars. He made him a part of the team.'

'I took some customers to Lehigh to see training camp, and they put us in a roped-off area. They don't understand the alumni. I know a lot of the alumni are crushed; they don't feel like they are treated like Eagles.'

'The Phillies take care of the alumni. They are a class act; they gave World Series rings to guys like Robin Roberts and Jim Bunning. It's a nice thing; that's how it's supposed to be done.'

'With my dad, the Mrs. Paul's alumni were members for life. They could always come home."

Bill Piszek

Another son of the founder of Mrs. Paul's, Bill worked with Bednarik when he was employed there.

"Chuck was a friend of my father. I remember my dad being a sports fan; he loved the Phillies and the Eagles. My dad being Polish, being a working man, was drawn to Chuck.'

"He's a throwback, the epitome of a middle linebacker. He's every bit that cantankerous, tough. As a kid, I was intimidated.'

'He and my dad became great friends and when we developed pierogies we thought of Chuck to market them. He figured it would be tough to say no to Chuck Bednarik.'

'Everybody knew Chuck, that pinkie. He would talk to the sales force; everybody wanted to know about the Gifford hit. That was Chuck; he really started the whole New York-Philadelphia rivalry, he made it fun.'

'He and my dad were buddies. They were similar men, they knew what they wanted. That mold is now broken.'

'People used to tell my dad that he couldn't do it, Poles couldn't do it. The Russians had kept the Poles down. It was tough to survive. Dad came from a big family, five sisters.'

'He got roughed up a bit, but he started the business and he deserves a lot of credit. He was hard working, loyal and dedicated.'

'That was a generation of hard work, and he and Chuck took to each other. We'd get on Chuck about the new generation of football players; we loved getting him worked up about Deion Sanders. Boy, did Deion set him off. You didn't want to mess with Chuck at 70.'

'He's the genuine article."

Paul Anthony

A supermarket owner in northeastern Pennsylvania, Anthony was a customer of Chuck Bednarik's when he was selling Mrs. Paul's pierogies.

"He comes here to visit a lot. I always enjoy seeing him and Emma. I started following him at Penn, and then I had season tickets to the Eagles. He's very religious. Sometimes I stop down and see him in church. We became good friends. My parents are from Czechoslovakia, the same village as Chuck's parents.'

'I saw him at a game in Buffalo and we got drunk with Howard Cosell. He was drunk, and he was sparking things up with Chuck. He said he had just come from a big fight, and he was talking about how he always has to tell it like it is.'

'I said to him, "How the hell can you tell it like it is, you don't know anything?"

'Chuck is panicked. He says, "Don't; Oh my God, you're gonna ruin me. He's going to destroy me on the air."

'Cosell goes up to the booth for the game and on the air he says to Gifford, "I just ran into Chuckles Bednarik; he really put you on your back."

'He came by my store when he used to sell pierogies for Mrs. Paul's. He'd stay at my house when he did demonstrations in my supermarket. We had the best sales with him there. He drew a terrific crowd.'

'He'd attract a great crowd. They'd be yelling, "Oh, go, yeah!" He'd cook the pierogies and sample them out.'

'He was giving demonstrations and for spite the Mrs. T's guys came in and pulled out their pierogies in front of him. Later they became the best of friends when Chuck was selling boxes. He went in to see them and Mrs. T's bought boxes from him."

Jim Andrew

The regional marketing director for Mrs. Paul's, Andrew sent Chuck Bednarik to football cities all over the country to promote the company's pierogies.

As sales manager for Mrs. Paul's, Jim Andrew supervised and worked with Chuck Bednarik, when the latter was employed to be a pierogie pitchman for the company.

"I was headquartered in LA at the time, the mid-to late 1970s, and was responsible for the Midwest sales for Mrs. Paul's. The Piszeks hired Chuck to do promotional and public relations work.'

'We'd schedule appointments for him in Midwestern cities, and whenever the buyers found out Chuck Bednarik was coming, the response was always, "Yeah, we'll see you there."

'Chuck was welcomed in the Midwest, especially the football cities—Kansas City, Dallas, Houston, Chicago, Milwaukee. These were not just 'get acquainted' functions; they were full presentations. They were set up to sell, and when Chuck was there we almost always increased business.'

'Chuck would spend a minimum 20, 30 minutes with the buyers. Other celebrity types might only spend 10, 15 minutes.'

> **"At the sales meetings, he would be talking, and he'd set in a football position with his feet about three or four feet apart and he'd stick out that right hand with those fingers. He was a rough-looking guy and it was like he was challenging guys to take hits at him."**

'He was a salesman, a natural in front of the trade, a big imposing man, a bruiser of a character.'

'One year, we were holding a national sales meeting in Philadelphia. The meeting ran from about eight in the morning to 3:30. We broke up and were scheduled to get together again about 7:00 p.m. for cocktails and dinner. Chuck said he was going to go home and would meet up with us later.'

'He shows up about 6:45, covered with bruises and scratches. "What happened to you?"

He tells us, "I was driving away from the hotel and couple of young guys in their 20's cut me off at a stop sign I got out of the car and we started fighting. One of them yelled out, "Hey that's Chuck Bednarik and they stopped. I told them that if it was only one of them I would have kicked his ass, but together they were pretty tough."

'He said that when he got home his wife started yelling at him, "You can't do this, you're 56 years old."

'I remember he could be foul-mouthed around the sales guys, and when his wife was around she'd tell him to cut it out.'

'At the sales meetings, he would be talking, and he'd set in a football position with his feet about three or four feet apart and he'd stick out that right hand with those fingers. He was a rough-looking guy and it was like he was challenging guys to take hits at him."

'He was 6' 4", 235, and carried himself like a big man; the trade loved him, especially in the NFL cities.'

'He was a real benefit to Mrs. Paul's; he more than earned his money. He generated real sales and increased profits. And he was just a good guy.'

'He didn't like softies, didn't like soft players, didn't like soft salespeople. If you didn't give 110%, you weren't his type of guy.'

'How could you not like a guy like Chuck? He was a storyteller, a natural salesman, a man's man—he carried a room.'

'One time, we were at a party at George Piszek's house. George would pick up small bottles of booze, and put them in baskets around the basement. He'd have a half dozen or more varieties.'

'One of the Mrs. Paul's guys was pocketing some of the booze. Chuck goes over to him and says, "Hey asshole; there's a sign there that says, "Food and drink must be consumed on the premises."

Chapter | fourteen

Chuck the Sportscaster

Chuck Bednarik was one of the first Philadelphia athletes to sit in front of a camera when he was hired by WFIL-TV (Channel 6) to handle the weekend sports reports and serve as a fill-in for lead sportscaster Les Keiter.

He wasn't naturally glib or relaxed, but no one worked harder at improving the craft. Most mornings, when his daughters came down for breakfast, Bednarik had five new words printed on cards that they all, himself included, had to pronounce with carefully defined precision.

There are those who believe he worked too hard at turning himself into one of the personality-free, monotone newsreaders of the day. If Bednarik had entered broadcasting later, when announcers were encouraged to blend their personality into their delivery, he may have developed into a Tom Brookshier-type sportscaster.

Bednarik tried too hard to be Chet Huntley and after a little more than two years on the job, he left at his choosing. One factor was money.

"'He left because it was getting to be too much driving back and forth to the studio," recalled Emma Bednarik. "They were only paying him something like $25 a shift. I had told him it wasn't worth it, but he kept saying, "It's good money." They wouldn't give him more money and he got tired and left."

He returned to the airways in 1976 when he and Al Meltzer served as the original hosts of the long-running HBO series, "Inside the NFL."

In addition to his sportscasts, Bednarik was also a frequent guest host on the popular after school kids' show, Sally Starr.

While his broadcast career was brief, Bednarik is well-remembered by those who worked with him.

Doing sports commentary on WKBS-TV channel 48

Al Meltzer

Veteran Philadelphia sportscaster, Al Meltzer, alongside Bednarik, was the first co-host of HBO's "Inside the NFL."

"Big Al" Meltzer and Chuck Bednarik were the first hosts of HBO's long running "Inside the NFL," which was the first cable television show devoted to sports. A long time sports anchor and announcer, Meltzer arrived in Philadelphia in 1964 and spent nearly 40 years on the local airwaves. Now retired, he splits the year between suburban Philadelphia and Florida.

"Chuck Bednarik was one of the greats. We worked together for the first season of "Inside the NFL" on HBO. Chuck had been doing the sports at Channel 6, so he was very familiar with the mechanics of TV.

'He understood the camera and he was just Chuck. He never tried to be anyone other than himself.'

"He was always the same on the air. He'd ask questions, give opinions, make predictions. He knew football more than any human being.'

'The show was unscripted and he always had the answers. It was a brand new show. It would open with a shot of us sitting there in bad suits. Chuck was always prepared, maybe over prepared. It might take him half an hour to say hello. If you wanted him to say something in half and hour, you allowed an hour.'

'I like him a great deal. He's a very honest guy and he has very strong feelings about things. He tells you exactly what he thinks even if it doesn't sit well with other people.'

'His feelings about things—his relationship with the Eagles—they come and go. He says he wants them to lose the Super Bowl, but he's proud to be part of the tradition.'

'He's as honest as anyone; you may not agree, but you're getting it straight.'

'Working with him on TV, I always found him to be a nice guy. I liked him; he was a hero, everyone in Philadelphia knew Chuck Bednarik.'

'We would give our predictions every week and he was always very definite about his selections. If I didn't pick the same winner as him, he took issue.'

'He is the most recognized athlete in Philadelphia. Chuck Bednarik is bigger than life in this city. A Hall of Famer, the 60 Minute Man, the best defensive player in the NFL.'

'He's been around so long, and he's so vocal. I had a memorable time sitting with him. He never hid his feelings. That's Chuck Bednarik. I was always very impressed to be sitting next to Chuck Bednarik.'

'He was much better on this type of spontaneous show than he was in a structured format. This was his element. He was comfortable. He was home. He was pro football.'

'I can tell you, he was 180 degrees different from what he was in a news studio. Given the right format and coaching, he could have been a great analyst like Brookie."

Francis Davis

A Drexel professor who was also the Channel 6 weatherman when Chuck Bednarik was doing sports reports for the station in the 1960s.

If anyone played the role of Professor Henry Higgins while Chuck Bednarik was a sportscaster for Channel 6 in Philadelphia, it was Francis Davis. Davis was the Philadelphia's first on-air meteorologist.

He also served as a meteorologist during World War II in the same branch of service as Bednarik, the Army Air Corp.

Davis was a professor at Drexel University and became the Dean of the College of Sciences during the time he was giving the weather forecasts at Channel 6. Bednarik had respect for Davis as a university professor. In an effort to improve his on-air performance, Bednarik often discussed vocabulary and pronunciation with Davis.

Davis is 91 years old and resides in Myrtle Beach, S.C.

"I remember Chuck Bednarik very well. He took great pleasure in coming up behind me and lifting me off the floor.'

'I worked with him on his English. He was very conscious of the way he spoke. He always tried to make sure he did things the right way. I sat down with him between shows to help him with his enunciation and pronunciation. I was very fond of him.'

'I was a college professor and he thought I could help him. To a slight degree he was self-conscious. He wanted to be sure he was right. He was never completely sure of himself. He was a husky, strong guy, but very gentle.'

'He was trying to shift the emphasis from football to public speaking and he looked to me for help. I guess you could say he looked to me as a mentor. He respected me as a college professor."

Larry Kane

As a young anchor man on WFIL-TV in the 1960s, Kane often shared the news set with sportscaster Chuck Bednarik.

Known as The Dean of Philadelphia Television Broadcasters, Larry Kane was 23 when he joined WFIL as an anchor in 1966. While he was new to the city, Kane was aware of the local legend who was doing weekend sports reports in the same studio. The young anchor and sportscaster Chuck Bednarik struck a friendship during those years at WFIL.

"I got to the station in 1966; I was 23 years old. Chuck had been there for about a year or two ahead of me. I was on the fast track as anchor and he was the weekend sports reporter, sitting in for Les Keiter.'

'Lew Klein, who had been two years behind Chuck at Penn, hired him to do sports. This was a time when stations were starting to bring athletes on to do the sports reports. '

'At first, Chuck was ill-equipped for what he did. He was rough around the edges, didn't know the mechanics of anchoring. He could talk sports, but he flubbed a lot. He would make it worse by getting angry at himself on the air.'

'I was young and scared and tended to crack up easily. Chuck didn't come off as being bright on the air. He wasn't fluent, somewhat gruff, but he is very bright. He had a lot of 'dese' and 'dose.''

'He massacred the English language, but that was what was great about him. He had only been on the air for one or two years, and nobody worked harder than him.'

'Running into him was one of my most delightful things. I learned his attitude about sports. He was a whirling dervish, full of energy. He was an imposing figure in the newsroom.'

'Working with Chuck Bednarik was very important to me; he was one of the great football players in the world.'

'He laughed a lot; he had a great sense of humor. He would prod me about being so serious about the news. To me the news was everything.'

'He called me "newsboy." I thought that was pretty funny.'

'In those days the newsrooms were really buttoned down and at time he felt uncomfortable. He was concerned that people might view him as less than adequate. He may have sometimes felt unworthy in the newsroom environment and he didn't always take input very well.'

'He knew his sports and he shined on the air when talking football. He had guests on the set like Jerry Wolman and Sonny Jurgensen, and he really shined in that element.'

'He was great when he was allowed to be himself, but they tried to make him be what they thought he should look like. They tried to turn him into something he wasn't—a polished sportscaster.'

'He would have been so much better if he had encouraged to talk like he talked. They wanted the All-American look in those days. They wanted everyone to look and sound the same.'

'I was Jewish; when I started there had never been a Jewish person on air in Philadelphia. They said I had a long nose, was too young-looking. Plastic surgery was suggested.'

'In those days he could have been sent to school to develop his own style. He could have been a forerunner to John Madden and Jimmy Johnson if he had been allowed to do his own thing. In those days you weren't allowed to develop your own act. A Terry Bradshaw or Howie Long would have never made it.'

'Chuck was gruff, tough—they should have said 'perfect', let him do his own thing. They didn't think of it in those days. Newsmen didn't even smile.'

'There were some big issues in the newsroom about how he was managed. He would throw some temper tantrums in the newsroom, not because he was a star or an egoist, but because of the way he was handled. He did not get the support that he needed.'

'He could get pissed off. One day I thought he was going to throw Rick Reedman across the room.'

'He would get upset with himself; he was competitive and wanted to be good at everything. He needed someone to guide him better. He should have been given his own weekly football show as a commentator/anchor. He should have been allowed to develop his skills with something he was comfortable with.'

'He was a vibrant, electrifying guy with football. He could have been one of the first great ones if he had been used as a football analyst."

Lew Klein

Lew Klein made his mark in local television as the executive producer of American Bandstand when it originated in Philadelphia. He was also program director of WFIL-TV from 1957-1969, during which time he was instrumental in hiring Chuck Bednarik to be a weekend sportscaster. Klein graduated from the University of Pennsylvania in 1949, the same year as Bednarik. He also taught at Temple for more than 50 years and the schools annually give the Lew Klein Alumni in Media Award to honor the achievements of the school's graduates.

"We needed someone to share the load with Les Keiter and Chuck came to Channel 6 to do weekend sports. I was involved in his hiring. He was a great name in Philadelphia, a sports icon. He and I had gone to Penn at the same time.'

operation. He wanted to be a success, wanted go do a good job.'

'He came into see me one day, not too long after he joined the station. He wanted to talk about a raise. He hadn't been there long, and while he was good, I wouldn't say he was a roaring success.'

'I asked him 'Why do you want a raise so soon?"

He said, "I'm not sure I should ask right now, but my wife Emma said I should."

'I got a kick out of him, "my wife said I deserve a raise." As big as he is, Emma was the boss.'

'He was a giant of a man, with a wife and five daughters. As great as he was he was, dominated by a house of females.'

'He lived in Abington, was friendly with Stan Lopata and Granny Hamner. He and

"We needed someone to share the load with Les Keiter and Chuck came to Channel 6 to do weekend sports. I was involved in his hiring. He was a great name in Philadelphia, a sports icon. He and I had gone to Penn at the same time."

'In an effort to boost the news, we felt that having a popular guy, identified with sports, was a good thing to do.'

'He had no training in broadcasting. He was inexperienced on the air, but we felt he was so sincere he would appeal to viewers. Things went well.'

'If you talk to people today, many of them don't know who he is, but he was a leading personality in the city at that time, and he was certainly well-received.'

'He was straightforward. He gave an honest, sincere, open effort and he came across well.

'Chuck is Chuck, and he sometimes mispronounced names, but he was very sincere at wanting to be good. He did not take it lightly and worked hard within the broadcast

Emma loved hosting parties; they loved company. '

"I always enjoyed being around him. Chuck was so likable. People take to him quickly and like having him around.'

'He worked hard at doing well. He worked at being a straight broadcaster. If he had come around later, he could have been a Madden, Vermiel, McCarver. If he had let his personality come out in his broadcasting, he would have been more successful in the long run. He could have made it on personality.'

'He tried to be a polished broadcaster because that was what was expected in the day. He tried to fit the mold. He wanted to be a success by the standards of the day, and being very competitive, he would get very upset with himself."

Sally Starr

This host of a popular after school television program remembers Chuck Bednarik as her favorite guest host.

The 1950s and '60s were the Golden Age of kids' afternoon television and Philadelphia boasted one the of the nation's most endearing hosts, the cowgirl, Sally Starr. In addition to providing moral guidance and stressing good behavior, she also introduced an eager generation to the likes of the Three Stooges and Popeye. She often invited special guests to spend the afternoon with a live audience and thousands of young viewers from Allentown to Cape May. Some of these guests included Dick Clark, Jerry Lewis, Larry Fine and even Colonel Sanders.

But, according to Our Gal Sal, her favorite guest host was Chuck Bednarik. In one of those timeless gifts of incongruity, Concrete Charlie was more Captain Kangaroo when he shared the stage with the woman who often wished "Love, Luck and Lollipops." The five Bednarik girls were born between 1950 and 1961, placing them square in the midst of this afterschool television generation. They often looked forward to accompanying their father to Sally Starr's show.

"Chuck Bednarik was always on the show. He would help me with the announcements.'

'Every year we used to celebrate my birthday on the show and one year Chuck

"He was very good with kids; he took time to talk to them on their level. He was better than any guest I had. He and I had a mutual feeling about the show."

and I took the cake to an orphanage. There were about 40 kids. They loved him.'

'Later on, one of the kids came to my house after he had grown up and still remembered Chuck.'

'Another time, we took kids to a ballgame on the bus. Chuck was a nice guy.'

'He was very good with kids; he took time to talk to them on their level. He was better than any guest I had. He and I had a mutual feeling about the show.'

'He used to announce the cartoons and one afternoon he got a real timid kid to come up and do the announcing. He said to the kid, "Maybe someday you can do what Aunt Sally does."

'He brought out the best in kids.'

'Kids used to ask him, "Why do they call you cement man?"

'He would tell them his name was 'Concrete Charlie, and explain the difference between concrete and cement."

Chapter | **fifteen**

The Media Remembers

W hile Chuck Bednarik was never regarded as a self-promoter who sought out media attention, he is remembered by sportswriters, columnists and sportscasters as a cooperative athlete who respected reporters and gave honest and thoughtful answers. Some, such as Steve Sabol of NFL Films, often found themselves spending excessive time in the editing room, as some of Bednarik's statements were a bit too blunt and earthy for everyday ears.

Photo: Michael Persico

Ray Didinger

This Hall of Fame football writer helped forge a détente between Chuck Bednarik and the Eagle's organization after the former complained about them not buying his first book.

R ay Didinger is a member of the Pro Football Hall of Fame for his distinguished work in covering Eagles for the Philadelphia Bulletin and Philadelphia Daily News. He was also an Emmy award wining writer and producer for NFL films. Currently he is seen and heard in the Philadelphia area on WIP radio and on Comcast Sportsnet.

He is also a passionate devotee of the history and tradition of professional football. He probably knows and understands Chuck Bednarik better than any media person.

A few years ago Chuck got himself exiled to the land of persona non grata with the Eagles. At the opening night celebration for Lincoln Financial Field, any reference to Chuck was conspicuously absent in the salute to the teams history. A supersized mural of him doing the Gifford hop hangs at the main entrance to the stadium, but on opening night when the teams' all-time greats were feted, Chuck was nowhere to be found. Things like that tend to happen when you publicly and continuously criticize the owner in most uncomplimentary terms for, among other things, passing on the opportunity to buy a copy of your book for all the members of the team.

Some public feedback was leveled at Chuck, "Why can't he be more gracious. Why is he so bitter, why doesn't he stop complaining."

An epiphany, primarily inspired by Emma and a friend, began to take a hold in Chuck. He decided to write

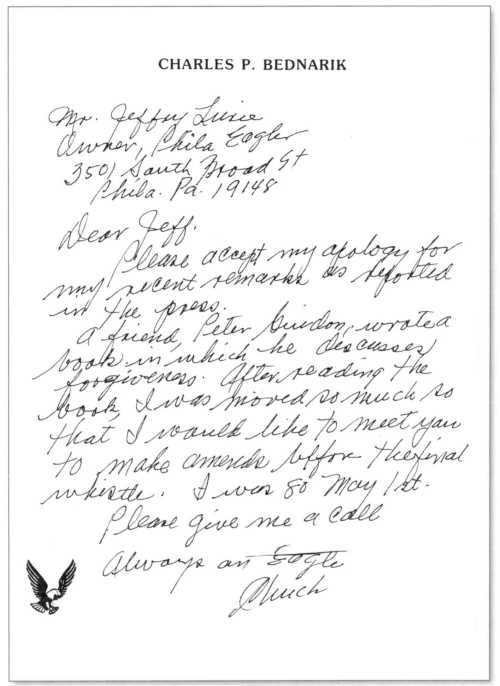

CHARLES P. BEDNARIK

Mr. Jeffry Lurie
Owner, Phila Eagles
3501 South Broad St
Phila. Pa. 19148

Dear Jeff,

Please accept my apology for my recent remarks as reported in the press.

A friend, Peter Gordon, wrote a book in which he discusses forgiveness. After reading the book, I was moved so much so that I would like to meet you to make amends before the final whistle. I was 80 May 1st.

Please give me a call

Always an Eagle

Chuck

Handwritten note delivered to Mr. Lurie by Ray Didinger

a letter in terms that were as apologetic and contrite as Charles Philip Bednarik can express. He tried to tell Jeff Lurie that he was truly sorry for his words.

The letter was placed in an envelope and sent certified to the Eagles office.

A few days later the letter was returned to sender, unopened.

Maybe it was a clerical error. Maybe some noticed the name on the return address and thought it best to not expose Lurie or an administrative person to what be an incendiary letter bomb. Whatever the reason, the letter was bounced back, the pin still in the grenade.

With the letter back in his hands, Bednarik believed he was now permanently, indelibly done with the team for good. They won't accept my apology; I'm through. His peace-seeking efforts were ignored.

Ernie Montella, a founder and active member of the Philadelphia's A's Historic Society, is one of the great sportsman this city has produced. He and most of the senior members of the Society preserve, protect and promote the tradition and history of all Philadelphia sports, not just baseball.

The story of the unopened letter was recounted to Montella during a casual conversation. Without assigning right or wrong, he understood that the situation should be remedied. The Legend can be gruff at times, but his old fans hate to see him estranged from the franchise he helped build.

Montella said there is only guy who can repair this unfortunate mess — Ray Didinger.

Didinger did not have to get involved; most people would probably think it wasn't worth the bother.

They might have also thought that Chuck had it coming; I'm not getting near this.

Without condoning this words or actions, Didinger understood as well as anyone that Chuck just says things. He also recognized what Bednarik meant to Eagles football and the city of Philadelphia, and took on the rule of détente negotiator.

> **"Chuck steps in and says, 'No, no, this is how you do it.' He sets up over the ball and launched a perfect snap back to the holder. He hadn't done it in I don't know how many years and the put the ball right on the money."**

He spoke to the Eagles, got them to accept the letter, and Bednarik was back in the family.

Eagles management chose the magnanimous route and in general has been well-received by the franchise in recent years. His picture can be found all over their offices at the NovaCare Center. Andy Reid still makes sure he gets a personal invitation to visit training camp. Harold Carmichael, head of the team's alumni organization, has openly praised Bednariks's importance to the history and tradition of the franchise.

Ray Didinger understood that it would not be right to have the book closed on Chuck Bednarik, with the guy who many consider to be "Mr. Eagle" standing in a bitter exile from the franchise that he so clearly defined.

"My first memories of Chuck Bednarik are of going to Eagles training camp in Hershey. I used to go up every summer with my parents and grandparents. We would make a mini-vacation of it and spend a few days.'

'We would time the visits around picture day. That was the day the team would come out in full uniform for press pictures. Things were much more open and accessible in those days and they would let the fans on the field with their cameras. When I was about 8 or 9 years old, I first got my picture taken with Chuck Bednarik, and after that I always got my picture taken with him.'

'He and Tommy McDonald were the most popular players, but they were all amazingly approachable. They were just working class guys who didn't view themselves as anything special. They were all very gracious.'

'As a professional, I met up with Chuck again in 1970. I was with the Bulletin and was assigned to cover training camp at Albright College. Chuck was brought in for few weeks during camp to work with the centers and linebackers. Jerry Williams was the coach, Pete Retzlaff the general manager, and they had been teammates with Chuck.'

'I have two vivid memories of that camp. The first was on the practice field. The centers were working on long snaps with the special teams.'

'Chuck steps in and says, "No, no, this is how you do it." He sets up over the ball and launched a perfect snap back to the holder. He hadn't done it in I don't know how many years and the put the ball right on the money.'

'Not only was it accurate, but he knew the rotation of the ball so well. The holder didn't have to spin the ball to get the laces lined up right when he set it down. He had been out of the game seven years, and I'm sure he didn't practice during that time. He was the best long snapper in camp.'

'My second memory of that camp was at the team hotel. He had the room next to me at Holiday Inn at Reading. I'm walking by his room one night and the door was open. He was watching the Phillies on television and he said, "Why don't you come in and watch the game with me."

'I'm watching the game with him; it's just me and the legend. I remembered meeting him as a kid and this was real thrill. He was larger than life.'

'He wasn't around the team after Williams was let go. I'm not sure what happened. He can perceive things as insults. Leonard Tose could be abrupt with people.'

'The team hadn't played well in recent years and it seemed that Tose cleaned house of the old Eagles.

'Williams, Retzlaff, Khayatt were all let go. These guys had been teammates of Chuck; they were the guys he was comfortable with.'

'Mike McCormack was brought in and he brought in guys with no Eagles history like Walt Michaels and John Sandusky. The entire staff was made up of guys with no Eagles history.'

'It might have bothered him that all of his friends were dissed. The new group had no relationship with him and may have not seen any value in having him around. The new staff never extended him an offer and you didn't see him around the team for three years.'

'In '76, Dick Vermiel came in and said we want you to be part of the family. Vermiel said, "You're Mr. Eagle, you're the glory of the franchise. You were with the last two championship teams and we want you around as someone the team can look up to."'

'He was at every game charting the plays for Vermiel. Dick had him speak to the team, tell them about himself.'

> **"In '76, Dick Vermiel came in and said we want you to be part of the family. Vermiel said, "You're Mr. Eagle, you're the glory of the franchise. You were with the last two championship teams and we want you around as someone the team can look up to."**

'One year during training camp at Widener, Vermiel had a family night and all the wives were invited for dinner. It was a nice affair, table cloths, silverware. Chuck brought his accordion and played music through the evening. Everyone got a kick out of that.'

'(Bill) Bergey always went up to Chuck before the game and put his arm around him. He would tell him that it was nice to have him around. The guys who got it understood what it meant to have Chuck around. It was a cool thing just having him there.'

'Bill's feelings about Chuck may have changed in later years because of some of the things that Chuck said, but at the time around '79-'81, Bill identified with Chuck. People talked about Bill being the reincarnation of Chuck and he liked the comparison.'

'It's not surprising that he might have rubbed some people the wrong way. He's a perfectionist and he cares deeply about the Eagles and about how the game should be played. You couldn't think that his emotions wouldn't surface. He is going to have the same reaction on the sideline that he had as a player. He was a most ferocious competitor.'

'I don't think Chuck made a lot of friends when he played, but he earned pure professional respect. Because he didn't make a lot friends, the guys who speak out about his ability do so out of real appreciation.'

'When Dick left, I think Chuck just had enough. After seven years he was tired. I don't know that it was a case of not wanting Chuck around. Tose could be moody and Chuck was outspoken. He was there because of Dick; his loyalty was to Dick.'

'Chuck also speaks very well of Andy Reid. He came from Green Bay where they do a good job of keeping guys in the flow; they bring the old guys back.'

'Where there's history, you look to Chuck. I give Andy credit. Especially with the Eagles training in Bethlehem, he's reached out to Chuck and offered him something to do. Even through his rifts with Jeff Lurie, Chuck always had good things to say about Andy.'

'I am glad to have played a part in rebuilding the bridge between Chuck and the Eagles. You wouldn't want to drive a tractor trailer across, but the bridge is up and you can walk over it.'

'It is good that Chuck can be around the Eagles and keep his head up and feel comfortable.'

'When you mention the all-time great players—any time, any position, any era—Chuck Bednarik is among the greatest who ever played.'

'When people retell things, the legends tend to get exaggerated. Chuck Bednarik is one of the very few cases where the actual accomplishments were greater than the legend. What's been lost is not just that he played two-ways, but how great he played.'

'He was almost playing out of position, but he made all the big plays in 1960 – knocking Hornung out of the championship game, causing Mel Triplett to fumble against the Giants, the Gifford hit, the final tackle on Taylor.'

'It's not just that he played two-ways; he made the plays that turned the season around. The plays he made were Roy Hobbs stuff. To do it at 25 years old would have been extraordinary; but to play 60 minutes at 35?'

'It was an amazing feat, even in that era. We'll never see it again. Think about it in context of today's game, as part of a championship season; it would never happen.'

'He looked larger that life to me at 8 and he looks the same today. It's interesting; it still excites people to see him, whether it's at the Hall of Fame in Canton, at the stadium, at training camp.'

> **"When you mention the all-time great players—any time, any position, any era—Chuck Bednarik is among the greatest who ever played."**

'It pained me to see him say some of things that he did in recent years. There were bad feelings there. It would have been terribly sad if he had passed away estranged from the Eagles.'

'I got involved in repairing things with the Eagles, because I felt it was important. I feel good that he is back on good terms and can talk to Jeff (Lurie).'

'He embodies the best part of this history of this team."

Steve Sabol

Steve Sabol has won 30 Emmy awards in appreciation of his presentations of the National Football League. He realized early on that Chuck Bednarik was one of the first players who understood the drama of the game and its hold on the public, and was able to discuss it basic elements with the flair of a showman.

'I have a couple of memories of the first game my father took me to in 1952 or '53. The Redskins were playing the Eagles at Shibe Park. The Redskins came out on the field and there were two things my father said to me.'

'The first was "See Number 33, that's Sammy Baugh." That was like pointing out the Washington Monument or the Lincoln Memorial. Even at age 10 or so, I knew what Sammy Baugh meant.'

'The second was when the Eagles were kicking off. He said, "See Number 60, he will kick off and make the tackle." How many guys kick off and make the tackle, but this was the early '50s. "Watch Number 60." He made the tackle and it made an incredible impression on me as a kid.'

'Longfellow said, "In this world a man must either be anvil or hammer." Chuck Bednarik was both; he could dish out and handle it.'

'In spite of the Gifford hit, Chuck was not really a big hit guy. Other than Gifford, he smothered, mashed guys with those powerful arms and big hands. The epitome was his tackle on Jim Taylor; he was more of a big, strong, bear hug guy.'

'Life was one long responsibility for him and he met all of them—growing up in Bethlehem, the war. When Bob Pellegrini goes, he steps in.'

'1960 was one long drama playing out in Philadelphia. It was larger than the game, Chuck Bednarik playing two ways every week.'

"My favorite photo of him, I remember that far out shot. Guys going in, guys going out and one guy standing on the field.'

'That performance in the 1960 champi-onship is close to a holy moment in pro football.'

'He was the last warrior with Ray Nitschke. He had a grandeur about him. When he left, something rode out with him that will never be present in football again. He took it with him.'

'Chuck Bednarik had a great passion for the sport. He also had a certain theatrical sense. He understood the x's and o's, but he also recognized the drama of the sport.'

'One of the first interviews we did at NFL Films was on linebackers. Our studio was still in Philadelphia and Chuck was there to be interviewed. We were having a problem with the cameras and had to delay the shooting. We had about a one hour wait, so we took Chuck to Bookbinder's for lunch. Of course he had a couple of martinis and that helped loosen him up.'

'We got him back in the studio and it was one of our most memorable interviews ever. He's talking about his state of mind in getting into the game. He's frothing at the mouth and he's talking about killer instinct. Kill him; put him in the ground. He's getting into it, and he holds up those crooked fingers. It was THE classic interview of linebacker play.'

'We had high school and college coaches calling up to request that tape. It was the definitive description of the state of mind needed to play linebacker—you have to build up hatred, you have to kill.'

'To this day it is one of the most memorable interviews ever. We loosened him up with a few drinks and there was no restraint on his personality. He knew his reputation and he knew that by being unrestrained. This was how he could hold on to his legacy.'

'He always gave his opinions and said things that he shouldn't have. He was always really animated and thoughtful. He always said one or two things that would border on the outrageous. He saw himself and didn't want to hold anything back.'

'I remember about 1968 or '69 doing a retrospective of the '60 championship team. We found a shot of him in the locker room smoking a cigar. The line I wrote to that picture that was read by John Facenda went 'The smoke he generated in the dressing room is only a pale reminder of what he left on the field."

"We got him back in the studio and it was one of our most memorable interviews ever. He's talking about his state of mind in getting into the game. He's frothing at the mouth and he's talking about killer instinct; kill him; put him in the ground. He's getting into it, and he holds up those crooked fingers. It was THE classic interview of linebacker play."

'That was one of the most memorable lines I ever wrote, especially with the way it was read by Facenda.'

'If there's a legacy of Steve Sabol, there it is.'

'The whole thing that Deion doesn't make contact was to demonstrate his own ferocity. It was part of his personality, what made him great. He was a showman.'

'After he quit, he found that he could stay in memories with his comments. His motivation for making those statements was to stay in the public eye. You may forget me as a player, but you'll remember me for what I say about modern players.'

"He's in a class by himself and he hasn't mellowed at all with age.'

'Chuck Bednarik starts at the highest tree branches of the universe as football players go. He's up there with the likes of Sammy Baugh, Otto Graham, Walter Payton, Jerry Rice and Johnny Unitas.'

'He's part of the football divinity. He holds a unique place in the game. His career achievements have only been enlarged with the passage of time.'

'Some players like Don Hutson, people say he may have been the greatest, but his achievements have been largely forgotten.'

'Chuck Bednarik is the opposite. As we look back on his career, his achievements, his personality appear bigger than life. There aren't many players you can say that about.'

'Controversy always seems to surround him and he has a lot of bitterness, but he's the ultimate hardscrabble tough guy."

Bob Lyons

This Philadelphia-based sportswriter and author was also the sports information director at LaSalle College when David Bednarik, Chuck's brother, was a member of the basketball team.

Robert S. Lyons covered professional and college sports for the Associated Press. He was also sports information director and director of the LaSalle University News Bureau. He co-authored 'The Eagles Encyclopedia' with Ray Didinger and also authored "Palestra Pandemonium: A History of the Big 5."

Lyons got to observe Chuck Bednarik up close when younger brother David Bednarik was a member of the LaSalle basketball team.

"I was a fan first, then got to know him casually when his younger brother David, played basketball at LaSalle in the 1960s while I was the sports information director.'

'When Dave was at LaSalle, Chuck used to come to practice and express his opinions and insights to the coaches, Joe Heyer and then Jim Harding. A lot of people thought Dave was Chuck's son, given the age difference, and were surprised to hear that he was a brother.'

'Dave was a brilliant young man; if he had played regularly he would have been an Academic All-American. He was very well-liked; one of the guys. Chuck was just a few years removed from playing in the championship and the guys were still in awe of him.'

'Around the same time Dave was at LaSalle, Carl Yastrzemski's younger brother, Rich, was playing baseball for us. It was interesting that we had the younger brothers of two all-time greats playing sports on campus at the same time.'

'Chuck would let people know what he was thinking. I do know that he played with the Eagles alumni basketball team; they played against the LaSalle faculty once. A friend of mine who was a member of the faculty team told me that Chuck didn't hold back under the boards.'

'He was an incredible football player, well deserving of all his accolades. The thought of him going both ways, epitomized by the 1960 championship, is amazing.'

'The game, from what I remember from afar, was more physical in those days. Players got away with a lot more on the field.'

> **"He was an incredible football player, well deserving of all his accolades. The thought of him going both ways, epitomized by the 1960 championship, is amazing."**

'I was with Chuck a few times recently, once at his house and another at the Philadelphia Sports Hall of Fame banque. His physical condition just amazes me. He's in tremendous physical shape; he's not limping like a lot of the others. He's taken care and kept himself in great shape.'

'I'm a big fan of "Inside the NFL" and there was one episode where Chuck was interviewed at his house. He talked about his life after football and I was struck by the paradox that here's this deeply religious guy who went out and killed people on Sundays. I always found that an interesting contradiction. I guess his rosaries were pressed to the limit."

Bill Campbell

Bill Campbell has been broadcasting sports in Philadelphia for nearly 70 years. He started in radio as a high school student in 1940. At various points in his career he has been the voice of the Eagles, Warriors, Sixers and Phillies. He was working in the broadcast booth for the Eagles during the championship 1960 season. A member of both the Philadelphia and Pennsylvania Sports Halls of Fame, Campbell can still be heard giving sports commentaries on KYW-1060 radio.

"You're writing a book about Chuck? I don't envy you; you have a tough job. I think he is spoiling his reputation because of his bitterness. Today many people only know him as a bitter old man.'

"I broadcast his games since [he played] at the University of Pennsylvania. Many of those teams would not have won without Chuck, but he did not get along with a lot of guys on some of those teams."

'His bitterness is more so than any great athlete and, it's unfortunate, because that many people don't know him for what he's done.'

"I broadcast his games since [he played] the University of Pennsylvania. Many of those teams would not have won without Chuck, but he did not get along with a lot of guys on some of those teams.'

'Chuck and Norm Van Brocklin did not like each other. Chuck held it against Van Brocklin and resented the publicity that Van Brocklin got.'

'I've been in broadcasting for 60 years and without a doubt Chuck Bednarik is one of the five greatest football players I've ever seen.'

'His resentment of modern day players makes him tough to listen to. It's unfortunate, his inability to be gracious. Many people don't rank him higher because of his personality'

'Chuck was not objectionable when he played for the Eagles. I feel sorry for him now. I've always wanted him to be a good guy. I feel badly that most people who remember him as a player, as Concrete Charlie, Number 60, have a negative view because of some of the things he's said in later years.'

'He's done some good things for me. In the '70s Dick Enberg was hosting a show in which they brought back members of the 1960 team. The show was being taped in Los Angeles and Chuck mentioned my name to the producer. They brought me out and put me up in Hollywood. I was part of the show all because of Chuck.'

'But, I just don't understand his bitterness at the NFL, the chip on his shoulder, and all his complaints."

Dave Anderson

Dave Anderson is most widely recognized as a Pulitzer Prize winning sports columnist for The New York Times. In 1960 he was Yankee Stadium providing sidebar coverage of the Eagles-Giants game for the New York Journal-American. He was one of the reporters who gathered around Chuck Bednarik to get his comments on the hit that dropped Frank Gifford. For a brief moment, Anderson thought he would suffer a fate similar to the Giants star.

"I was never around Bednarik much, but I was assigned to do a sidebar for The Journal-American the day he hit Gifford.'

'He was sitting on a stool in the locker room after game and I was standing next to him. He was still in full uniform with his shoulder pads, and I believe his shoes on. I remember asking him to show us how he hit Gifford.'

'He stood up and, with his pads and cleats on, he looked 10' tall. I wasn't a small guy, about 5'11", but he was towering above me. I'm thinking for a moment, "My god, he's going to hit me like he did Frank," and he lowered his shoulder pad into me to show me how he hit Gifford.'

"He stood up and, with his pads and cleats on, he looked 10' tall. I wasn't a small guy, about 5'11", but he was towering above me. I'm thinking for a moment, "My god, he's going to hit me like he did Frank," and he lowered his shoulder pad into me to show me how hit Gifford."

'He said, "Hey, I just tackled him…I wasn't celebrating him being hurt, I was happy because we won the game."

'At the time I didn't think it was a cheap hit. He buried his shoulder into him; he was doing what he was supposed to do and I didn't take it that he was gloating.'

'I remember when they took Gifford out of the locker room on a stretcher with and ice pack on his forehead. I can still see that.'

'I saw both sides after the game. It became such a big incident that was added to by the players being who they were. Frank was the popular star of the New York Giants and Bednarik was the ultimate hitter. When he hit you, he hit you. That's what people remember."

Dave Klein

Dave Klein observed the Eagles while serving as the Giants beat writer for the Newark Star Ledger from 1961-1996.

One of four sportswriters to cover every Super Bowl, Dave Klein was the Giants beat writer for the Star Ledger of New Jersey from 1961-1996. He owns and operates the Giants on-line newsletter, E-Giants.

"I got to know Frank Gifford after he got out of the hospital in 1960. You know he refused to let the nurses answer any phone calls from Chuck Bednarik while he was in the hospital. The Giants were going to be playing the Eagles again the following week. He wanted to make Chuck squirm and worry so that he wouldn't be able to concentrate.'

"Bednarik was someone who made people nervous. The Giants used to comment on him coming to town. Not the Eagles, "We're playing Bednarik next.""

'I started covering the Giants in '61 and don't recall any talk about revenge against Bednarik. They had a new head coach that year, Allie Sherman, and I know the Giants finished first and beat the Eagles twice during the season.'

'I remember Bednarik as the best of the old school middle linebackers. He didn't have the most foot speed, but he was much bigger than the other linebackers of the era. His experience as an offensive lineman helped in reading plays.'

'He had a certain vicious approach to the game; he played hard and tough. He was the best I saw for that time and place, better than Bill George, Ray Nitschke or Joe Schmidt.'

'Bednarik was someone who made people nervous. The Giants used to comment on him coming to town; not the Eagles; "We're playing Bednarik next.'

'I don't think he could play as well today, because the game is much bigger and faster, but he was huge for his time. Remember Rosie Brown? He seemed massive on the field, but the never weighed more than 250. Andy Robustelli, a Hall of Fame defensive end, played at 235, max.'

'I've been involved with the charity, the Valerie Fund. One year we roasted Frank Gifford and you couldn't have a Gifford roast without inviting Chuck Bednarik.'

'Without telling anyone, Chuck made a deal with the hotel manager to have the lights turned out for about 30 seconds when he got up to speak. No one knew what was going on.'

'The lights go on and you hear Chuck say, "Frank, was that familiar?"'

'Everyone laughed including, Frank. His wife Kathie Lee didn't get it, and watching her was almost as much fun.'

'Chuck was a good guy. The hit on Gifford was clean, he just tackled as hard as he could. I asked him once if he was celebrating in the photo, and he said, "Hell no, I was calling for someone to help." Gifford always said it wasn't the hit that caused his injuries, but his head crashing on the hard ground.'

'For his time, Bednarik was the best linebacker in football. Sam Huff was the poster boy for the New York media, but he wasn't as good as Chuck. They used to say, 'You know why you see Number 70 in so many pictures? It's because he was always the last man to the ball."

Larry Merchant

While serving as sports editor of the Philadelphia Daily News in 1958, Merchant never received a wedding gift from Bednarik and Brookshier because it got dumped in a hotel swimming pool in California.

The voice of HBO boxing since 1978, Larry Merchant was a sports editor and columnist for the Philadelphia Daily News during the late 1950s and early 1960s. He was one of the 'new breed' of sportswriters who asked probing questions and often covered the games and players in less than worshipful manner.

"When I first saw him, Chuck Bednarik was already larger than life. He had been a celebrated college player at Penn. Many of the players in college football at that time were men. They had been in the service and were older guys.'

'Chuck Bednarik fit that mold – a vein of anthracite in a coal mine, a chunk of steel from mill – that was my image of him.'

'He came to the Eagles and they won a championship early in his career. He became a force very quickly.'

"Chuck Bednarik fit that mold– a vein of anthracite in a coal mine, a chunk of steel from mill– that was my image of him."

'I showed up in Philadelphia in the late '50s and he was already Concrete Charlie. He was a figure to be reckoned with in terms of his stature within the game. In hindsight, he came to epitomize the new breed of big, dominant inside linebackers. He was the prototype for what would be the common player at that position in years to come.'

'What he did in that '60 championship game is memorable, remarkable. That was the last two-way performance that we'll see.'

'I still have an image of Chuck standing on the field, with everyone else racing on and off. He had a pigeon-toed look about him. Forty-three other players would be in motion all around him. It is an image that is still very strong in my mind.'

'I think it was interesting that he let Van Brocklin take over the team. I didn't know enough to investigate, but Van Brocklin came in and was the unquestioned leader.'

'He was brought in to do what he did. He had an extraordinary presence. He had won a championship, was a war veteran, and everyone knew he would become a coach.'

'The Eagles turned the team, the game plan, over to him. He was even consulted on trades. The Eagles were a primitive organization in those days compared to the Browns, the Rams. Those teams foretold the corporate image that was to come.'

'At the draft, which was held in Philly, the Eagles showed up with four guys, some file cards and a few magazines. 'The Browns and the Rams sent a full staff. They had scouted players. They held meetings.'

'Players were brought in at Van Brocklin's request. The safety, Don Burroughs. There was a guard.'

'Van Brocklin knew the guys from the Western Division who the Eagles didn't see much of.'

Van Brocklin was a coach on the field. I think he was responsible for McDonald and Retzlaff becoming great players at new postions – McDonald from halfback to wide receiver and Retzlaff from wide receiver to tight end. With Van Brocklin getting them the ball, they became the main offensive forces on the team.'

'Bednarik intuited Van Brocklin's presence. He didn't poke his nose into the offense. He sensed that Van Brocklin had a chance to bring them a championship.'

'Given Bednarik's personality, he wanted, needed people, to recognize how great he was. I find it interesting that he grasped on, told himself "don't interfere." There were a lot of strong personalities on that field, Brookshier comes to mind, but they sensed it was the right thing to do, to let Van Brocklin take over.'

'A couple of personal things about Bednarik; in his presence you knew he had those huge gnarled hands. His whole body, whole presence seemed gnarled. He played with a torn muscle in his arm; it looked like someone tucked a baseball in it, but you couldn't stop him. When it came to him, nothing I saw surprised me.'

'The second thing; I was married in 1959 and spent part of my honeymoon on the West Coast. The Eagles were playing the 49ers in an exhibition game and we were staying in Palo Alto, near Stanford. It was a real California style hotel with a pool and plants.'

'As a kind of initiation, a practical joke, they threw me into the pool. Bednarik and Brookshier were the leaders.'

> **"I still have an image of Chuck standing on the field, with everyone else racing on and off. He had a pigeon-toed look about him. Forty-three other players would be in motion all around him. It is an image that is still very strong in my mind."**

'I could be tough or kind to them; I had no personal relationship with anybody. I was part of the new generation of sportswriters— find the story and poke around.'

'My wife thought they were doing something bad to me. She was upset, but I was flattered by the attention.'

'A few seasons later, '61 or '62, I wrote a column about Bednarik not being Bednarik any more. While I flattered and praised him for what he had been, he was no longer what he was. He took great exception and told people that I wrote this because he had thrown me in the pool.'

'He is a great man in football history, larger than life. He made all the big plays–Taylor, Gifford. He played bigger, stronger, better than most people. No one ever said of him that was just playing football.'

'John Bateman was an assistant coach at Penn while Chuck was with the Eagles. He told me that when he coached at Columbia and they played against Penn they would devise all kinds of schemes to misdirect Bednarik. They had fakes on the line, fakes in the backfield, all designed to lead him away from the ball.'

'He said it was never successful; he always smelled where the ball was going. He had an intelligence that doesn't show on tests. He had a football intelligence of a higher order.'

'Of course he was bigger than most linemen. There were very few linebackers who were that big and on top of that he could smell everything out.'

'That motor nerve. He could see, react. Along with his physical endowments, his desire to win—he was a great package.'

'In 1960, even though it was recognized what he was accomplishing, the attitude was, 'well it's Chuck Bednarik,' if anybody can do, he can. He was already a larger than life figure.'

'The 1960 season for Bednarik, I think it was like somebody who had a last great achievement in his career. It was like a writer or an artist coming up with a big one after people thought they were done.'

'Hemingway, everyone thought he had nothing left, couldn't come up with the big one, then he writes the "Old Man and the Sea', as if to say "See, I still have my fastball." 1960 was Bednarik's "Old Man and the Sea."

'The drama of the season, the come from behind wins, the championship – it was a fitting new ending, a climactic ending to his career.'

> **"It has always interested me since that time that whenever his name popped up it was about how much money the players are making and how great he was. There was a melancholy, a bitterness about protecting his reputation. That bitterness served him well while he was playing."**

'It has always interested me since that time that whenever his name popped up it was about how much money the players are making and how great he was. There was a melancholy, a bitterness about protecting his reputation. That bitterness served him well while he was playing.'

'Joe Paterno once said of one his players, "He is what God had in his mind when he made a football player."

'That bubbles in my mind when I think of Chuck Bednarik.'

Gordon Forbes

Before becoming a national football columnist for USA Today, Forbes was the Eagles beat writer for the Philadelphia Inquirer.

Gordon Forbes was the Eagles beat writer for the Philadelphia Inquirer from 1967-1982, a period he remembers as mostly "terrible years [where] the team usually won four or five games." He got to know Chuck Bednarik when he hung around the team during those early years and later when Dick Vermiel invited him back to the team.

Forbes left the Inquirer when USA Today offered him "an extra $25 a week,' and became one of the best known football columnists while writing for the daily national paper.

"I started covering the Eagles in 1967, and in those days Jerry Williams and Eddie Khayatt coached the Eagles, guys who had played with Chuck Bednarik. When I asked guys like them and others who played with and against Chuck what made him such a tremendous player, they would talk about his size and vicious attitude.'

'It's become an overused cliché, but they said he was one of those guys who made everybody around him better. He made you want to be part of the Eagles way—fire and brimstone.'

"The NFL featured a mostly running game and Chuck's greatest attribute was his ability to smell out a run and make a tackle. He loved contact."

"When Chuck was a player, it was largely a running game. Only about 40% of the plays were passes. You'd get the third and long, the play action pass.'

'The NFL featured a mostly running game and Chuck's greatest attribute was his ability to smell out a run and make a tackle. He loved contact.'

'He did a little freelancing. Coaches today would probably frown on his style, but Chuck had the ability to freelance and get to the ball. He could get away with that because the offenses were much simpler in those days. Now the playbook is the size of a phone book and teams runs counters and misdirections.'

'He could definitely play today. He might not be as dominant, but certainly a Pro Bowl player, and I'm sure he'd be screaming if they took him out on third and long. He could probably play any position.'

'You know how I would like to see him play?...Today, the way they use players on short yardage; I'd love to see him carry the ball.'

'When I was working in Philadelphia, I sometimes went over to Penn for pickup basketball games. Sometimes Chuck would be there and when he was on the court, you could feel the elbows then.'

'The Gifford tackle was clean, though the Giant fans and players didn't think so. I have a Gifford story; there was a charity roast for Frank and Chuck was invited. He said, "I came up with a great idea. I told the people who were running the hall that when I'm introduced lower the lights for five or ten seconds on my cue. When the lights went out, I said, "Frank, does that ring a bell?"

'Frank laughed, but Kathie Lee didn't get it.'

'The other tackle Chuck is famous for is Jim Taylor in the title game at Franklin Field. Chuck got credit for it, but Bobby Jackson made the first contact. He was the nickelback; you know Jerry Williams invented the nickel back, but George Allen always took credit for it.'

'At present, Chuck is bitter about today's players and salaries. I told him it's the same way with sportswriters. I never made the money that the guys make today. It was long hours and terrible play.'

'I remember when Dick Vermiel brought him back as honorary coach. In a game against Denver there was a pass interference play away from the ball. Chuck was ranting and raving on the sidelines. He yelled out "That was a horseshit call." The official yelled back him, 'Buddy, you have a horseshit team."

'He was a great player; they don't make them like that. He's from the days of the running game and low salaries."

Jack Whitaker

A nationally-renowned sportscaster, Whitaker recalls being awed by Chuck Bednarik's punting ability while covering his first Eagles pre-season game in 1954.

A native of Philadelphia and graduate of Northeast Catholic High School and St. Joseph's University, Jack Whitaker is one of the most esteemed broadcasters in the history of televised sports. He started his career in Philadelphia before joining CBS Sports in 1961, and later ABC Sports. He was one of the Eagles announcers through most of the 1950s.

"The first things I remember about Chuck Bednarik are the stories that I heard about him at the Univeristy of Pennsylvania while I was growing up in Philadelphia.'

'My first personal memory of him is what a great punter he was. The first game I did for the Eagles was a preseason game in Little Rock against the Cardinals. I had heard what a great player Bednarik was on offense and defense, but I'm watching the warm-ups and he's booming 50 and 60 yard punts, perfect spirals. I didn't even know he could kick.'

'My second memory is 1960; both ways, the last 60 Minute Man.'

'We were amazed. I remember when he was sent in to center the first game against the Giants. They were getting to Van Brocklin, putting him on his back. He was very upset that the Giants were getting to him. Chuck was sent in to center, the pass rush stopped and the Eagles won.'

"I remember the excitement when Gifford was hit. Everyone was very happy, but only because that was the end of the game, and it was a pivotal game. We didn't know how bad he was hurt. He said that it was the hard ground in Yankee Stadium that caused the injuries, not the hit.'

'Years later, I did a series "Where Are They Now." I went down to Philadelphia to interview Chuck when Dick Vermiel was the coach. Chuck wanted to make a point about how the game had changed. He said that in 1960 his job was to drive Buck Shaw home every afternoon at 2 pm. He said now, Dick Vermiel sleeps in his office four or five times a week.'

'Oh sure, we were surprised how well the team did in 1960. We lost to Cleveland the

first week, then almost lost to Dallas, and this was their first year in the league.'

'We won the next couple of games, then beat Cleveland on a last second field goal by Bobby Walston.'

'The first Giants game, we're losing 10-0, when Tim Brown sucks Sam Huff in for a touchdown.'

'That team went a long way with not great talent. Van Brocklin was great at reading defenses; Tommy McDonald made big catches, and of course Chuck going two ways.'

'We were happy, but surprised; the Giants and Cleveland had better talent.'

'We were on the bus going to the game in St.Louis in the snow. Maxie Baughn was sitting behind Chuck and he said "Snow, I never saw snow before." Chuck looks at him and growls, "How old are you? When I was your age I was fighting Germans in Europe."

'Chuck Bednarik was indestructible; one of a kind; concrete.'

'It seemed only fitting that Chuck would make that last tackle on Jim Taylor. He had been such a big part of the championship team."

Bill Lyon

A longtime Philadelphia Inquirer sports columnist, Lyon profiled Bednarik in a book.

A native of the Midwest, Bill Lyon started covering sports for the Philadelphia Inquirer in 1972 and stayed on the job for 32 years. Among many honors, he was named Pennsylvania Sportswriter of the Year six times. While he never covered Chuck Bednarik as an active player, he became acquainted with him on the local sports circuit. Bednarik was one of 20 subjects in Lyon's book, "When the Clock Runs Out," and in preparation he spent time in the Bednarik home.

"I came to Philadelphia in 1972. I was in the Midwest when he was playing. If he doesn't have the best nickname in sports, it's up there.'

'I spent time at his home when I was doing the book, "When the Clock Runs Out," about 10 years ago. You know how he is, gruff and cantankerous. Deion was playing at the time. Chuck was 73, and maybe 10 pounds over his playing weight.'

'He talked about going out and playing. He said he might get the snot kicked out of him, but he could make more money in one game than the made in his entire career.'

"He went into a room and came out with two shopping bags full of fan letters and autograph requests. He said he answers them all and doesn't charge anyone."

'He said, "If they just let me go out one game and snap the ball, I won't even block anybody." Emma looked over and said, "Oh yes you would." And he said, 'You're right, I probably would."

'The enduring image of Chuck is him and what we thought was a lifeless Gifford. I also spent time with Tom Brookshier for the book and Brookie said "He cleated Frank." He had a big blown up picture of the hit in his den and he said, "Look at this, you can't see the shoe." You look closely and see that the shoe is hanging off of what appears to be one toe.'

'I was at this house the better part of the day. His grandchildren were running around and of course Emma was there. He got out his accordion. It was a real hot day.'

'He went into a room and came out with two shopping bags full of fan letters and autograph requests. He said he answers them all and doesn't charge anyone.'

'He stands up for his convictions; there's no doubt where he stands on things. You don't have to ask; he'll tell you anyway.'

'He says some things not in a diplomatic way. That's the way he is. I prefer someone like that than a hypocrite.'

'No one can say that Chuck Bednarik is a hypocrite. He has convictions and he stands up for them. He's stubborn and sometimes there's not much difference between stubborn and steadfast.'

'He's like everybody's gruff old uncle. He certainly commands a room."

'His image hasn't been tarnished at all with his fans. The great mystique still lives on…the last of the 60 minute men.'

'That's a great thing to put on his tombstone—'The Last of the 60 Minute Men.'

'What he says is true, it's all specialists today. He was a specialist – a specialist at playing every damn play of a game.'

'A generation today may not understand what he accomplished. I remember he said, "Thank God for fathers and grandfathers, they keep me alive."

Stan Hochman

Stan Hochman was hired by sports editor Larry Merchant to cover sports for the Philadelphia Daily News in 1959 and has been on the job ever since. One of his early assignments was to spend all day with Chuck Bednarik on what was supposed to be his last day in an Eagles uniform. He later dealt face-to-face with Boxing Commissioner Bednarik when he tried to intercede in setting up a Joe Frazier-Muhammad Ali fight.

"My one unhappy experience with Chuck was through the State Athletic Commission. Muhammad Ali was in exile after he didn't step forward for the draft. New York took away his boxing license, as did subsequently every other state.'

'Ali was living on City Line Avenue at Major Coxon's house at the time. There was talk that they could put together an Ali-Frazier fight on an Indian reservation in Oklahoma. Oklahoma didn't have a boxing commission so there was a need for another state to step in and sanction the fight.'

'Gene Kilroy, who was Ali's business manager and did a lot of jobs in taking care of him, sensed that since Ali lived in Pennsylvania and Frazier was more or less established and recognized as a resident, that they might be able to get a license to fight in Pennsylvania. Kilroy asked me to help.'

'Chuck was one of the three members of the boxing commission. I called Chuck and asked him how he felt about the fight.'

"Over my dead body," was his response.

'I guess I could understand. He had served in the war; Ali didn't step forward and that ruled him out. The decision had to be unanimous and without Chuck's support the idea died. Frazier was for it, his company Cloverlay would have backed the fight.'

'The fight died. I understand Chuck's feelings in light of his background, but that was my one unhappy experience with him.'

"Other than that, we got along well. He trusted me enough to allow me to follow him for a day when he was going to retire.'

'I felt that Chuck was respected by the defense. Van Brocklin was the leader who set the tone for the offense. Van Brocklin could be mean and demanding. The defensive guys gravitated to Chuck. There may have been a little bit of tension as to who was the leader of the team.'

'Chuck may have felt that he didn't get credit for all he accomplished. He went both ways, and he probably didn't get the credit he deserved.'

'He was vital to that championship. He probably should have been the MVP of the championship game. Even then we tended to give the quarterback too much credit. That may have been part of the pattern of him being overlooked. It gives you some understanding of his bitterness.'

'It was an incredible feat. He wasn't just ordinary in either position. He was terrific at center and linebacker. He could have been Pro Bowl at either position. It was remarkable and he didn't get the credit he deserved.'

'Chuck got angry when Deion Sanders was promoted as a two-way player. That was understandable, the "Deion couldn't tackle my wife" quotes. Sanders was an overrated media creation and Chuck doesn't hide or disguise his feelings.'

'He's a one-of-a-kind guy. He has no thermostat to gauge how what he says sounds, or looks in print.'

'Some of the stuff has been awkward publicly — his row against the Eagles about not buying his book. Something should have told him not to say the things he said. Eagles fans don't like to see one of their legends rooting against the team.'

'He's was always decent with the media. He didn't hide from writers or insult them. Diplomacy didn't come naturally to Chuck, but he treated the media fairly."

Chapter | **sixteen**

Other Voices From Around the City

With an ongoing presence that has touched the Philadelphia sports scene for more than 60 years, Chuck Bednarik has left an impression on many local sportsmen that extends beyond the football field. He is a charter member of the Philadelphia Sports Hall of Fame. The Maxwell Club presents a national collegiate football award in his name. Bednarik has also been a guest at several functions of the Philadelphia A's Historic Society. There are many experienced voices who believe his legacy has been as important to the City of Philadelphia as any athlete's who ever performed there.

Merrill Reese

The radio "Voice of the Eagles" since 1976, Reese was a young fan in the stands when the Eagles won the NFL championship in 1960.

Merrill Reese has been the radio voice of the Eagles since 1976, the year Chuck Bednarik rejoined the team as a special assistant to Dick Vermiel. A native of Philadelphia, Reese was a lifelong Eagles fan and relished the opportunity to spend time with one of his boyhood heroes when he was involved with the team.

"He was one of the greatest Eagles of all-time. I watched him as a kid. I was at the '60 championship game in the corner of the end zone. He was always very nice to me and it was a lot of fun to talk to a hero from that championship team.'

'The two greatest Eagles of all were Chuck Bednarik and Steve Van Buren.'

'Chuck Bednarik. Two ways. I have always enjoyed seeing him over the years. He's always been nice to me. He comes to training camp at Lehigh, it's close for him.'

"He's still strong and looks formidable. He looks like he could step in and play today.'

'It's amazing, he really was Concrete Charlie. With some guys the legend is built up. With him, the legend grows and he has exceeded it. He was one of the great players in the game; his reputation wasn't inflated.'

'I think the city has a great tradition, but the young fans don't have knowledge of even the '80s and '90s. But in any sense of Eagles history, Chuck Bednarik occupies a prominent role. If they don't know everything about him, they know his name.'

'Every time I visit the NovaCare Center, there are four pictures that I see—Tommy McDonald, Steve Van Buren, Reggie White, and Chuck Bednarik.'

'I see him in his stance and he looks like a force, you can see the power he exuded.'

'He draws attention wherever he goes.'

'He has always been passionate about football. I remember one game in Dallas when he was helping Dick Vermiel and he drew a penalty for yelling at an official."

Ed Snider

Snider was Vice President of the Eagles in the late 1960s and always welcomed Chuck Bednarik's presence around the organization.

Chuck Bednarik had minimal involvement with the Eagles following his retirement in 1962. Ed Snider was part of the group that purchased the team with Jerry Wolman in 1963. As executive vice president of the team, Snider reached out to Bednarik in 1965.

Bednarik recalls Snider telling him, "Chuck, you should always be part of the Eagles." Ed Snider told me that I would have a role with the team as long as he was involved. He said that I should always act like I "belonged" with the Eagles."

Snider created an all-purpose position for Bednarik that included helping out at training camp with centers and linebackers, scouting, and making public appearances for the team. Bednarik stayed active with the team until it was purchased by Leonard Tose in 1969. He went into another period of estrangement from the team, until invited back by Dick Vermiel in 1976.

Bednarik has remained grateful that Snider and Wolman made him feel part of the Eagles 'family,' as Dick Vermiel and Andy Reid would do in later years.

Snider moved on to become the most successful combination sports and entertainment mogul in Philadelphia history. He was responsible for bring the Flyers to the city in 1966. He also created Spectacor which later merged and is now known as Comcast-Spectacor.

"We took over the team in 1964 and I know Chuck had not been around the team much the past few years, and I thought he should be.'

'We weren't part of whatever reasons that had existed to keep him away from the team, but we wanted a strong alumni presence around and no one personifies the Eagles more than Chuck Bednarik. I've always been a great admirer of his and I wanted him to be part of the team.'

'I had struck up a friendship with Chuck and always thought highly of him and his importance in the history of the Eagles.'

'He was great, the last of the two-way players and I'm one of his biggest admirers. He's right up near the top in Philadelphia sports history; a legend.'

'It's amazing what a great player he was, the last of a breed. And those hands, those fingers going in every direction."

"He was great, the last of the two-way players and I'm one of his biggest admirers. He's right up near the top in Philadelphia sports history; a legend."

Bob Clark

The Maxwell Football Club was founded by Bert Bell in 1935 to honor football excellence and to serve the community. Bob Clark has been involved with the club since 1955 and has served as executive director since 1965. He was elected to the Pennsylvania Sports Hall of Fame in 1993. Chuck Bednarik has a long association with the club, having won the Maxwell Award for Outstanding College Player of the Year in 1948. In 1995, the club instituted the Chuck Bednarik for College Defensive Player of the Year and it is now recognized as a major national award.

"The story behind the creation of the Chuck Bednarik Award goes back to ESPN. We (the Maxwell Club) had a deal to do a TV show to announce the winner of our Player of the Year Award. Our award went primarily to offensive players and ESPN said they would like to have an award that represents defensive players be part of the show.'

'The offered us the opportunity to sponsor the award and we elected to name the award for Chuck. He was known primarily for his offense in college, but of course he played both ways and had been a great defensive player. He was really the only semi-local guy who was outstanding enough to have an award named for him.'

'He has been associated with the Maxwell Club for many years and was the first lineman to win our award when he was a senior at Penn in 1948. He's been a dues-paying member of the club and he always participated in our banquets, golf outings and TV shows.'

'When he's not on one of his tirades, he's one of the nicest, quietest guys around. He was a hell of a football player, but he probably would have been better off if he hadn't made some of the comments that he's made over the years.'

'It's unfortunate; if you polled most of the football players in the NFL today, most of them wouldn't know who he was. The exceptions from that era are guys like Mike Ditka, and that's only because they see him on TV. Today a player wins the Doak Walker Award, and says "Who?" Today, the only thing they care about is today...no allegiance or interest in tradition."

Dave Jordan

"As a season ticket holder during the four years Chuck Bednarik played for Penn, actually my father had the season tickets but I went to all the games with him, ages 10 to 13, I saw just about all of his college games. Penn played almost all home games then, although I guess I may have missed two or three away games. He was certainly a dominant star as a center, as a linebacker, as a punter, even as a runner from fake punt formation at times. Several years ago, when Chuck was at the A's Historical Society museum, I mentioned to him that I saw the famous 17-14 upset of Penn by Princeton in 1946. Chuck growled a little, then said, "Yeah, but we kicked their ass up there the next year!" I saw that game in Palmer Stadium, as well. And of course my last memory of Bednarik as a player came on December 26, 1960, or whatever the date of that NFC championship game was. We were sitting in the next to last row in the center of the upper deck at the rounded end zone of Franklin Field, with the Packers driving for what would have been a title-winning touchdown. I watched Bednarik take down Jimmy Taylor, the Packers' fullback, short of the end zone and then sit on him while staring up at the clock as it rolled off the final seconds. Then, when the gun sounded, he let Taylor up.

This may not be anything you can use, but I'm glad to see you're doing a work on the man I still think was the greatest football player I ever saw."

John Chaney

The legendary Temple basketball coach remembers Chuck Bednarik and Jim Brown as the being the best football players of his lifetime.

The Hall of Fame basketball coach for Temple University, John Chaney grew up in Philadelphia as a fan of all the local teams. He has met Chuck Bednarik on a number of occasions and is also a member of the Philadelphia Sports Hall of Fame. A legend himself, Chaney has a strong appreciation for other legends of sport.

'There are only two football players that I rank in the top tier of the game in my lifetime. Chuck Bednarik and Jim Brown are the greatest players who ever lived.'

'If Chuck Bednarik played today, he would still be great. He would be even better with today's technology. He played two-ways in a time when the equipment was bad.'

'He had sheer toughness, didn't cut corners. He'd go to work after football to sell concrete to make an extra dollar. My mother always said if you have two jobs, something is wrong with your first job.'

> **"If Chuck Bednarik played today, he would still be great. He would be even better with today's technology. He played two-ways in a time when the equipment was bad."**

'He was not rewarded for his accomplishments. He was born in an era when large financial rewards did not exist. He survived and was par excellence on the field.'

'I don't know where he ranks in the national hall of fame, but he ranks at the top in Philadelphia.'

'I couldn't imagine, not in my world, this man—a superman—at a time and era when many people would suggest he was inhuman.'

'How strong, big and cut he was for such a long time. I would never bet against him.'

'The most amazing thing about him, I would like to find out what drove him; what was he made of. There was courage found in his heart and mind. I wish we could find some way to dissect him.'

'There is nothing you can say in a negative way about Concrete Charlie. He came from the steel mills, in that very tough era. Like Ted Williams was the best in baseball, Concrete Charlie represented that in football.'

'He came from a time when many great athletes chose to, or were told to, go to war. Too much of life is spent, or misspent, in war.'

'It's a shame that so much of what he is and what he was was missed by the world. We are local in what we have here, always have been. We have been privileged in what our heroes accomplished. Unfortunately word doesn't get out around the world.'

'We have to get word out through the media. Philadelphia is like a bunch of crabs in a basket when it comes to our great people. Every time one crab tries to pull itself out, it gets pulled back in by the others. We trivialize many of our athletes; that's the culture in this area.'

'Mike Schmidt was booed here. In other areas, people talk about how great our guys are and were.'

'We should argue that our guys don't get enough credit, that the outside world doesn't think they are as great as we think they are.'

'In this city we lost sight of what made them great, and we don't reward them.'

'Here again we find someone special; there should be a statue of Concrete Charlie. We should take down the Rocky statue and put him up. He is a true giant, a true miracle...he is the real Rocky, we should take Rocky down. I wish I was in charge.'

'If he isn't someone you can talk about to youngsters, no one is. What a perfect model for a human being.'

'Nobody can imagine a guy like this today; all these specialists.'

'I don't think anyone could strike fear into an offense like Chuck Bednarik. Why can't we clone guys like him. He is special, at the top of the list.'

'When Chuck Bednarik and Jim Brown played, I was down in Jacksonville for some of those years. We had no TV; we had to 'look' at the radio to get games from Philadelphia. Those are the guys I remember. That was football.'

'We used to get out stats in the newspapers. You went to school and read the current events in the newspaper. That is a tragic downfall today, no one especially young people are reading, or writing. Everyone is involved with technology.'

"I don't think anyone could strike fear into an offense like Chuck Bednarik. Why can't we clone guys like him. He is special, at the top of the list."

'So much has been lost. We find ourselves forgetting about the struggle to be great; that is what Chuck Bednarik represents. His was a great life story that suggested he wanted to be great.'

'Discipline is a key element in learning. Too many people think of it as punishment, but you have to run if you want to be great.'

'You have to choose the way to be a great player. When I was young, I wasn't sure what I wanted, but I knew what I didn't want. I knew that if I would work hard, it would take me away from what I didn't want.'

'Chuck Bednarik was so disciplined. It's no wonder why he was so great. It took dedication; those helmets, what were they made of cloth? And no facemask.'

'His is a story that needs to be told with an asterisk around all the great things he did. He was like Wilt Chamberlin. Wilt was disciplined as well as something special.'

'Chuck Bednarik and Wilt Chamberlin were real heroes in Philadelphia sports. Everyone else can stand in line behind them.'

'Tell Chuck that I'm thinking about him and be kind to that great man. I love him in spite of everybody.'

'Let him know that there is one guy would take his bucket of water up the hill for him anytime."

Ken Avallon

A native of Philadelphia, Ken Avallon is president of the Philadelphia Sports Hall of Fame, of which Chuck Bednarik is a member of the charter class. A graduate of LaSalle University, Avallon is a technology consultant and lives in Wyncotte, PA with his wife and three children.

"From a personal perspective, I never saw Chuck play, as I was born in the early 1960s. However, even as a young boy, I read a lot, mainly about World War II and football. I first became aware of Chuck while reading "Great Defensive Players of the NFL," one of the many books I read from The Punt, Pass and Kick Library. As a decorated World War II vet and one of football's all-time greats, Chuck seemed a mythic figure, combined of my two greatest interests, heady stuff for a 9 or 10 year old for whom heroes still existed. To me he was football's version of Ted Williams.

Chuck Bednarik is the embodiment of a true Philadelphia sports legend. He joins only Tom Gola and Paul Arizin as an All-American for a local college (Penn), a champion for a local pro team (1948, 1960 Eagles) and a Hall-of-Famer in his sport (Pro Football Hall of Fame). All three are Charter Members of the Philadelphia Sports Hall of Fame.

Today, almost 50 years after his final game, Chuck still presents a commanding figure. As a special guest at all Hall of Fame events, it is amazing to see the crowds that surround Chuck. Crowds made up of grandfathers, fathers, sons and 9-10 year old grandsons who never saw him play but who want to shake the gnarled hand of the still mythic figure."

"Chuck Bednarik is the embodiment of a true Philadelphia sports legend."

Mickey Minnich

The long time director of the Big 33 Football Classic, Minnich always considered Chuck Bednarik to be one of the program's best supporters.

The Big 33 football game, played annually, is one of the most tradition-rich high school football games in the country. For more than 50 years it has been the true showcase of Pennsylvania's great football heritage.

Over the years, honorees have included Joe Montana, Dan Marino, Joe Paterno, Dave Wannstedt, Frank Kush, Ted Kwalick, Rocket Ishmael and Tony Dorsett, with the latter bringing out a classic Bednarik moment.

Mickey Minnich was the executive director of the Big 33 for 22 years. He estimates that during that time Bednarik was present for about 15 of them.

"Chuck has been a big part of the program. He and Lenny Moore were probably the most consistent guys in coming out and supporting us. Of course they never got to play in the game; they were already pros when this was started, but at our 50th anniversary we made them honorary team members. We gave them watches and trophies. NFL Films helped us put together a highlight film showing how great they were.'

'He (Bednarik) spoke to our team a number of times. He could be very blunt.'

'The kids would get a kick; he would sign their t-shirts with the unedited version of what he said to Gifford'.

> **"I don't know that overall we have ever really appreciated Chuck, how they played football in his day, the missions that he flew in World War II, his versatility."**

'One year, Tony Dorsett was the honorary captain. He was a no-show for the banquet and Chuck stepped in as featured speaker.'

'But, he did get us nervous and we had to tone him down. He was saying "I'm gonna tell people what a no-good son-of-a-bitch this guy is."

'We had to tell him, Chuck please don't do that. Like a lot of guys of his generation, he had a chip on his shoulder toward current players.'

'He gave a great speech. He was inspiring; he was funny. He had everyone in the audience eating out of his hand.'

'The sponsors all loved him. They bought his game jersey and had him sign it. He was great with them.'

'He always brought his wife with him. He loves Emma and always talks about her.'

'Chuck became a big fan of the Big 33. He was very loyal to us, but he was a traditionalist.

'Sometime I would tinker around, looking for ways to make the game more interesting. One year Chuck and Frank Kush were at the game. Sometimes the kickers never got on the field during the game, never kicked at all. They would come to the game with their parents and I wanted to get them in.'

'So I arranged for them to kick before the half. Let them try to score for their team.'

'Kush and Bednarik beat me up. They went nuts, "How can you do this, you have to keep the game pure."

'Outside of the Big 33, we always tried to help Pennsylvania football. Paul Posluzny won the Bednarik award from the Maxwell Club a couple of times, but Chuck was never there to present it. Paul was thrilled to win this award. It meant so much to him, but he wanted to meet Chuck.'

'We held an event at the Radisson in Harrisburg, I believe in '06. Paul was there and we sent a driver for Chuck. It was such a thrill for Paul. Everyone took pictures and it was a great day.'

'I don't know that overall we have ever really appreciated Chuck, how they played football in his day, the missions that he flew in World War II, his versatility.'

'They don't make them like Chuck and Frank Kush anymore. Kush was one of like 15 kids from a coal mining family in Winder–old school, hard core guys, who were also very giving people.'

'You look at their backgrounds and all that toughness, but they are very bright, articulate people. No prima donnas.'

'They know what it means to these high school kids when they come back."

Sonny Hill

Known as "Mr. Basketball" in Philadelphia, Sonny Hill has made many contributions in a distinguished career dedicated to that sport, including the establishment of the renowned Sonny Hill League summer program. Hill also played touch football while growing up in Philadelphia and one his favorite early players was Chuck Bednarik. Hill later joined Bednarik as a member of the Philadelphia Sports Hall of Fame.

'In the early part of his career at Penn, Chuck Bednarik was larger than life. In those days, college football was bigger than anything other than baseball and boxing. The NFL didn't really get on the sports map until the Colts and Giants in 1958.'

'During the mid-1940s, in our neighborhood in North Philly, we played rough touch and two-hand touch and we were always emulating the names in the news. In those days, we got our news on the radio and assembled information from newspapers. Sometimes the papers might be a few days old, but old news was new news to us.'

'Playing football, we emulated the names we heard, the real players. Chuck Bednarik was the largest name, the legend.'

'Today, he is larger than sport, an icon, a legend. We are very fortunate in Philadelphia to have one of the all-time great players.'

'He was a rare player, the only player in Philly sports who was so good across the board. A dynamic linebacker, an offensive center, the last of the two-way players.'

'In the history of the Eagles franchise, there are two players in the pantheon, Number 60 and Number 15. There are others striving to get there, but the purists will tell that these are the guys who had an impact, Chuck Bednarik and Steve Van Buren.'

'That was the era of two-way players. Young guys didn't understand that kind of football. You explain it to them and they are enamored that it was done. Chuck was the last two-way player in the NFL and one of the greatest at both positions.'

'He was out there. Butkus is nowhere near the linebacker, can't do anything like Chuck Bednarik.'

'Chuck Bednarik was the baddest dude in the NFL; let's rumble. He could settle any dispute on the field.'

'The only comparable in Philadelphia is Wilt Chamberlin. Wilt was even more dynamic, enormous. His impact was international, universal.'

'Chuck and Wilt crossed all boundaries, all ethnicities. They were heroes in our midst. People identify with athletes who had an impact."

Stan Kotzen

One of the nation's best known sports artists, Stan Kotzen is a graduate of the University of Pennsylvania. His work has been commissioned by such groups as the Baseball Hall of Fame, Maxwell Club, Philadelphia Sports Hall of Fame, and the University of Pennsylvania. Chuck Bednarik has been part of several of his group and team collages. Kotzen followed Bednarik's career at both Penn and with the Eagles, and got to observe him up close around the Penn campus in later years.

'When I think of Chuck, I think of the Palestra. I was at Penn from 1952-'56. Every Friday afternoon we'd play three-on-three basketball and Chuck would be there. He was a good player.'

'In the fall of '56 or '57, I scouted for Penn. Chuck had played with Paul Rabbic and he would help scout and work with the linebackers.

'One time he was working with one of the linebackers and he grabs the kid and tells him you have to move here to get a better angle to the ball. And being the typical Ivy Leaguer, the kids says "Why?"

'Chuck explodes, he says "What do you mean why? Because that's where you should be."

'He was so instinctive. He often didn't have to think about what he was doing.'

'About 15 years ago, I was listening to the Penn-Princeton game on WXPN. It was a big football game and the XPN announcer interviewed Chuck. He asked a pregnant, stupid question; "You played both ways in the NFL, could you play both ways today?"

"I was laughing as I pictured the look on Chuck's face, "Are you kidding me, of I course I play both ways."

From Stan Kotzen print "Eagles Memories"

Harold Serfass

This Pennsylvania horse trainer raised a colt named "Concrete Charlie" who was a money winner from his first race.

At the end of the movie 'Beau Geste,' at least the classic 1939 version, the aristocratic Lady Patricia Brandon, when informed about the death of Beau, states, "Beau Geste...gallant gesture. We didn't name him wrong, did we."

Pennsylvania horse trainer Harold Serfass of Serfass Farms could have made a similar statement when remembering one of his colts. Serfass raised a successful racehorse who was christened Concrete Charlie as a result of a random golf course conversation.

Concrete Charlie was a champion from his first race and shared many character traits with his namesake.

"It was a Saturday, April 8, 1995, Easter weekend. My veterinarian called and said that his father was visiting and asked me to play golf with them at Fox Hollow.'

'We get up to the first tee and Chuck Bednarik is in the group in front of us. We were making small talk and

MAIDEN / PURSE $16,000
5½ Furlongs-1:05
Po Dunk, 2nd   Harold Serfass Jr & Robert Richards, Owners
Gold Collector, 3rd   Steve Rowan, Trainer
COPYRIGHT   *Concrete Charlie*   Jeff Lloyd, Up
Arvicom Pictures   May 11, 1999
                                            PHILADELPHIA PARK

Chuck asked about the horse business. He said wouldn't it be great if we could have a horse named Concrete Charlie.'

'I told him that I had one more mare expecting and, if it had a colt, I would name it after him. Well, on April 11, it had a colt and we named it Concrete Charlie.'

'I contacted the jockey club to register the name and at first they said you can't use it, there was another Concrete Charlie. It turned out that the other Concrete Charlie was more than 25 years old, and after 25 years, the registered name expires. So, I submitted the papers and we got Concrete Charlie.'

'Chuck came up to the farm in Barto to see him regularly. He came up with Emma when he was a yearling, when he was two years old. He kept coming up to see Concrete Charlie.'

'I don't like to run two year olds. We didn't enter him in his first race until May 11, 1999 at Philadelphia Park. He was four years, one month old, and he won his first race.'

'The announcers played it up and made a big thing about Concrete Charlie. They kept saying keep your eyes open for Concrete Charlie. They were asking if Chuck was going to be there, but he didn't make it. I think he had a golf outing.'

'But Chuck met us a few days later at the Limeport Inn and signed pictures for everybody.'

'Concrete Charlie won a $16,000 purse that first race. Jeff Lloyd, a veteran, was the jockey. He was the favorite and won by two lengths; he beat a horse named Podunk.'

'Charlie had a short career. He raced some more after he was five years old. He ran about 10-12 races and won about $40,000-$50,000. His heart was in every race; that horse doesn't owe me anything.'

'He's presently a show horse. He's a solid horse, just like Chuck, rock solid. I know he won his last show at Stroudsburg. He also won an equestrian event.'

'Many times it's tough to take a horse from track to show. He didn't need any time to wind down from racing. In about three-to-six months he was a show horse. He also did some jumping.'

'We had a lot of fun; he was really put together. His chest is as big as Chuck's hand. He's a real competitor, like Chuck. He was knocking on the door from his first race.'

"It's such a coincidence. The name came out of a conversation on the golf course and the mare had a colt three days later.'

'If there is such a thing as "this is what it was supposed to be," this is it. If the colt had been a filly, there would be no story. It was like this is supposed to happen. Chuck asked about naming the horse, and boy oh boy, what a coincidence. This was the right horse for the right name."

Pat Williams

A senior vice president for the Orlando Magic, Pat Williams has been an NBA executive for more than 45 years. He was a senior executive with the 76ers when they won their last NBA title in 1983. Williams grew up in Wilmington, DE, a passionate fan of all the Philadelphia teams. He recalls being fascinated by news reports that Chuck Bednarik might become a two-sport star by signing on as catcher with the A's.

"My story is typical of that generation that grew up in the Delaware Valley during the 40s and '50s. I grew up in Wilmington and was a sports fan from age seven or eight. The A's, Phillies, Warriors, Eagles.'

'Chuck Bednarik is a name that we grew up with. I admired him from afar, glued to my black and white TV. Between the flicker, I remember Number 60.'

'My most vivid memory: I was home from Wake Forest for Christmas and I had two tickets with my father to the championship game in 1960. One of the five great moments in Philadelphia sports history–Chuck Bednarik sitting on Jim Taylor, counting down the clock, "OK Jim, you can get up now."

'I loved the A's. I grew up in Shibe Park. We would hear reports through the newspapers that Chuck Bednarik was working out with the A's. He used to take batting practice with them and the reports were that he was good enough to play for the team. I was intrigued by the fact that he could play baseball too.'

'I would read the quips in the paper and it fascinated me that Chuck Bednarik could be catching for the A's in a Sunday doubleheader. They said he was a prospect, this big, large football player.'

'I was intrigued by those newspaper articles, that Chuck was at the ballpark and that he was good enough to play. It fascinated me.'

'I see him now in his eighties, and he's still a force, an aura that is intimidating."

Bob Levy

Robert P. Levy has been a vital and a contributing principal within the Philadelphia sports and charitable communities for more than 60 years. He founded the Little Quakers football program, has been chairman of the Philadelphia Sports Congress, and had been honored with every conceivable local award that honor service to the community. He has also been a very successful breeder of horses with his Robert P. Levy Stables. His horse, Twice A Bet, won the Belmont Stakes in 1987.

'We were always good friends. We played golf at Whitemarsh. Ray Dooney and I would be hitting a driver and he would be hitting a four wood. When we were hitting a wood, he would hit an 8 iron.'

'He was always good with kids. You could bring him and Reds Bagnell to high school functions. They didn't always know who he was, but he was great with them.'

'At some of the Penn dinners he sometimes talked too long, but he was great. A good colorful speaker.'

'He's a great guy and I like him very much. One year the Little Quakers football team when to Florida. He and Tommy McDonald came along with the kids. This was 30 or 40 years ago, and they all knew who he was. We had a lot of fun on that trip."

Upton Bell

The youngest son of Bert Bell, Upton grew up in Philadelphia and followed his father to University of Pennsylvania and Philadelphia Eagles football games. His entire family had strong affection for Chuck Bednarik and Bell recalls the thoughtful speech that Bednarik gave at a dedication to Bert Bell in Narberth, PA a few years ago.

'The first time I saw Chuck Bednarik play was when he was at Penn. Penn was a powerhouse in those days and the games were on television. I remember the Thanksgiving Day game of 1948 against Cornell.'

'Penn needed to win that game and not only did he play his usual two-way positions, he also played fullback that day. That amazed me about him; the modern day athlete would never do that.'

'From the perspective of a kid, I was in awe. It just wouldn't happen today. Penn needed him at fullback and he played there. He was a great athlete; he could play anywhere.'

'When he joined the Eagles, I knew this guy would play right away. In those days, they brought rookies along slowly, but you knew this guy would play from the start. He was gregarious, outgoing, a leader from the beginning.'

'He had a ferocity for the game and was a tremendously coordinated athlete. He could do it all. Today they talk about how tough, big and fast the players are, but I believe it was a much tougher game then.'

'He is one of only two guys I think could have played both ways. Chuck was the precursor to Dick Butkus and I'm not even sure Butkus could have gone two ways.'

'Some aspects of the game haven't changed, but we'll never see the likes of Chuck Bednarik again. It's not only that he was the 60 Minute Man, but he could play any position on the field. He was very smart and understood football.'

'When Paul Brown started the Bengals, his first draft choice was Bob Johnson, a center. He caught a lot of criticism, but he said the center has to be the smartest guys on field and he wanted to start his franchise with a center.'

'Chuck understood offense and defense;

he knew the game. He was a guy who could take over the game; you couldn't take your eyes off him. He looks like he could still play the game today.'

'I started with the Colts in the days of Ewbank and Shula. You had to learn the playbook, some college students couldn't. Some could learn the playbook, but couldn't make split decisions on the field.'

'Besides being bright, Chuck was very instinctive. He always knew where the play was coming from. He started as a rookie and looked like he had been out there for 10 years. They hardly played rookies then. You had a lot of rough guys and they hazed the young guys, but Chuck was so driven. He was a man when he came in; World War II, flying over Germany.'

'Today they have different technology, better equipment, the players are quicker and faster and stronger; but none of these kids are men. Look at the Packers, a lot of those players who made up the core of the great teams were products of World War II and the Korean War. What could they be afraid of?'

'Those players – their pads provided the bare minimum of protection. There equipment was nothing like what you find in today's game, but they had a toughness. When I hired Bucko Kilroy with the Patriots, he still had a big cleat mark on his face. My father lost all his teeth playing at Penn in 1917.'

'Paul Brown was one of the first to have the players use a facemask. There was no protection for the players. The first ones were made of plastic and shattered.'

'There's no question the collisions are greater in today's game. The guys in Chuck's era may not have been as big, but it was a much rougher game. Dick Syzmanski said they used to tell players, "Wherever you are on the field, drop off if you don't you will get hit."

'When I went to the Colts in 1961, everyone worked another job. That may have been the start of the modern era, but it's amazing when you think of today and compare it to how difficult those guys had it.'

'Today Monday comes around and the players spend the rest of the week recovering. But those guys would take a beating and get up Monday morning and go to work. They had jobs to go to even during the season.'

'My father used to go to the training camps to speak to the players every summer. When he got to the Eagles, Chuck used to say, "Here he comes." They all had his speech down pat. He always emphasized two things: one – stay away from the gambling and the booze; and two – use football as a means to prepare for later life. He constantly preached to the players to use football to set yourselves up for the rest of your life.'

'Chuck took care of himself. It amazes me to see him at 84, looking like he could still put on a uniform. He looks like he could still line up anywhere.'

'The National Football League today would not be around without the Bednariks. They should take care of those guys. My father died a young man by today's standards to keep his league going 24 hours a day.'

'One difference from today, the guys had fun in that era. When I think of football, I think of Chuck Bednarik. He'll always be remembered as the 60 Minute Man; everyone knows him.'

'After my father died, my brother moved to New York with the Rozelle group. He was at both games in 1960 when the Eagles played the Giants back-to-back. He had the binoculars trained on Chuck when he hit Gifford. He never believed it was vicious. It was a very rough game back then and the players did not have great protection. If it had not been Gifford, the 'Golden Boy' in New York, the hit would not have been known.'

'The taunting on the field is worse than ever today; it's bad. They could not get away with the taunting that they do today in Chuck's era. Imagine if they tried to do that in his day. Like Bill Parcells says, "Act like

"Some aspects of the game haven't changed, but we'll never see the likes of Chuck Bednarik again. It's not only that he was the 60 Minute Man, but he could play any position on the field. He was very smart and understood football."

you've been there." It's not the same today. It was privilege to watch Chuck play.'

'I was home watching the game the day Chuck had his fight with Chuck Noll. I was later with Chuck (Noll) at Baltimore. I recommended him to the Steelers, though I'm sure I wasn't the only one. I thought he would be a great coach.'

'I remember watching the fight on TV and I'm not sure what was said in the meeting when my father called Chuck (Bednarik) in, but I know what his concerns would have been. He was always trying to be careful about the image of the league.'

'The league had sued Life Magazaine over an article that had come out about five years earlier that said the league was brutal, nothing but mayhem.'

'My father had some of the players testify and he won that case. After that, he always remained concerned about how the game was seen on TV. He didn't want it associated with wrestling, didn't want the league to be viewed in infamy.'

'I'm sure my father wasn't too tough on Chuck; he loved the guy. He probably handled it like he did when he fined Bucko Kilroy. He told Bucko that if he behaved himself the rest of the season, he wouldn't give the money back to him, but would give it to his wife to buy a new coat after the season.'

'Chuck Bednarik was a big hit with all of the Bell family. I wish there were more like him. He's gotten himself in trouble with some of his comments, but it was never intentional. He's said things, but he never hurt anyone.'

'He was at the ceremony when they dedicated a plaque to my father in Narberth. He gave a great speech. He said that all of the owners who have made fortunes out of football should thank Bert Bell for all the money that he put in their pockets.'

Tom Ridge

A request was e-mailed to the attention of Susan Nix in the office of former Pennsylvania Governor Tom Ridge, requesting his participation in a new book about Chuck Bednarik. A short time later the following was received from Ms. Nix.

"I merely mentioned Chuck's name and Governor Ridge began citing his many incredible accomplishments. When he was done I was able to mention your request and he said he'd love to chat."

A few days later a booming voice gushed through the phone and a man, who is so well regarded by Chuck and Emma Bednarik that he is one of the few Republicans they have ever supported, was reminiscing about Number 60.

"I believe that Chuck Bednarik reflects the best qualities that America had to offer while he was growing up—the 'whatever it takes' attitude. He's a hardworking ethnic kid with a 'what do you want me to do coach attitude, even when he was 35 years old."

If there has been a politician or government official from Pennsylvania whose upbringing most paralleled that of Bednarik, Ridge is the guy.

He was raised on the other side of the state. While Bednarik came from Bethlehem, Ridge was born in Pittsburgh's Steel Valley. His maternal grandparents emigrated from Czechoslovakia. He is decorated Army veteran who served in Vietnam.

Ridge served in the United States House of Representatives from 1983-1995, was elected governor in 1995 and served in that position until 2001 when he was named the United States' first Secretary of Homeland Security. Ridges is the founder of Ridge Global, a security consulting firm based in Washington, D.C.

"He was one of those that I admired as young kid growing up and meeting him as Governor gave me a great thrill. He is iconic.'

'You know I'm from the other part of the state and we grew up watching the Steelers and the Browns, but I remember that championship game and the hit on Gifford.'

'My appreciation for his athletic achievements grew as I learned more about him.'

'Sixty minutes; no one will ever do that again. Today, football is more technical, more specialized, the players more pampered. Today's players might have the talent, but they're not conditioned to go both ways.'

'With Chuck, like Ronald Reagan, his legend grew with time. '

'This is a rough analogy but, with life in general, whether its sports, politics, government—we don't appreciate what we have, when we have it.'

'Like Reagan, his legacy grew. Now that we have time to reflect, damn he was good.'

'The thing I noticed when I first met Chuck was that he was a big guy; but not a monster like you see today. Then you notice those hands, man he must have broken every one of his fingers.'

'He loved to play, you bet he did. And he looks like he could still play.'

'I believe that Chuck Bednarik reflects the best qualities that America had to offer while he was growing up— the 'whatever it takes' attitude. He's a hardworking ethnic kid with a 'what do you want me to do coach attitude, even when he was 35 years old.'

'You look at today's game, the equipment, the medical support, the salaries, and you realize that Chuck was just knocking around and playing. He is from a different breed.'

'One thing about him, his language is very clear. You never walk away from a conversation with him not being sure of what he just said.'

'That's just his nature; what's fair is fair; what's right is right.'

'He has a very clear set of principals and they have guided him morally and ethically. He follows his convictions and has a very principled, incredible work ethic.'

'He's the guy I would want with me in a foxhole.'

'I have enormous admiration for people who have lived a tough life and live by principle. He has lived by his parents' principles on and off the field. There is much to be admired of both Chuck and his wife.'

'I am always very happy to talk about a guy I admire so much.'

'You know the football stadium was built while I was in office and I've never been there. I would love to go to a game with Chuck Bednarik."

Ed Rendell

The governor of Pennsylvania and former mayor of Philadelphia is a huge fan of the Philadelphia Eagles. He is a regular panelist on the Eagles post show on Comcast Sportsnet. He first developed an appreciation for Chuck Bednarik while growing up a Giants fan in New York.

Rendell took time from a state budget planning meeting to discuss Bednarik. As governor, Rendell has honored Bednarik in Harrisburg and has reappointed him to the State Athletic Commission several times.

"I grew up in New York and I was there at Yankee Stadium the day he hit Gifford. We were more stunned than angry. We weren't sure if Frank was hurt.'

'Chuck Bednarik's importance to the NFL is that he was one of the people who brought the sports into its incredible popularity. Part of the allure of football is hard hits—like crashes in Nascar. He was a master of the hard hit. He was tough, no nonsense. And he has those fingers that point every way.'

'He helped usher in the era of terrific fan excitement. People may love offense, but it's defense that wins games. Philly fans understand and love defense.'

'To the Eagles, Chuck is the epitome, the prototype of what Philly fans want a football player to be. He's tough,100% gusto and zest, a true blue collar, lunch pail guy. He's the last two-way player. [He] never worried about salary, endorsement, public relations or TV.'

'He was the consummate hard hitter. He is the embodiment of Philadelphia, a force that gripped the town.'

'The linebackers I would compare him to are Dick Butkus and Sam Huff, but Chuck was a better hitter than Huff. Huff was more of a strategic middle linebacker. In

> **"Chuck Bednarik's importance to the NFL is that he was one of the people who brought the sports into its incredible popularity. Part of the allure of football is hard hits— like crashes in Nascar. He was a master of the hard hit. He was tough, no nonsense. And he has those fingers that point every way."**

terms of hitting, Butkus was the only one in the same league as Chuck.'

'I've met him several times; it has always been my pleasure to reappoint him to the State Athletic Commission. He is every bit as blunt in those meetings as he is everywhere else. He is plainspoken on boxing issues.'

'It's refreshing in this day and age for someone to have someone who is so blunt and straightspeaking.

'That's life and some people don't like what he's saying. He doesn't pull punches and he's not politically correct.'

'You have to admire his direct honesty, even when he steps on toes.'

'There's that new saying going around, "It is what it is." Well Chuck Bednarik 'is what he is' with five exclamation points behind it. There's something really to be said about his honesty in this day and age.'

'He's a good guy behind the gruff exterior. He has a kind heart and does a lot for people. It doesn't matter to him – white, black, rich poor.'

'I know the old-timers get him. He's Andy's (Reid) type of football player. The modern day players, I wonder what goes through their heads when they think about Chuck Bednarik.'

'We're never going see the likes of him again. When you think about what records in sports won't be broken— Cy Young's 511 vicotries—he's right up there. It's a different era now.'

'He's always going to remain the last two-way player and he's a fine, fine man; no question."

Bert Bell, Jr.

The eldest son of the former NFL commissioner; Bert Jr. worked for his father when the league offices were in Philadelphia. He continued with the league when Pete Rozelle succeeded his father and moved the offices to New York.

'The big thing about Chuck Bednarik is that when he entered the University of Pennsylvania, the Ivy League was falling on hard times and he gave the league a new status. He went both ways and brought a toughness to the league.'

'To describe him among all of the players I have known, I wouldn't call him a brain, but he always knew where the ball was going on the field. He had a sixth sense. He understood things that you can't learn in a playbook or on a blackboard. He was not a cerebral type- and he was always in the right place at the right time.'

'It was a very fitting ending to the 1960 season that it was him lying on Jim Taylor at the seven or eight yard line. He was always where he needed to be.'

'This guy stood out above all of them. Many guys need to ride the gravy train of a championship game; not Chuck Bednarik, he drove the train.'

'He knocked out Frank Gifford for a year. The tackle was not brutalizing, just efficient. He had great instincts and it was just the way he hit. He was in the right spot at the right time.'

"He knocked out Frank Gifford for a year. The tackle was not brutalizing, just efficient. He had great instincts and it was just the way he hit. He was in the right spot at the right time."

'Of all the great middle linebackers, he was far greater than any of them. Joe Schmidt was small; Sam Huff played in defensive system that allowed him to roam to the ball. Chuck made the plays on his own and he was not bad at center, either. He was an amazing player.'

'My dad was quite proud of him. Having gone to the University of Pennsylvania himself, it meant a lot to him that Chuck was also from Penn. When the Eagles came and desecrated the hallowed ground of Franklin Field, he was right at home. He was at most of the games and he died at Franklin Field during a game.'

'He had a very stern father. I found an 1898 Spalding Guide that showed that my grandfather was on the collegiate rules committee. He was second in seniority to Walter Camp. My dad had gone to Episcopal Academy in Haverford and when he was looking at colleges, his father told him, "You can to Penn, or you can go to hell."'

'Dad later coached at Penn with John Heisman. His real name was DeBenneville. Looking back in history players couldn't say DeBenneville. I don't know how he chose 'Bert,' but it was a more appropriate football name.'

'Dad absolutely had a warm feeling for Chuck. We all knew that there was a great player amongst us. My brother and I were both very instinctive about who could play, and we picked him out early. He and I, and Fred Schubach, who was the equipment manager for the Eagles and Colts, really knew personnel.'

'When my brother and I were with the Colts, we hated when coaches came near the draft. Art Rooney also used to hate having the coaches in the draft room. Dan Rooney and Chuck Noll had a fistfight once because Rooney wanted to pick Franco Harris and Noll wanted Robert Newhouse. Dan Rooney had the same instinct for football players as his father had about horses.'

'When it comes to Chuck Bednarik, I have just the greatest memories. He was one of the greatest players of all time and he saved two franchises—he put Penn back on the football map and he brought the NFL championship back to Philadelphia.'

'I watched them all in the 1950s, and what else saved football was the facemask. Tackling was poor and the facemask gave people courage. Guys were worried about their face and now with protection they lost their fear. Facemasks improved tackling and improved the game.'

'You know how Paul Brown made all of his money; he invented the facemask. He was a brilliant mind. At a banquet in Philadelphia, someone asked my dad who he thought should be commissioner if he weren't around. Without hesitation, Dad said Paul Brown.'

'Norm Van Brocklin didn't want to come to the Eagles when he was traded there. Dad got him to come to Philly. He wanted out of Los Angeles because he thought he was better than Bob Waterfield, and he was, but he did also want to play in Philadelphia. He and Chuck brought the championship back to Philadelphia.'

'There is absolutely no doubt at all that Chuck Bednarik could play today. He had such a nose for the ball. There is not a coach who wouldn't put him out there. I don't know that he could play both ways; there weren't a lot of finely conditioned linemen back then. In fact, a lot of them were fat. Plus, they only played 12 or 14 games.'

'When I see Chuck Bednarik today, I see the same kid I did 50 years ago. He is classic football. Like my dad, he lived for football."

Chapter | **seventeen**

Good Neighbor Chuck

As much as he might try to blend into the traditional fabric of suburban living, there is nothing mundane about being a neighbor of Chuck Bednarik. The world's most famous ring announcer grew up in Abington, PA, and he remembers a particular neighbor on Canterbury Road who had a unique style of reminding teenage drivers that a gradual roll does not constitute full suspension of movement at a stop sign. Bednarik has often also referred to himself as the "Patron Saint of Dead Animals" for all of the roadkill he has conducted decent burials for. A good friend of his young daughters remembers the particular compassion the great linebacker showed when her pet cat did not make it's way home one afternoon.

(L-R) Twins Pam and Carol, Charlene, Jackie, Chuck, Emma, Donna, and poogie

Patty Burns

Patricia Burns, an advertising executive in Chicago, has told many people over the years the story about how her neighbor, a famous NFL linebacker, showed great compassion when her pet cat was killed in a traffic accident. Growing up in Abington, Burns was best friends with the Bednarik twins, Pam and Carol.

My family moved to Abington when I was 8 years old. We moved to a new home on Hemlock Circle. Hemlock Circle was literally a circle street that intersected twice on Canterbury Rd. where the Bednarik family lived. I don't remember exactly how I met the family, but my best guess is that I was probably riding my bike to an original hamburger fast food restaurant called Gino's. It was right around the corner from the Bednarik's home. So, I guess I met the twins on the way. Being a little kid on a bike, I remember meeting the twins in the driveway and wound up going inside their home.

I met Mrs. Bednarik, the other sisters, and Mr. Bednarik. I remember when Mr.

> **"I saw a very overwhelmed face and maybe a tear or two. He explained to me that while he was taking a walk, he saw a mail truck hit George and that George had to go to heaven."**

Bednarik asked me where I lived, all about me and stuff, and I told him my family just moved around the corner on Hemlock Circle. I remember seeing his twisted little pinky and asked him why his finger was like that. I was only 9. Mr. Bednarik asked me if I knew anything about football and of course, I answered "no." So, he invited me into their home, along with Pam and Carol, and took me down into the lower level of the house where all of "Concrete Charlie's" awards, trophies and photos were. I thought it was a game room with all the things around. I didn't know he was a famous football star with the Philadelphia Eagles. He then explained that the reason he had a crooked pinky was from wearing his NFL rings. "Patty, they were too heavy for my pinky and that's why my pinky is twisted." OMG – I kind of believed him but still didn't understand being a little gal only 9 years old! Guess I then realized that Mr. Bednarik was

famous but I certainly didn't get how famous he was. It didn't matter to me. What mattered was that I was friends with Pam and Carol; that was more important to me then.

I am going to save my best memory of Mr. Bednarik for last. Besides the pinky story, I have another one that I will never forget, but it's not the last and best.

Pam and Carol invited me over for a barbeque. Mrs. Bednarik was bringing out the food for the grill, which was outside in the back, off the kitchen, and it started to rain. I was confused about how they were going to grill our dinner when it started to rain. Mr. Bednarik laughed at me in a good way and told me that "we can still grill in the rain because we have an awning." Phewww, I remember thinking. I was hungry and I wondered why I didn't think about an awning.

While I was getting to know the Bednarik family, I remembered teasing Mr. Bednarik that he and his wife didn't have a son…thought he may have wanted a "little Chuck" that may play football. Obviously, I finally understood that he was a big time player in the NFL. When I asked him if he was upset about not having a son, his response was magnificent. "Patty, I have a beautiful wife who gave me 5 beautiful daughters…what else can I want besides this wonderful family."

I thought back then that he may have wanted a son, but he was thrilled with his beautiful wife, Emma, and their daughters.

As I mentioned, I am saving the best story for last. This is the story about Mr. Bednarik that I have never, ever forgotten. I was nine years old and my Mom got me a little kitten that I named George. It was my first kitten. My parents told me things I needed to learn about having a kitten – feeding, play time, and of course, it was my job to clean the litter box. George and I were inseparable. I took him everywhere with me. We were the best of friends. I didn't know then that I shouldn't have let George outside, but it

seemed normal for him to roam around the neighborhood and he always came home to me. One evening in the summer, I saw Mr. Benarik talking to my parents in the back yard and they were all appeared upset. I didn't know why. Mr. Bednarik came into the house from the back patio and when he saw me, I saw a very overwhelmed face and maybe a tear or two. He explained to me that while he was taking a walk, he saw a mail truck hit George and that George had to go to heaven. Of course, I asked if George had died and Mr. Bednarik told me that he picked George up and had buried him in our back yard. That's why he was talking to my parents. Mr. Bednarik wanted to tell me and

not my parents because he was there and just wanted to tell me himself about George. I immediately started crying and Mr. Bednarik threw his arms around me and told me that George was gonna be OK but that I wouldn't be able to see him again. I cried myself to sleep. However, I have never forgotten what he did for me regarding George. Here was this big man that totally had a huge heart and was incredibly sensitive.

This is my story about Mr. Bednarik. I could never call him "Chuck" or "Concrete Charlie." He was my best friend's parent and my neighbor. He will always be Mr. Bednarik to me.

At the Bednarik home in Abington, PA Back (L-R): Charlene, Donna, Carol, Pam, Jackie. Front: Emma with poogie and Chuck.

Michael Buffer

The "Let's Get Ready to Rumble" boxing announcer grew up in Abington, PA and, as a teenager, had his car stopped by Chuck Bednarik when the rolled through a stop near Bednarik's house.

"Growing up in the Roslyn, PA suburbs of Philadelphia during the '50s, I remember my local sports heroes were Robin Roberts and Del Ennis of the Phillies, and the Eagles' Chuck Bednarik, AKA Concrete Charlie.

'When I was nine or ten years old, my mother took me to a sporting goods store having it's grand opening in neighboring Willow Grove, PA. Now in those days, there were two stores that a ten year old lost sleep over the prospects of visiting: a hobby shop and sporting goods. This visit had some special added excitement as the new owner may actually be there and he was none other than Chuck Bednarik of my beloved Eagles. I was assured, that if I behaved (not my strongest ability in those days), I would be allowed to buy something within a reasonable price. That was great but would we actually get to meet Mr. Bednarik?

'As I try to remember that day, now over half a century ago, one thing stands out as forever unforgettable. After choosing a royal blue football helmet with a gold stripe, three or four very large men emerged from, I presume, the back. The largest one picked me up as though I were a pillow to be fluffed, placed me on the counter and tapped the helmet now on my head, which I planned on wearing out of the store and, in this gruff but raspy smooth voice, said something now faded with time. Yes, it was Mr. Bednarik. I had never seen a man this big in person before. He had the broadest shoulders, the thickest neck and biggest hands in the world. Besides all that, he was as handsome as The Lone Ranger, Roy Rogers and Buster Crabbe. Maybe even better looking because they didn't have a really cool, football player-style broken nose.

What a day that was! The other large men were teammates whose names I don't recall, their autographs now tucked away with Mr. Bednarik's. That day, though, will never be tucked away. When I see actor/comedian Billy Crystal speak of his childhood meeting with Mickey Mantle and his eyes glaze with the memory of his youth and his hero, I know exactly how he feels. It's a wonderful feeling.

A FEW YEARS LATER...

In 1997, I was invited to the Pro Football Hall Of Fame to introduce the new inductees at the luncheon held the day before the big ceremony. On induction day, there's a big breakfast before the parade and it is packed with all the hall of famers, past and present, many with their wives and/or family members. Well, lo and behold, the legendary Mr. Bednarik and his wife were there. Chuck, a long time fight fan and PA Boxing Commissioner, knew who I was and we chatted for awhile. I didn't mention the previous story because I didn't want to seem like too big of a Concrete Charlie geek, but I did tell them a story from my high school days.

**"When I see actor/comedian
Billy Crystal speak of his
childhood meeting with Mickey
Mantle and his eyes glaze
with the memory of his
youth and his hero,
I know exactly how he feels.
It's a wonderful feeling."**

The Bednariks had a beautiful home on Canterbury Drive in Abington Township, PA. I attended Abington High School, which was about four blocks from their home and one my classmates actually lived next door to them, so everybody knew where they lived. One of the hazards of living near a high school is that teenage idiots drive through your neighborhood more than you'd like. The Bednariks had four daughters who, of course, would ride their bikes and play on the street like all kids in the neighborhood. I'm sure there were more than a couple times when some moron in his hot rod came roaring down the street. There was a stop sign a few houses down from the Bednariks and coming to a complete stop was repeatedly ignored by most of the high schoolers. The rolling-stop was the usual way of acknowledging the sign. This did not sit too well with the father of four recognized by many as one of the toughest men on the planet.

One early summer evening in 1962 or '63, with a date sitting next to me, I committed the sin of not coming to a complete stop at that stop sign on Canterbury. Out of the bushes sprang the large, broad-shouldered legend of professional football to the front of my '55 Chevy with a baseball bat, as if he needed it, barking something like, "Hold it right there!" In a split second he was at my window letting me know that stop means STOP and I better remember it and make sure all my friends remember it. I somehow didn't soil my pants and remember saying at least a dozen times, "I'm sorry Mister Bednarik!"

After telling the story, they both had a pretty good laugh and Mrs. B. said, "Oh yes, I remember that. He was crazy when it came to that stop sign." What a great way to bring to a close, after thirty plus years, one of the most embarrassing and depressing moments in my life...when I was chewed out by my hero, Concrete Charlie."

Frank Unger

A neighbor of the Bednariks in Abington, PA.

The Unger family were neighbors of the Bednariks in Abington, Pennsylvania during the '50s and early '60s, Bednarik's prime years. For the Ungers, one of the biggest sports stars in town was just another guy in the neighborhood.

"Our yards backed up to each other. We lived on Edmund. He was a good guy and a good neighbor, but he couldn't take any kidding, especially about having five daughters and no sons.'

'He wanted a son, oh, he wanted a son. He didn't talk to me for about three months when my son was born. He was a very proud guy.'

'People in the neighborhood didn't make much fuss about him, but after I moved to Ocean City, Chuck and Emma came to visit us one day. Word got out that he was here, and kids were bringing footballs for him to sign all day. He was very obliging. The woman who owned the Asbury Avenue sports store said she sold more footballs that day than any other.'

'Do you know what he did with his first bonus? He put in a bathroom in his mother and father's house in Bethlehem. They had never had a bathroom.'

'We got to know each other in those days through our wives. Our wives ran our social lives.'

'When he moved to Canterbury Road, he lived one lot away from Old York Road. It was a busy street even in those days and he used to complain about the traffic."

Stan Lopata

Stan Lopata was a catcher with the Phillies for parts of 11 seasons. A two-time All-Star selection, Lopata was a neighbor of the Bednariks in Abington, PA.

"Chuck and I were neighbors in Abington. We enjoyed life together; there were a lot of parties. He is a heck of a man and he's always been a real good friend.'

'He never lost his temper around his friends. We enjoyed getting together with our wives. We had a group in the area that included Johnny Callison, Curt Simmons and Robin Roberts. Emma is the godmother to one of my children and I'm the godfather to their daughter Jackie.'

'He and I had some good time. He was just a regular neighbor.'

'Through him, I got a job in the concrete business. He asked me if I was interested in being in concrete sales. He set up a dinner with Mr. Morrisey, of the Morrisey Company. I worked four or five years in sales and eventually became the sales manager.'

'Being an athlete in Philadelphia opened a lot of doors. I was originally from Detroit, but I made my name in Philadelphia."

Chapter | eighteen

Scrapbook

Breakfast with the girls – (L-R) Donna, Pam, Chuck, Carol, Charlene, (standing) Emma

Emma, Emma, Sr., Margaret, Stephen, Willie

Bill Margetich on leave from Navy, 1943

Chuck stading in the backyard

Charles Sr. in front of Chuck's trophies

David, Richie, Mary, Jeep, Chuck, Betty, Mom and Pop Bednarik

Emma age 17

/8 YRS OLD

1. BASIC TRAINING.
   GREENSBORO N.C. —

2. ASSIGNED CREW BOISE IDAHO —
   GOWEN FIELD

3. FLEW PLANE TO ENGLAND
   STOPS AT VALLEY WALES

4. BASE WAS RACKHEATH ENG
   467th BOMB GRP 788 SQUADRON

5. COMMANDER WAS COL. AL SHOWER

6. CREW DEAN MORROW STILL IN CONTACT
   CO PILOT   CALIF.

7. SOME MISSIONS BERLIN 3 TIMES
   3 X COLOGNE INSBRUCK
   BOMBED   STUTTGART
   FACTORIES AND RAIL ROAD —

9. AFTER 30th KISSED GROUND
   NEVER WANT TO FLY AGAIN

10. AIR MEDAL 5 OAK LEAF CLUSTERS
    MEDAL - 5 BATTLE STARS

11. DISCHARGED FROM GREENSBORO N.C.

12. ENTERED UNIV. of PENNA.
    ALL AMERICAN - HALL OF FAME

13. EAGLES 14 YRS - PRO HOF

14. MARRIED 58 YRS TO EMMA —

Co-Captains ... by Pap'

FALCONE SHARES THE HONOR OF CAPTAINING PENN WITH CHUCK BEDNARIK!!

Carmen

FALCONE IS A FINE BLOCKER AND AN EXCELLENT DEFENSIVE PLAYER

I'LL RUN IT BACK

CHUCK DOES THE PUNTING AND CARRIES THE BALL ON FAKE KICKS

Chuck BEDNARIK —THE QUAKERS' ALL-AMERICAN CENTER

AP Newsfeatures 220

UNIVERSITY of PENNSYLVANIA

PHILADELPHIA 19104

Department of Physical Education
205 HUTCHINSON GYMNASIUM
GEORGE A. MUNGER, *Director*

October 1, 1969

Charles "Chuck" Bednarik
Philadelphia, Pennsylvania

Dear Chuck:

Your many loyal and longtime friends in Bethlehem continue to always do the right thing. If I had it over, I would hope that I, too, could have been born in Bethlehem! I suppose in another few years they will buy up the home you were born in and turn it into a national Bednarik Shrine.

Today many young men reject the old values on which you were raised and have continued to live by—loyalty, honor, respect for authority, hard work, dedication, love of family and self-discipline—all qualities we admire and hope every young man will have in abundance as you have had. With all your success, you have continued to be just "Chuck". We all admire you for this and are happy to be part of this testimonial party in your honor.

Sincerely,

George Munger

George A. Munger

THE NATIONAL FOOTBALL FOUNDATION
AND HALL OF FAME

NEW BRUNSWICK   NEW JERSEY

CHESTER J. LaRoche, *President*   EARL H. BLAIK, *Vice President*   WALLACE S. GIRLING, *Vice President*
THOMAS J. HAMILTON, *Vice President*   VINCENT DRADDY, *Vice President*   ROBERT A. HALL, *Secretary*
EDGAR W. GARBISCH, *Vice President*   CLINTON E. FRANK, *Vice President*   JOSEPH D. TOOKER, JR., *Treasurer*
ROGER M. BLOUGH, *Chairman, National Advisory Board*   HARVEY HARMAN, *Executive Director*
                                                        ROBERT HARRON, *Assistant to the President*

NEW BRUNSWICK OFFICE
137 CHURCH STREET
NEW BRUNSWICK, N. J. 08901
CHarter 7-1766

April 22, 1969

Mr. Charles P. Bednarik

Dear Chuck:

As Chairman of the Honors Court of the National Football
Foundation, I have the honor of notifying you that you have
been elected to the National Football Foundation's Hall of
Fame.

This is the greatest honor that can come to a former college
player or coach, and I wish to congratulate you. This will
be released to the newspapers in a short time, and I request
you to withhold the release of this information until the
story has broken in the papers.

You will be inducted into the Hall of Fame at its annual
Awards Dinner next December 9th at the Waldorf Astoria Hotel
in New York. You will be hearing from Executive Director
Harvey Harman and Dinner Chairman Vincent DePaul Draddy about
this occasion.

With best wishes, I am

Cordially yours,

Fred Russell

Fred Russell
Honors Court Chairman

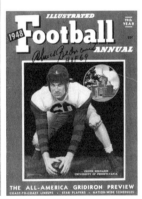

The Eagles defensive front in the 1950s was known as The Suicide Seven. From the left are: E, Norm Willie; LB Bednarik; T, Mike Jarmoluk; NG Bucko Kilroy; LB Wayne Robinson; T, Jesse Richardson; E, Tom Scott.

Chuck signs a contract with Vince McNally

Bednarik to Make 11th Season His Last

Bednarik donates his uniform to the Pro Football Hall of Fame after final game.

Walking off the field, Paul Hornung, Bednarik, and Jim Taylor.

PHILADELPHIA **EAGLES** GREEN BAY **PACKERS**

NATIONAL FOOTBALL LEAGUE
WORLD CHAMPIONSHIP GAME
FRANKLIN FIELD · PHILADELPHIA · DECEMBER 26, 1960

50¢

Time Out

Bednarik Prefers to Quit While He's on Top

By JOHN DELL

WHEN Ted Williams visited Philadelphia last winter he sat across a dinner table and told why he expected to have a good season. The 40-year-old man's reasoning was simple: "I can still do everything I've ever been able to do: swing a bat, run, throw and field. I can do every-

to say then, as he does now, "I feel I'm just as active and spry as any one of these 22 or 23-year-old kids are."

"The big reason I want to quit now is that I don't want to become a bum. I want to quit while I'm still good. I don't want to hang around so long that people get to saying 'that guy should have quit long ago.'

"Look at Pellegrini. He's only been playing linebacker two-three years and already he's complaining. I say to him, 'What are you going to do after 10 years?' And he says, 'Go to offense.' So you can see what's harder."

• • •

Chuck at Greasy Neale's HOF Induction

Greasy Neale's thank you note to Chuck

Chuck with golfers Ed McMahon, Johnny Carson

Chuck with Rocky Marciano

Signing for the military

ART ROONEY

FRANK GIFFORD

BOBBY LANE

1977

DANTE LAVELLI

BOBBY BELL

NIGHT TRAIN LANE

LEROY KELLY

PAUL WARFIELD H.O.F.

VAN BUREN WOJIE ? WISTERT LINDS
HOT SPRINGS ARK — 1949 — ROOKIE YEAR

GIFFORD KATHY LEE
NITSCHKE CUDY

JIM TAYLOR GREEN BAY PACKER

Eagles 75th Anniversary Team

JEFFREY LURIE
CHAIRMAN AND CEO

Dear Chuck,

I want to express my gratitude for your gracious gift. The Eagles shirt are beautifully crafted and unique. Your thinking of me is most appreciated. Hope you and your family are doing well.

I look forward to seeing you.

Best Wishes,

Jeffrey

Chuck — Thanks for The Friendship Andy Reid

Index